US Hegemony and the

In this book, Arturo Santa-Cruz advances an understanding of power as a social relationship and applies it consistently to the economic realm in United States relations with other countries of the Western Hemisphere. Following the academic and popular debate on the ebb and flow of US hegemony, this work centers the analysis in a critical case for the exercise of US power through its economic statecraft: the Americas—its historical zone of influence. The rationale for the regional focus is methodological: if it can be shown that Washington's sway has decreased in the area since the early 1970s, when the discussion about this matter started, it can be safely assumed that the same has occurred in other latitudes. The analysis focuses on three regions: North America, Central America and South America. Since each region contains countries that have at times maintained very different relationships with the United States, the findings contribute to a better understanding of the practice of US power in the sub-region in question, adding greater variability to the overall results.

US Hegemony and the Americas: Power and Economic Statecraft in International Relations is an invaluable resource for students and scholars interested in Latin American History and Politics, North American Regional Integration, International Relations, Economic Statecraft, Political Economy and Comparative Politics.

Arturo Santa-Cruz (PhD, Cornell University) is Professor at the Pacific Rim Department and Director of the North American Studies Center, at the University of Guadalajara, México. He is the author of *Mexico–United States Relations: The Semantics of Sovereignty* (2012) and *International Election Monitoring, Sovereignty, and the Western Hemisphere Idea: The Emergence of an International Norm* (2005); he is co-author of *América del Norte*, Volume 1 in the series "Historia de las relaciones internacionales de México, 1821–2010" (2011). He is editor or co-editor of, among other works, *Introducción a las Relaciones Internacionales: América Latina y la Política Global* (2013), *The State and Security in Mexico: Transformation and Crisis in Regional Perspective* (2012), *La Política Sin Fronteras, O la Ubicuidad de lo Distintivo* (2012), and *El Constructivismo y las Relaciones Internacionales* (2009). He has contributed many book chapters, and has published in specialized journals such as *International Organization, Journal of Latin American Studies, Estudios Internacionales* and *Foro Internacional*.

"This carefully crafted and lucidly written book covers history (case studies of 1971–1989, 1990–2000, 2001–2016), theory (a discussion of hegemony, power and statecraft), and different facets of the Americas (case studies of Canada, México, Central America and South America). A marvel of clear thought about history, theory and the Americas it is one of the best works, probing the rise and falls of American power."

—*Peter J. Katzenstein, Walter S. Carpenter Jr. Professor of International Studies, Cornell University*

"Arturo Santa-Cruz has written a definitive book on US hegemony in the Americas. Perhaps for the first time, an analysis of the Western Hemisphere en masse has been situated in the broader International Relations literature. Santa-Cruz walks us through four decades beginning in 1971, all the while tackling big questions concerning power, hegemony and political and economic statecraft. He argues that the nature of US hegemony in the Western Hemisphere was based largely on economic statecraft and intact all the way up to the 2016 election of Donald Trump. Since 2016, Washington's hostility toward the entire region and its attempts to pose China as a threat to US hegemony in the Americas, could well turn out to be a self-fulfilling prophecy. This sophisticated book offers a full explanation of how the US got from here to there."

—*Carol Wise, School of International Relations, University of Southern California*

"Arturo Santa-Cruz's book is a timely re-examination of the pivotal issues facing the Americas. Moving beyond both simplistic notions of hegemony, as well as a narrow geographic ambit, Santa-Cruz combines sophisticated conceptualization with detailed case studies. His conclusions offer valuable insights about the trajectory of power, and the nature and impact of shifts concerning US economic statecraft in the time of the Trump presidency. The book deserves a wide readership among students and scholars both of comparative regional orders and the Western Hemisphere more specially."

—*Andrew F. Cooper, Professor, the Balsillie School of International Affairs and the Department of Political Science, University of Waterloo*

"Arturo Santa-Cruz explores whether the degree of US hegemony (or of asymmetric power) is declining, increasing or holding steady with reference to specific countries and in Latin America as a whole. Other discussions of this question are often ideological and/or polemic. Santa-Cruz tackles the issue lucidly by clarifying concepts, reviewing and comparing data, and taking into account variations among cases and over time."

—*Abraham F. Lowenthal, Professor Emeritus, University of Southern California*

US Hegemony and the Americas

Power and Economic Statecraft in International Relations

Arturo Santa-Cruz

Routledge
Taylor & Francis Group

NEW YORK AND LONDON

First published 2020
by Routledge
52 Vanderbilt Avenue, New York, NY 10017

and by Routledge
2 Park Square, Milton Park, Abingdon, Oxon, OX14 4RN

Routledge is an imprint of the Taylor & Francis Group, an informa business

Library of Congress Cataloging-in-Publication Data
A catalog record for this title has been requested

ISBN: 978-0-8153-8109-9 (hbk)
ISBN: 978-0-8153-8110-5 (pbk)
ISBN: 978-1-351-21122-2 (ebk)

Typeset in Bembo
by Deanta Global Publishing Services, Chennai, India

To Brigit, Hannah, and Diego

Ten Pysk

Contents

Abbreviations

AIG	American International Group
ALBA	Bolivarian Alliance of the Americas
ATPA	Andean Trade Preference Act
ATPDEA	Andean Trade Promotion and Drug Eradication Act
BRIC	Brazil, Russia, India, and China
CAFTA	Central America Free Trade Agreement
CARICOM	Caribbean Community
CBI	Caribbean Basin Initiative
CBTPA	Caribbean Basin Trade Partnership Act
CCCT	Joint Commission for Trade and Transactions
CD	Certificates of Deposit
CELAC	Community of Latin American and Caribbean States
CIA	Central Intelligence Agency
CUSFTA	Canada–United States Free Trade Agreement
DFAIT	Department of Foreign Affairs and International Trade
DR-CAFTA	Dominican Republic–Central America Free Trade Agreement
EEC	European Economic Community
EXIM BANK	Export-Import Bank
FEP	Foreign Economic Policy
FIRA	Foreign Investment Review Agency
FMCSA	Federal Motor Carrier Safety Administration
FMLN	Farabundo Martí National Liberation Front
FRC	Family Resemblance Concepts
FTA	Free Trade Agreement
FTAA	Free Trade Area of the Americas
G7	Group of Seven
GATT	General Agreement on Tariffs and Trade
GDP	Gross Domestic Product
GSP	Generalized System of Preferences
HLED	High Level Economic Dialogue
HST	Hegemonic Stability Theory

IADC	Inter-American Democratic Charter
IMF	International Monetary Fund
IPE	International Political Economy
IR	International Relations
MFN	Most Favored Nation
NAFA	North American Framework Agreement
NAFTA	North American Free Trade Agreement
NATO	North Atlantic Treaty Organization
NEP	National Energy Program
NORAD	North American Aerospace Defense Command
OAS	Organization of American States
PAN	National Action Party
SPP	Security and Prosperity Partnership
SRE	Secretariat of Foreign Affairs
TPP	Trans-Pacific Partnership
UN	United Nations
USAID	United States Agency for International Development
USSR	Union of Soviet Socialist Republics
USTR	United States Trade Representative
WB	World Bank
WHI	Western Hemisphere Idea
WTO	World Trade Organization

Introduction

For over four decades now, scholars and the media have been discussing the ebb and flow of US hegemony. First in the context of the Nixon Shock and the oil crisis, talk about US decline mushroomed; a decade later, with the retreat and eventual demise of the Soviet Union, the discussion shifted in the opposite direction: Washington was presented as the New Rome. Around the turn of the millennium, with the emergence of the BRICs in general, and China in particular, the debate shifted back again.

The pendular nature of the discussion on US hegemony has evinced both a shifting focus of the issue with regards to the areas under consideration, and, more importantly, an erratic conception of the concept that underlies it: power. Different definitions and parameters of it have been used, which makes evaluating competing claims difficult. Basically, two broad understandings of power have been (more or less explicitly) advanced: one conceives of it as a property; the other one regards power as a social relation. Careful consideration of the alternative understandings of power, as well as a consistent use of the term in a clearly demarcated issue area, should shed some light on the changing position of the United States in the international system. As suggested above, three distinct phases on the debate of US hegemony can be distinguished: 1971–1989, that is, from what was considered to be the end of the Bretton Woods system to the end of the Cold War; 1990–2000, which corresponds to the interregnum or "unipolar moment," and 2001–2016, a period that stretches from the alleged "rise" of China (as symbolized by its entrance into the World Trade Organization), and (practically) until the end of the Obama era in Washington.

This work centers the analysis in what would be a critical case for the exercise of US hegemony: the Americas—its historical zone of influence. The rationale for the regional focus is methodological: if it can be shown that Washington's sway has decreased in the area since the early 1970s, when the discussion about this matter started, it can be safely assumed that the same has occurred in other latitudes. The Western Hemisphere would thus be a "crucial case study"; as it has been well established in the literature, these cases are useful to test both hypotheses and theories.[1] The analysis focuses on three regions: North America, Central America and South America. Since each region contains countries that have at times maintained very different relationships with the United States, the findings should contribute to a better understanding of US power in the sub-region in question, adding greater variability to the overall results. That is, methodologically, this work also relies on the comparative method, in order to bolster the findings from the diverse cases.[2] The advantage of resorting to the (multiple and comparative) case study method is that this methodology excels at focusing on process, which is precisely what is needed when assessing the wax and wane of power in international politics. Given the nature of the inquiry, the approach taken here is mostly state-centric, but on occasions it delves into domestic politics.

The analysis will center on the economic relationship between the United States and the hemispheric countries under study. The economy is a field that sits between matters traditionally considered the realm of hard power and/or high politics, such as security, about which sociologically oriented approaches and conceptions of power usually say little, and soft power and/or low politics, such as diplomacy or normative change, on which mainstream theories have shown little interest. Since both approaches have something to contribute to the debate on the economy as a power arena, it should serve as meeting place for them. In order to further specify the concept of power and operationalize it, the focus will be on economic statecraft, understood not only as a repertoire of tools to which policymakers resort to exercise power, but also as a more structural component, related to the identity of the power wielder, i.e., the United States. The aim is to "thicken" the concept of economic statecraft, looking at it as a deeply embedded and quotidian social practice that is not limited to the use of special techniques in extraordinary circumstances.

Structure of the Book

This work is divided into eight chapters (plus a concluding one); the first half deals mainly with conceptual and historical matters, while the second presents analytical narratives of the empirical cases. Chapter 1 reviews the debate on the decline of US hegemony. In order to contextualize the academic discussion, the chapter also looks at the initial conditions around which the debate has revolved, and considers the means through which Washington achieved hegemonic status in the aftermath of World War II. The previous considerations serve to re-examine the phases the debate in question has gone through since the 1970s; the argument focuses on the Western Hemisphere, and particularly on Latin America, in order to introduce the analytical debate to the region this work is concerned with. A final section frames the overall discussion in terms of anarchy versus hierarchy, contending that the underlying theme in the various stages of the debate is the type of order that exists in international politics.

Chapter 2 develops the nature of hierarchical regional orders, focusing on the Western Hemisphere. It elaborates on the significance of regions in world politics, and then focuses on the workings of hierarchical relations in the Americas, considering the cases of Canada and Latin America separately. Chapter 3 offers an examination of the concept of power, as it underlies the idea of hegemony and is pervasive both in the specialized field of International Relations (IR), and in Political Science in general. It reviews different understandings of power used in the discipline, and advocates the adoption of a social relational one. The chapter discusses the notion of power as an attribute, then takes on the understanding of power as a relation, in both its "thin" and "thick" variants, and deals with the operationalization issues that come about when doing power-centered empirical analysis.

Chapter 4 concludes the analytical section of the book. It is about thick economic statecraft and the political economy of US power. It connects the previous discussion on the concept of power to its actual exercise in the economic realm; the purpose here is to display a sphere where diverse theoretical understandings of power can partially converge, and thus have a more focused discussion on the matter of how US power has waxed and waned during the last five decades in the Western Hemisphere. The chapter starts by focusing on economic statecraft as an academic field—making the case for what I call "thick" economic statecraft—and then reviews the political and power dimensions of US economic statecraft. It subsequently deals with the practice of US economic statecraft in general, and tracks the evolution of US trade policy since the 1970s—it is here where matters of domestic politics come in. The chapter closes by discussing the operationalization of the concept of power in the economic domain, as understood by a thick economic statecraft approach.

Chapter 5, the first of the four empirical chapters, is also the first of the two devoted to the North American region; the rationale for having two chapters on the immediate vicinity of the United States is that Canada and México have the most intense relationship with it and, therefore, figure more prominently in its economic statecraft—arguably even receiving differentiated treatment. The chapter reviews some aspects of United States' economic statecraft toward Canada since the early 1970s; it is divided into the three sub-periods noted before (1971–1989, 1990–2000, 2001–2016), and covers both tranquil economic relations as well as the more contentious moments in the Canada–United States political economy. Amid the instances reviewed here are Washington's reaction to Ottawa's nationalist economic policies in the 1970s, the negotiation of the bilateral free trade agreement in the 1980s, the normalcy of economic relations in the 1990s, and the more confrontational cases of softwood lumber and the Keystone pipeline.

Chapter 6 considers United States' economic statecraft toward México in an analogous fashion. The chapter is likewise divided into the three noted sub-periods, covering both regular and critical economic interactions. Among the cases reviewed are Washington's reaction to México's first attempt at GATT membership in the late 1970s, the negotiations leading to the North American

Free Trade Agreement (NAFTA) in the early 1990s, and the discussions regarding cross-border trucking access in the first decade and a half of this century.

Chapter 7 deals with United States' statecraft toward Central America; the Colossus of the North has established a sort of patron–client relationship with the countries of the region, which has largely been treated by it as a unit.[3] Like the previous chapters, it is divided into three sections, each corresponding to one of the established sub-periods. Among other subjects, the chapter reviews Washington's policy of economic coercion toward Sandinista Nicaragua, the creation of the one-way free trade program known as Caribbean Basin Initiative (CBI), the subdued foreign economic policy toward the region in the 1990s, and the negotiations leading to the Dominican Republic–Central America Free Trade Agreement (DR–CAFTA).

Chapter 8, in turn, covers United States' statecraft toward South America. Historically not at the center of Washington's priorities, the region has nevertheless fallen within Washington's premise of hemispheric hegemony. This chapter is also partitioned into three sections, each corresponding to one of the above-mentioned sub-periods. The chapter deals with US foreign economic policy toward Chile during the administration of Salvador Allende; Washington's response to the debt crisis of the 1980s, particularly its reaction to the challenge on the matter presented by Peruvian president Alan García; the passage of the Andean Trade Promotion Act (ATPA), also a one-way free trade program; the establishment of the free trade agreement with Chile; the response to the Argentinian crisis of the early 2000s, and the relationship with Brazil in the context of the negotiation of the Free Trade Area of the Americas (FTAA).

Although the empirical chapters focus on the exercise of US economic statecraft toward the countries of the Americas, the analytical narratives presented in them also point to a wider context and claims in which the economic relationship was embedded; the reason for this is to make the broader, relational and social components that allow economic statecraft to be an arena of power relations explicit. In the concluding chapter, I revisit the exercise of US power through its foreign economic policy in the different countries and regions covered in the analytical narratives in each of the three sub-periods; I go back to the discussion on the nature of power, regional orders and economic statecraft, and, finally, I ponder on the prospects of US hegemony since Donald Trump's arrival into the White House.

As with all academic work, the crafting of this book was a collective enterprise—even if it is signed by one author, who is responsible for all the errors and omissions contained herein. I would thus like to acknowledge the support of different kinds I received from colleagues, family and friends. Since each of them knows what kind of assistance they provided and how grateful I am for their help, I will just list them here in alphabetical order: Antonio Ortiz-Mena,

Arturo Sotomayor, Athanasios Hristoulas, Brigit Baur, Carlos Pérez Ricart, Charlie Baker, Christian Cabrera (special mention for excellent research assistance!), Clare Seelke, Craig Deare, Dagoberto Amparo, Diego Santa Cruz, Fernando Osuna, Gonzalo Paz, Gustavo Vega, Hannah Santa Cruz, Héctor Raúl Solís, Jeff Hornbeck, John Feeley, Jon Luckhurst, Karla Planter, Kevin Delgadillo, Marcela López Vallejo, Melba Falck, Miguel Híjar, Miguel Sigala, Natalja Mortensen, Roberto Hernández, Santiago Aceves, Stella Villagrán, Thiago Rodriguez, and Tom Legler; I would also like to thank Routledge's anonymous reviewers of both the project proposal and the final manuscript. Someone who doesn't know about the assistance he provided for this work—because we have never met or communicated—is David A. Baldwin, so I want to thank him explicitly for the enormous intellectual support the lucidity and sharpness of his works meant. At the institutional level, I would like to acknowledge the University of Guadalajara for the working environment which has made the making of this work possible. This book is dedicated to Brigit, Hannah and Diego, whose presence makes the ebb and flow of life so enjoyable.

Notes

1 Eckstein 1975; Lijphart 1975; George, 1979; Gerring, 2007.
2 Lijphart 1971; Ragin 1987; Collier 1993; Kohli et al. 1995; Peters 1998.
3 "Colossus of the North" is not a contemptuous or derogatory term synonymous with "imperialist power," as it is often assumed in Latin America; Thomas Jefferson used it to refer to his country. See Van Tassell 1997: 243. Note that Jefferson used the term well before the United States was a country of "immense size or power" (Merriam-Webster) in the Western Hemisphere.

References

Collier, D. (1993). The comparative method. In A. W. Finiter (Ed.), *Political science: The state of the discipline II* (pp. 105–119). Washington, DC: APSA.

Eckstein, H. (1975). Case study and theory in political science. In F. I. Greenstein & N. W. Poslby (Eds.), *Handbook of political science* (pp. 79–137). Reading, MA: Addison-Wesley.

George, A. L. (1979). Case studies and theory development: The method of structured, focused, comparison. In P. Gordon (Ed.), *Diplomacy: New approaches in history, theory and policy* (pp. 43–68). New York: Free Press.

Gerring, J. (2007). *Case study research: Principles and practices.* Cambridge: Cambridge University Press.

Kohli, A., Evans, P., Katzenstein, P. J., Przeworski, A., Rudolph, S. H., Scott, J. C., & Skocpol, T. (1995). The role of theory in comparative politics: A symposium. *World Politics, 48*(1), 1–49.

Lijphart, A. (1971). Comparative politics and the comparative method. *American Political Science Review, 65*(3), 682–693.

Lijphart, A. (1975). The comparable-cases strategy in comparative research. *Comparative Political Studies, 8*(2), 158–175.

Peters, G. (1998). *Comparative politics: Theory and methods*. New York: New York University Press.

Ragin, C. C. (1987). *The comparative method*. Berkeley, CA: University of California Press.

Van Tassell, D. (1997). Operational code evolution: How Central America came to be our "Backyard" in US culture. In V. M. Hudson (Ed.), *Culture & Foreign Policy* (pp. 231–261). Boulder, CO: Lynne Riener.

Chapter 1

Five Decades and Still Going
The Debate on the Decline of US Hegemony

Politics is politics is politics—be it domestic or international. The alleged demarcation principle of the latter—anarchy—is not, in fact, its most significant feature. Instead, hierarchy figures prominently in both the domestic and international realms;[1] it is, as it were, the "General Theory" (*per* Keynes) of politics, with anarchy being a special case. Hierarchical orders can of course take many forms, and their metrics vary, but all of them imply stratification as the milieu in which power relations take place. Thus, in an analogous fashion to the post-war II dominant party systems that emerged in countries such as Italy, Japan and Sweden, where one political faction became hegemonic, the post-war international system exhibited a particular feature: United States' hegemony.[2] After all, as Helen Milner noted right when the Cold War had finished and the "unipolar moment" emerged: "The essence of international politics is identical with its domestic counterpart."[3]

If the two compartmentalized realms of politics are, at bottom, so similar, it should come as no surprise that the intellectual puzzles they generate are also alike; one of them has to do with the sustainability and eventual decline of an established (hierarchical) order. Thus, just as in dominant party systems, in the post-war international system the question of the durability of the political faction in power became an issue from the get-go. Not long after Washington's hegemony had been established as a social fact, debate started about its eventual demise; over time, the topic would become a veritable cottage industry in the International Relations (IR) literature. This chapter presents a brief overview of the wax and wane of the debate on US hegemonic decline, and argues that part of the reason for its recursiveness has to do with the different referents and standards used in the discussion; this account serves to lay the way for delineating the framework I will be using in this work, as well as to focus the debate on the concepts that will be discussed and made operational in the empirical section of the book.

This chapter is divided into six further sections: the first one sketches the debate on the decline of the United States as a world hegemonic power; the second takes a step back and looks at the initial conditions around which the debate revolved. The third section considers the means through which

Washington achieved hegemonic status in the aftermath of World War II, and was able to sustain it during the Cold War, according to different approaches. This account in turn serves to re-examine, in the fourth section, the phases the debate in question has gone through since it became salient, in the 1970s; here the discussion focuses on the Western Hemisphere, and particularly on Latin America, in order to introduce the theoretical debate to the region this work is concerned with. Section five frames the discussion in terms of anarchy versus hierarchy, as it argues that the underlying theme in the various stages of the debate is the type of order that exists in international politics. In the last section I briefly recap the discussion presented.

1) The United States as Hegemon

With little hyperbole, it could be said that the decline of US hegemony in world politics has been a matter for consideration from the moment it was established. The 1949 Soviet nuclear test made analysts—as well as Washington's leadership—ponder the endurance of the still novel US privileged position in world politics. After all, as Stephen Walt has noted, "When a state stands alone at the pinnacle of power (...) there is nowhere to go but down."[4] On a rather intermittent fashion, the issue never left the public and scholarly debate, with developments such as Soviet ventures beyond Eurasia in the 1960s, or United States economic (e.g., trade deficit, end of Gold Standard) and military troubles (Vietnam) the following decade infusing it with renewed relevance. But the topic became established in the IR literature in the late 1970s and early 1980s. Since that time, as Adam Quinn has written, debate about US decline "has been through enough iterations for articles noting that the debate is cyclical to be themselves a feature of the cycle."[5]

For all the valuable insights that greatly influential works such as Richard Rosecrance's edited volume *America as an Ordinary Country* (1976), Robert Cox's "Social Forces, States and World Orders" (1981), Robert Gilpin's *War and Change in World Politics* (1981), Robert Keohane's *After Hegemony* (1984), and Paul Kennedy's *Rise and Fall of the Great Powers* (1988), contributed to the debate, more often than not their authors were talking past each other. This was of course something to be expected, as the "debate" was in part something of a misnomer—as many of its contributors were not really speaking to each other—reminiscent of the "first" Idealism–Realism debate in the discipline.[6] That is, the writers were not necessarily addressing the exact same questions; for instance, while Keohane was concerned with the resilience of international regimes after the eventual demise of US hegemony, Kennedy centered on imperial overstretch over a 500-year-long historical period. Furthermore, although the position that during the first decade or two of the academic discussion seemed to prevail was the obsolescence of US hegemony, the verdict was reached, as Ian Clark has observed "on a number of quite disparate grounds."[7]

These discrepancies have to do in part with the indicators used to estimate the hegemony Washington has exercised at different times since the end of World War II. Thus, for instance, whereas for some it was material resources that mattered, for others it was structural power or leadership.[8] The differences of opinion also had to do with the degree or quantity of attributes the United States had to evince in order to qualify as hegemonic. However, the dissonant character of the exchange that has been taking place in the academic literature for six decades now has a more fundamental reason: there are multiple understandings of hegemony itself.[9] Looking first at the way the different perspectives claim Washington achieved hegemonic status might shed some light in this regard.

2) Initial Conditions around which the Debate Revolved

The question is then: what made it possible for Washington to become an hegemonic power in the aftermath of World War II? For some, the answer lies in the accumulation of material resources, particularly economic ones. Thus, for instance, William Zartman states that "The United States arrived at a hegemonic position through the exercise of its enormous economic power."[10] Similarly, for Guy Poitras, US hegemony was "derived from economic and military resources,"[11] whereas for Quinn overall US power is explained by its "possession of a preponderance of material resources."[12] For others, the conditions of possibility are more diffuse. Susan Strange, for example, argued that US hegemony had to do with its "structural power," that is, "the power to choose and to shape the structures of the global political economy within which others states, their political institutions, their economic enterprises, and (no least) their professional people have to operate."[13]

From a more sociological perspective, Clark has argued that the emergence of US hegemony can be explained by the special recognition conferred on Washington by its allies. As he puts it,

> It was not the cumulative institutions of the second half of the 1940s that created an inadvertent US hegemony: rather those secondary institutions became possible because a group of states had already opted to accept a hegemonic principle for their sphere of international society … on the hegemon, there was conferred a certain status with various rights.[14]

These rights were of course not given *carte blanch* to the United States; Washington had varying degrees of leeway depending on the issue area, and it was not always able to elicit support from its allies and followers on a series of policy matters that were important to it.[15] Similarly, drawing on Antonio Gramsci, for Cox, hegemony was related to material capabilities (suggested sometimes to be coterminous with power), institutions and ideas; he maintained that American hegemony "commanded a wide measure of consent."[16] Furthermore, to some extent anticipating Clark's argument, Cox noted "a close connection between institutionalism and what Gramsci called hegemony," observing that, in an institutionalized milieu, "the weak accept the prevailing power relations as legitimate," while the leading powers "make concessions that will secure the weak's acquiescence."[17] Along the same lines, authors such as Robert Keohane and Christian Reus-Smit have stressed the rule-making function Washington was able to assume in the post-war period.[18]

It should thus be clear that while some have equated US hegemony with primacy, others have made it synonymous with leadership or rule-setting. However, I would argue that there has been in fact some unacknowledged commonality—a sort of intervening variable, that is, a "variable that explains a relation or provides a causal link between other variables"[19]—at play in the different accounts of the ups and downs of US hegemony: legitimacy. While this factor is evident in the more sociological accounts, it is rather hidden in the materially laden perspectives. The argument is not that legitimacy "causes" the possession of resources, but that the latter cannot be successfully put to use without the former; that is, material primacy is a poor representation of (social) power. Authors who emphasize material resources know that even if they exist "out there," their instantiation as power does not: it is something that is created by social interaction. That is, such authors know that political processes mediate between initial conditions and outcomes; they would probably argue that their simplified model provides "a quick sketch, a representation that is easy to compute, convenient, and just accurate enough to be used in guiding behavior."[20] The problem is that assets per se (be they economic or military) are not a very useful proxy of power. Let's briefly consider how the different accounts have dealt with this issue when analyzing the different phases of US hegemony.

3) US Hegemony: Phases

There has been widespread agreement that the United States emerged from World War II as a hegemonic power, and that this situation lasted for about 25 years.[21] During this period Washington was instrumental, both in setting the fundamental institutions of the post-war order (United Nations, NATO, World Bank, International Monetary Fund, to name only a few) as well as in leading them; furthermore, it accounted for an unequaled amount of material resources, and a widespread network of alliances. The United States' cherished economic doctrine was extrapolated onto one of the two blocs that coalesced during the Cold War, in what became known as "embedded liberalism"—that is, Keynesianism at home and free trade abroad.[22] All accounts in the hegemonic decline literature agree, albeit to different extents, that during this period Washington enjoyed both material superiority and rule-making leadership in a wide array of issue areas (security, finance, trade, diplomacy). Significantly, though, it was not only a matter of superiority. As John Gerard Ruggie put it in his analysis of the emergence of multilateralism after World War II, what mattered "was less the fact of American *hegemony* [...] than it was the fact of *American* hegemony."[23]

The turning point, according to many analysts, came in the early 1970s. The successful economic reconstruction of its allies, particularly of Germany and Japan, the increasing competition the USSR and its bloc represented, along with the current account problems the United States faced, led many to conclude that Washington's hegemony had come to an end about two and a half decades after the end of World War II.[24] As suggested, Kennedy had pointed to imperial overstretch (i.e., that empires acquire military obligations that turn out to be unsustainable burdens in the long run). Similarly, in the 1980s, Gilpin wrote of "the fading hegemony of the United States," noting that the country had become a "'predatory hegemon,'"[25] while Cox observed that the economic crisis of the 1970s suggested "the disintegration of hegemony in world order" analogous to the "long period of decomposition of the liberal world order in the late nineteenth century".[26] According to Cox, such decomposition was a reflection of the deteriorating "material foundation" of the leading country; for him—following Gramsci—"power based on dominance over production is *rationalized* through an ideology incorporating compromise or consensus between dominant and subordinate groups."[27] For Lawrence Whitehead, the reasons behind the demise of US hegemony were also fundamentally material; for him, it was, indeed, "hardly possible to reverse the (...) long-term decline in the United States' relative strength."[28] On this perspective, the decreased share of American resources (somehow) had brought with it a comparable decrease in its ability to exercise political leadership. The thesis on the expiration of US hegemony during the 1970s became prevalent.[29]

There were, of course, dissenters. In 1986, a year after Keohane's volume on a post-hegemonic world appeared, Bruce Russett argued that in the debate over US hegemonic decline, "The puzzle stems from trying to explain a phenomenon that has not really occurred."[30] Similarly, a couple of years later Susan Strange took issue with the declinist position. Based on a conception of what she called "structural power," she argued that US hegemonic decline was a "myth."[31] For her, the United States in the 1970s was still prevalent in the four components of structural power: "the security structure, the production structure, the credit (or financial) structure, and the knowledge structure."[32] Also on the anti–declinist front, Samuel Huntington argued that since the U.S. was still among the top in "almost all sources of national power," it was able to confront setbacks in one by drawing on the others; for him, more than being threatened by decline, Washington faced the challenging prospect of "renewal."[33] Still, by the end of the 1980s the decline perspective was still on the winning side— thanks in part to the appearance in 1988 of Kennedy's above-mentioned book (a similar thesis, using the analogy of British decline, but from a world system perspective, appeared at around the same time in Boswell and Bergesen 1987).[34]

As Strange noted: "it looks as though the "school of decline" as it has been called has thus far got the best of the intellectual joust."[35]

But things started to change in the 1990s. By that time, not only had substantive decline (in real or absolute terms) of the United States failed to materialize, but the collapse of the Soviet Bloc, and with it the end of the Cold War, brought with it a diametrically opposed political and academic discourse.[36] Thus, in January 1991, president Bush delivered an address to Congress in which he spoke of his country leading the world in the creation of a "new world order."[37] In a more scholastic tone, inspired by Hegel's philosophy, Francis Fukuyama (1990) claimed that since market capitalism and liberal democracy faced no credible alternative, history had virtually come to an end. Around the same time, Charles Krauthammer proclaimed the upshot of the recently acquired US global primacy: "Now is the unipolar moment."[38] Joseph Nye, for his part, forcefully argued against what had been the prevailing position just a few years before, claiming instead that the United States was, as the title of his 1991 book put it, *Bound to Lead.*

And so it seemed: the outcome achieved by the widespread international coalition put together by the Bush administration to fight Sadam Hussein's forces in Kuwait in 1990–1991 signaled an important victory for his country in the political and military fronts, just as the widespread diffusion of the so-called Washington Consensus would in the economic one a few years later.[39] It was therefore not all that surprising when the French Minister of Foreign Affairs, Hubert Védrine, came up with the term "hyperpower" to describe the situation the United States found itself in the new world order ("a country that is dominant or predominant in all categories").[40] Paramount among the reasons cited for Washington's alleged re-claimed position was its material primacy. As William Wohlforth put it at the century's close: "the system is unambiguously unipolar"; furthermore, for him, the disparity in material capabilities between the United States and other states was so large that the new international order was "not only peaceful but durable."[41] But there was also ample recognition that the institutional architecture of the post-Cold War order had Washington's imprint.[42] Thus, as Michael Cox put it 2002, "there is no practical or theoretical reason why the 21st century should not be just as American as the 20th."[43] At the dawn of the third millennium, the anti-declinists of yesteryear seemed vindicated.

But the pendulum would swing fast. The economic emergence of the so-called BRICs (Brazil, Russia, India and China; South Africa would be added a few years later) in general, and of China in particular, plus the unilateralist instincts of the George W. Bush administration, specifically its military adventure in Iraq in the early 00s, led once again to the widespread questioning of Washington's hegemony—both on material and political grounds.[44] The United States was squandering its legitimacy. This would lead to what Christian Reus-Smit called "a central paradox of our time": the fact that the unipolar power could not obtain the influence it desired.[45]

The 2007 US-initiated global financial crisis would only compound Washington's leadership troubles. For Jonathan Kirshner, the financial crisis had "brought about an end to what I call the "second US post-war order" (which I define as the period of US hegemony *after* the Cold War and associated with its project of domestic and international financial deregulation), due to a collapse of its international legitimacy."[46] As Henry Paulson—US Treasury Secretary at the time of the financial crisis—would later recount, in 2008 Chinese vice minister Wang Qishan had this to tell him about US leadership in economic affairs: "You were my teacher [...] look at your system, Hank. We aren't sure we should be learning from you anymore."[47] Hence, perceiving that "On every dimension other than military power—industrial, financial, social, cultural—the distribution of power [was] shifting, moving away from U.S. dominance" Fareed Zakaria concluded that the international order was mutating into a "post-American world."[48]

The momentum seemed to have shifted back to the declinist camp. David Calleo, a seasoned participant in the debate, noted in 2010: "Taking a long view, stretching back to the Second World War, it seems indisputable that America's relative economic position has declined. An obvious indicator is its diminishing share of the world's gross output."[49] Quinn likewise has noted that "US primacy shows all the signs of being unsustainable,"[50] and Christopher Layne, who only a few years before considered the possibility that unipolarity could last still one or two more decades, wrote in 2012: "the 'unipolar moment' is over, and the Pax Americana—the era of American ascendancy in international politics that began in 1945—is fast winding down";[51] thus, for him, "The debate about unipolarity is over."[52] So, four decades after the academic debate on US hegemonic decline became salient, it came full circle.

4) US Hegemony in the Western Hemisphere: A Teaser

When the wider debate on the decline of US hegemony started in the 1970s, the perceived new state of affairs did not go unnoticed in the Western Hemisphere. As Alfred Stepan put it in the late 1970s: with "the diminishing international financial, technological and military power of the United States, the relationship between the United States and Latin America has changed profoundly."[53] Similarly, north of the US border, David Dewitt and John Kirton argued that Canada could become a "principal" player in international relations "as the pre-eminent America that catalyzed its [the post-war order's] creation and enforced its effectiveness has experienced a massive decline."[54] The debate about US hegemonic decay regarding the Western Hemisphere, and particularly concerning Latin America, followed a dynamic that to some extent paralleled the overall argument—but not at every turn. There are historical reasons for this. Ever since the early 19th century, with the proclamation of the Monroe Doctrine, the region has been widely considered as Washington's area of influence *par excellence*. For James Kurth, it constitutes "almost an ideal type" of an hegemonic system.[55] Similarly, in the late 1980s Strange considered Latin America "the most solid part of the American empire."[56]

Interestingly, scholarly emphasis on the importance of US material superiority as the basis of its hegemony was more pronounced when it came to Latin America than in other areas of the world. As Jan Triska put it in a work comparing the US and Soviet spheres of influence:

> The unequal relationships within the two regions are perceived differently: Latin Americans claim mainly economic exploitation (in terms of national resources, short-term investments, cheap labor, large US assets in Latin America), while Soviet exploitation of Eastern Europe is principally political and security-oriented.[57]

Thus, influenced more by the Marxist than the Realist IR tradition, from early on the more influential analyses of the area stressed Washington's exploitation of its southern neighbors, focusing on what in this perspective were simply objective conditions;[58] this was clear, for instance, in the Dependency school—the most prominent approach in IR theory to emerge from the region.[59] This is not to suggest that all or most Latin American observers, or Latin Americanists from other latitudes, were of a Marxist inclination; interestingly, however, the stress on the economic component was a constant in the specialized literature. As Alan Knight would later put it: "to the central question—'what is the basis of U.S. imperialism hegemony in Latin America?'—the principal answer must be the old and familiar one: 'It's the economy, stupid.'"[60] Likewise, in Canada, an important strand of the literature on the country's relations with the United States has emphasized its vertical component, particularly in a division of labor between the two countries in which Canada is, of course, the subordinate.[61]

In any case, by the early 1980s, the decline of US hegemony in the region was widely accepted.[62] Observers who had a wider understanding of hegemony included more caveats in their analysis, but most of them concurred that Washington had been losing its traditional role in the region since the early 1970s.[63] Only a few scholars took a contrary position. One of them was Peter Smith, who considered that the "notion of declining hegemony rests on dubious assumptions," and argued instead that "U.S. hegemony [had] climbed to an all-time high" starting in the mid-1980s.[64] For him, however, this was not due to changes in US capabilities or behavior—it was simply an instance of "hegemony by default," explained "because outside powers withdrew from the Americas and directed their attention elsewhere."[65] Once again, Washington's ascendance in the region was in the final analysis understood in terms of the *distribution* of capabilities (or of attention *led* by capabilities).

Whether or not it was a change in attention, capabilities, or both, the fact is that the Western Hemisphere's milieu changed in the 1990s—as did the academic discussion on the matter of US hegemony in the region during those years. Thus, for instance, David Lake remarked on the increased degree of US hegemony in the area at the time.[66] A large part of the explanation had to do, as in the wider debate, with the end of the Cold War, as noted in Smith's argument. But, interestingly, the focus this time was again placed on economic matters—even if not in the customary, material exploitation (e.g., via extractive industries) form. This time around, the focus was much more on the realm of economic ideas: the already alluded to Washington Consensus—a new understanding regarding economic policies, such as balanced budgets, deregulation, privatization, and trade liberalization (more on this in Chapter 4); all these items became buzzwords among academics, politicians and policymakers in the region during the 1990s. It is worth noting that what became, as suggested, a global economic doctrine, saw its beginnings in the Western Hemisphere.[67] Part of the change in the hemispheric milieu involved the northernmost country, Canada. In 1988, Ottawa entered into a trade deal, the Canada–United States Free Trade Agreement, with Washington (more on this in Chapter 5). Furthermore, two years later, in 1990, Canada became a member of the Organization of American States.

Around the time when talk about the BRICs started, which for some suggested once again the decline of US hegemony, or at least the arrival of a multipolar world, Latin America's relations with Washington were starting to change.[68] At the dawn of the new century, a series of electoral victories of left-leaning candidates in the region prompted political commentators to notice that a "resurgent left" was replacing the Washington Consensus of the previous decade. The political turn in several countries of the region—the "pink wave"—was accompanied by efforts to promote Latin America-only integration. Thus, in the late 00s, a corpus of literature on "post-hegemonic" (or "post-liberal") regionalism—claiming the "partial displacement of dominant forms of US-led neoliberal governance"—emerged.[69]

Nevertheless, contrary to both wider political developments and the state of the debate on the global decline of US hegemony, what appears to be the end of the left turn in Latin America in the second decade of the 21st century has made the academic consensus move away—once again—from what only a few years ago was the prevalent position: that Washington was no longer the region's hegemon. As Juan Gabriel Tokatlian has noted, "the United States never 'left' the region"—it is, like in Aníbal Troilo's tango, "always arriving".[70] In Canada, on the other hand, Chrétien's government grew distant from Washington, particularly over the issue of president Bush's military intervention Iraq. However, still with Bush in the White House, under the leadership of Stephen Harper, relations between Canada and the United States warmed up substantially—suggesting that Washington was also always arriving north of its border. As Ottawa's representative to the OAS, Paul D. Durand, acknowledged in 2002, "we look for leadership" from Washington on international trade matters.[71]

5) Anarchy vs. Hierarchy

IR's fixation with anarchy as the defining concept of the discipline started only a few years after the US-decline debate emerged. This is intriguing because arguing over a hegemonic actor—whether it is in decline or not, and regardless of the basis of its hegemony—went against the grain of what had become orthodoxy in the field. Indeed, the dominant literature in IR takes anarchy as the ordering principle in world affairs.[72] As Kenneth Waltz argued in his 1979 classic, *Theory of International Politics* (one of the influential works in the IR literature), it is from this basic feature of the international system that the self-help behavior of its units derives.[73] Anarchy thus serves to demarcate what goes on in the international realm from what transpires inside its constituent entities. Significantly, the literature on hegemony, by presenting hierarchy as a feature of the international system, departs in this regard from mainstream IR theory—but this genre did not become ... hegemonic in the discipline. Anyhow, the centrality of anarchy in the discipline is rather recent, dating from the 1980s.[74]

Leaving aside the wider theoretical consequences of the equivocal meaning of anarchy in the literature (sometimes it is taken to mean some sort of state of nature and sometimes simply a lack of international government), what matters for my discussion here are a couple of assumptions that are made when taking anarchy as the fundamental concept in the discipline: 1) that it is the polar opposite of hierarchy, and 2) that it is the defining characteristic of the relationship between states. These suppositions are important because they impinge on the understanding of the exercise of hegemony in international affairs—be it at the global or regional level.

Regarding the first assumption: as Jack Donnelly makes clear, anarchy is not the opposite of hierarchy; it is "archy" that stands in the antipodes of anarchy (with hegemony as a point in the anarchy–empire continuum).[75] Hierarchy does not mean total control of one actor over other. As Lake puts it,

> Hierarchy exists when one actor possesses authority over a second. Authority is never total, of course, but varies in extent. A may possess authority over B and issue commands, regulating possible actions 1–5 but not on actions 6–n, which remain 'private' to B or beyond A's ability to expect compliance.[76]

It follows that, theoretically, the dichotomy between international and domestic politics, or between the anarchy of the conventional literature and the hierarchy of the literature on hegemony, is one of degree, not a clear-cut one.

Regarding the second assumption, that anarchy is the defining characteristic of the relationship between states, the historical record shows that anarchy has not been the rule, even in the modern state system.[77] To name just one case that is germane to this work: thanks to the already mentioned Monroe Doctrine, by the early 20th century the Western Hemisphere was widely recognized as the "sphere of influence" of the United States. Thus, for instance, at Versailles, the European powers sanctioned Washington's manifesto.[78] This recognition of course implied that the United States was in a position of authority and therefore enjoyed certain rights in the Americas. Over a longer historical period, as Donnelly documents, hierarchy and not anarchy has been the rule in international systems.[79] Hence the analogy at the beginning of the chapter between hierarchy and an underperforming economic system: both would be the normal state of affairs, the former in politics (domestic or international), and the latter in market economies.

Furthermore, from an analytical stand, as John Hobson has argued, the theoretical edifice of IR rests on a "hierarchical conception" (implicit, for instance, in the Eurocentric standard of civilization) that renders the "sovereign equality" purportedly produced by international anarchy problematic.[80] At the same time, however, the undeniable fact that "some states are more equal than others" has been explicitly recognized in the discipline. Thus, no other than Waltz wrote that states "of greatest capability take on special responsibilities"—pointing not only to some kind of functional differentiation among the units of the international system, but also to some sort of hierarchy in the international realm; for him, "the inequality of nations is still the dominant *political* fact of international life."[81] Interestingly, however, this authoritative component of world politics plays no role in his theoretical apparatus.

Gilpin also openly acknowledges that all actors are not the same in the international system, and that this has effects for the nature of the latter; thus, he writes: "the character of the international system is largely determined by the type of state-actor."[82] For my purposes, the relevant difference between the two accounts is that Gilpin incorporates the hierarchical nature of the international system. But the sense of uneasiness with the paramount role assigned to anarchy in the discipline is of course not confined to (neo) realist authors such as the ones just mentioned; liberals like Milner, already quoted in this regard, or Lake; constructivists like Reus-Smit or Alexander Wendt; and critical theorists like Richard Ashley and Robert Walker, have for a long time questioned the centrality of the concept in the discipline.[83]

Thus, if anarchy—even in its minimalist meaning of the lack of government—is not the opposite of hierarchy, and the latter is both common historically and an acknowledged feature of the international system theoretically, it follows that hegemonic systems, as suggested before, might be more frequent than generally accepted. The significance of this rests not so much on the brute fact of the unequal attributes of the units that make up the system as on authoritative relationships that are established amongst them. It is important to highlight that the distribution of capabilities per se, à-la Waltz, does not produce politically stratified relations—that is, domination, a kind of power imbued with authority.[84]

This is important because a political order—be it domestic or international—that lacks legitimacy cannot endure.[85] And legitimacy is not an inherent attribute of actors, but rather a quality conferred by others, *de jure* and/or *de facto*;[86] that is, legitimacy is a social fact (more on this in the next chapter). Having to do with norms and mores, social facts are not categorical. Hence the utility of thinking of the notion of legitimacy, as Rapkin and Braaten suggest, in terms of "family resemblance concepts" (FRC). As they point out, FRC are "multidimensional," encompassing several meanings (e.g., values, procedures and outcomes), and "multilevel," involving various indicators.[87] This approach goes beyond the traditional focus on substantive and procedural sources of legitimacy, and considers performance (outcome) as a secondary source of legitimacy; thus, for the IR literature on hegemony, the provision of public goods would be a source of outcome legitimacy.[88] The important point for the argument here is that by considering legitimacy—or authority, or power—as an FRC (instead of an ideal type), we can more easily think of it as a gradation, and therefore find more instances of it in the "real world."[89] As Michael Zürn, Martin Binder and Matthias Ecker-Ehrhardt have noted, "authority may be legitimate to varying degrees."[90]

It follows that the influence an actor has over others does not depend solely on the material capabilities at her command, but also on the extent to which other relevant actors accept her.[91] As Rousseau commented on the supposed "right of the strongest": "Force is a physical power, and I fail to see what moral effect it can have. To yield to force is an act of necessity, not of will—at the most, an act of prudence. In what sense can it be duty?"[92] And, of course, for there is an ontological gap between an agent's will or sense of duty and the brute fact of physical control; the former is embedded in authoritative relationships produced and reproduced through social norms and institutions, the latter is alien to it.[93] Hence, in contrast to the *modus operandi* of a political regime (or state system) that rested exclusively on material capabilities, to wit, coercion or force, the *modus operandi* of domination is legitimacy and persuasion.

Similarly, a resource-based understanding of hegemony does not produce politically stratified relations. In the conventional literature on the matter, the starting point is a materialist conception of ascendancy, usually economic or military capabilities.[94] An inference is then usually made: there is a connection between this brute fact and two social ones: responsibility and influence. But again, the latter are of a different nature. That is why the *with great power comes great responsibility* motto—so dear to different strands of theories of international politics, such as Hegemonic Stability Theory (HST) and its liberal version—is problematic.

In the hegemony literature, great (material) power *cum* responsibility is supposed to be actualized through the provision of public goods. Thus, whereas in HST the relevant public good might be the provision of international security through military alliances, in a liberal perspective, it could be the establishment of international economic institutions.[95] These rationalist perspectives generally conceive of the hegemon as a benevolent leader who acts on its enlightened self-interest.[96] However, the exercise of leadership, even if it is for the common good, is not frictionless; hegemons must at times resort to coercion to assure that others pay their share in the production of social order.[97]

But coercion should be used sparingly by the hegemon. As mentioned before, legitimacy and not coercion is the *modus operandi* of an authoritative regime, for the frequent use of the latter would reveal the subordinate actors' lack of acceptance of the prevalent social order. Thus, the litmus test of the hegemon's leadership is the socialization of its values and interests; when this happens contestation of the political order is minimized.

It should come as no surprise that norms and institutions play an important role in the international realm, one in which—as we saw—hierarchical relations are more than a mere practical and theoretical possibility. Authors associated with the English School wrote about this long ago. Foreshadowing the constructivist literature, Hedley Bull recognized both the malleability and endurance of the normative element in international relations; for instance, he noted that "States change the rules by demonstrating, through their words or their actions, that they are withdrawing their consent from old rules and bestowing it upon new ones, and thus altering the content of custom or established practice," while acknowledging that "rules are not infinitely malleable.[98] Furthermore, Bull was interested in "international society," which he thought came into existence "when a group of states, conscious of certain common interests and common values, form a society in the sense that they conceive themselves to be bound by a common set of rules in their relations to one another";[99] this normative bond was in turn strengthened by the emergence of five international institutions (international law, the diplomatic system, the balance of power, the notion of "great power," and war).[100] These institutions were no mere historical accident or epiphenomena; they explained the quotidian practices of international society.[101] As suggested by most of the institutional architecture of international politics, relations between states were politically and materially hierarchical.

Thus, hegemony as a hierarchic order might, as suggested before, be thought of as a halfway house between anarchy (in the sense of an absence of rule, not only in the sense of an absence of government), and empire;[102] henceforth, the existence of authoritative relations is a key component of it. That is why in a hegemonic system subordinate states recognize the right of the dominant state to play an exceptional role in it.[103] Among other things, this means that the hegemonic state has special responsibilities; that is, in hegemonic systems, not only the distribution of capabilities is unequal, but so is the distribution of responsibilities—itself a veritable source of power.[104] This is no mere definitional discussion. Hegemony has real effects on the manner international affairs are conducted. It is of course not the same to be part of an empire than to be the purported atomistic state of mainstream theory than to be a constitutive unit of a hegemonic order (be it in as superordinate or subordinate position)—institutional arrangements matter. Furthermore, it should be noted that no single ordering principle exists in hegemonic systems;[105] what obtains is a gradation of authority.

What makes hierarchical systems analytically interesting lies precisely in such gradation, for actors continually renegotiate and move along this continuum. Furthermore, the political (as opposed to material) basis of hegemony means that the bargaining, contestation and trade-offs between the superordinate and subordinate states takes place through (constitutive and regulative) norms and institutions.[106] What this means in investigational practice is that there is no such thing as *an* hegemonic order—and therefore no way in which the decline of a world hegemon would be instantiated uniformly across regions or issue areas. Both relations of authority and their concomitant effects are bound to vary across different instantiations of hegemony. Thus, as Donnelly has suggested, the task ahead is to look into the different kinds of hierarchical systems.[107]

6) Summary

As noted at the start, politics has to do with stratification, and knows no boundaries. Since the 1940s, the United States structured a great part of the international system along hierarchical lines, an order on which it projected the ordering principles of its own political economy. About three decades later, though, among both academics and the wider public (and practitioners), a lively debate initiated on the demise of US hegemony. This debate turned cacophonic at times because the understanding of the bases and meanings of hegemony varied—some accounts gave more importance to material factors and others to normative ones. Although to different degrees, most of them rested, though, in the recognition that Washington enjoyed international legitimacy. But whatever the bases of analyses, three phases can be established in the debate on the wax and wane of US hegemony: 1971–1989, the last two decades of the Cold War; 1990–2000, the interregnum or unipolar moment; 2001–2013, the emergence of the BRICs, but particularly of China.

In the Western Hemisphere, the United States-led order predated the wider one (i.e., the one in the Western bloc) by more than a century, as the global recognition of the 1823 Monroe Doctrine achieved attests. In the particular hierarchical system established in the region, both material and normative factors have figured prominently; as the paradigmatic case of US hegemony, the Americas are thus an interesting case for considering the debate on the decline of US hegemony. In the next chapter, after briefly considering the salience and meaning of regional compacts for international politics, I delve into the workings of hierarchical relations in a particular region—the Western Hemisphere.

Notes

1   Sartori 1987: 131.
2   Pempel 1990.
3   Milner 1991: 79.
4   Walt 2011.

5   Quinn, 2011; 804; see also Calleo 2010: 215, Cox 2007: 644.
6   Long 1995; Wilson 1995.
7   Clark 2011: 129.
8   Cf. Waltz 1979; Strange 1987; Gilpin 1981.
9   Russett 1985: 209–210.
10 Zartman 2009: 5.
11 Poitras 1990: 2.
12 Quinn 2011: 812.
13 Strange 1987: 565.
14 Clark 2011: 143.
15 Ibid.: 237; Ikenberry, Mastaduno and Wohlforth 2011, 71; Walt 2011.
16 Cox 1981: 144.
17 Ibid.: 137.
18 Reus-Smit 2004; Keohane 1984.
19 Danish 2017: 50.
20 Graziano 2013: 28.
21 Calleo 1984: 442; Wallerstein 2007: 51; Clark 2011: 125; Kurth 2010: 61.
22 Kahler 1980: 461; Ruggie 1982; Rodman, 1995: 105.
23 Ruggie 1992: 568.
24 Calleo and Rowland 1973: 3–4; Kahler 1980: 458; Greenberg 1990: 109; Hartlyn,
    Schoultz and Varas 1992: 70.
25 Gilpin 1987: 154, 345 (quoting John Coynbeare).
26 Cox 1987: 270.
27 Ibid.: 394. Cox 1977: 387, italics mine; Cox seems to make legitimacy simply a matter
    rationalization.
28 Whitehead 1986: 99.
29 Cox 2002: 54.
30 Russett, 1985: 230–231.
31 Strange 1987: 551.
32 Ibid.: 571.
33 Huntington 1988.
34 Destler 2005: 48.
35 Strange 1988: 2.
36 Cronin 2001: 104; Cox 2002: 60.
37 Bush 1991.
38 Krauthammer 1990: 24.
39 Ikenberry 2011: 236.
40 International Herald Tribune 1999; see also Boniface 2001: 157.
41 Wohlforth 1999: 7, 8; cf. Layne 2009: 172.
42 Wohlforth 1999: 33; Ikenberry 2011: 238.
43 Cox 2002: 67.
44 Wallerstein 2007: 50.
45 Reus-Smit 2004: 2.
46 Kirshner 2014: 7; italics original. The first US post-war order was the one of embedded
    liberalism mentioned above. Cf. Dabat and Leal 2013: 83; Fernandes 2015: 8.
47 Paulson 2015: 240.
48 Zakaria 2008.
49 Calleo 2010: 216.
50 Quinn, 2011: 807.
51 Layne 2012: 203.
52 Ibid.: 212.
53 Stepan 1979: 659.

54 Dewitt and Kirton 1983: 3.
55 Kurth 2010: 63.
56 Strange 1988: 16.
57 Triska 1986: 9.
58 Wesson 1982: 2.
59 For example Marini 1973; Cardoso 1972; cf. Palma 1978.
60 Knight 2008: 44–45.
61 Smythe 1980: 140-144.
62 Smith 1999: 223; see also Lowenthal 1983: 311; Whitehead 1986: 92–93.
63 Poitras 1990: 179; Gill 1986: 207.
64 Smith 1999: 224.
65 Ibid.: 225.
66 Lake 2009: 48.
67 Williamson 1994: 15, Dominguez 1997: 26–27.
68 O'Keefe 2018: 1
69 Riggirozzi and Tussie 2012: 12. Cf. Legler 2013.
70 Tokatlian 2013.
71 OEA 2002.
72 Mattern and Zarakol 2016: 626.
73 Waltz 1979: 111; Donnelly 2015: 394; Ricks 2014.
74 Donnelly 2015: 393.
75 Donnelly 2006: 162.
76 Lake 2009: 38.
77 Hobson and Sharman 2005: 64; Donnelly 2006: 145; Mattern and Zarakol 2016: 624.
78 González 2010: 234.
79 Donnelly 2015: 408.
80 Hobson 2014: 558.
81 Waltz 1979: 198, 152; italics mine.
82 Gilpin 1981: 26.
83 Mattern and Zarakol 2016: 628-629; Milner 1991; Lake 2009; Reus-Smit 1999; Wendt 1992; Ashley 1988; Walker 1991.
84 Weber 1978: 53, 212–213, 946.
85 Sartori 1987: 144.
86 Friedman 1990: 60–62.
87 Rapkin and Braaten 2009: 115.
88 Ibid.: 124; cf. Zürn et al. 2012: 84–85; cf. Sartori 1987: 144.
89 Rapkin and Braaten 2009: 134.
90 Zürn et al. 2012: 85.
91 Reus-Smit 2004: 4.
92 In Hobson and Sharman 2005: 68.
93 Donnelly 2012: 625.
94 Prys 2010: 487.
95 Gilpin 1981; Ikenberry 2005.
96 Katzenstein, Keohane and Krasner 1998; Kindleberger 1981; Keohane 1984.
97 Lanoszka 2013: 398.
98 Bull 1977: 73; 45.
99 Ibid.: 13.
100 Ibid.: 37, 74.
101 Bull 1966: 48.
102 Lake 2009: 39.
103 Hobson and Sharman 2005: 69.
104 Bukovansky et al. 2012: 9.

105   Hobson and Sharman 2005: 93; Donnelly 2015: 414.
106   Mattern and Zarakol 2016: 637.
107   Donnelly 2015: 419.

References

Ashley, R. (1988). Untying the sovereign state: A double reading of the anarchy problematique. *Millennium*, *17*(2), 227–262.

Boniface, P. (2001). The specter of unilateralism. *Washington Quarterly*, *24*(3), 155–162.

Boswell, T., & Bergesen, A. (1987). *America's changing role in the world-system*. New York: Praeger.

Bukovansky, M., Clark, I., Eckersley, R., Price, R., Reus-Smit, C., & Wheeler, N. (2012). *Special responsibilities: Global powers and American power*. Cambridge: Cambridge University Press.

Bull, H. (1966). Society and anarchy in international relations. In H. Butterfield & M. Wight (Eds.), *Diplomatic investigations: Essays in the theory of international politics*. Cambridge, MA: Harvard University Press.

Bull, H. (1977). *The anarchical society: A study of order in world politics*. London: Macmillan.

Bush, G. H. W. (1991, January 29). *Address before a joint session of the congress on the state of the union*. Online by Gerhard Peters and John T. Woolley, *The American Presidency Project*. Retrieved from http://www.presidency.ucsb.edu/ws/?pid=19253

Calleo, D. P. (1984). Since 1961: American power in a new world economy. In W. H. Becker & S. F. Wells (Eds.), *Economics and world power: An assessment of American diplomacy since 1789* (pp. 391–457). New York: Columbia University Press.

Calleo, D. P. (2010). American decline revisited. *Survival*, *52*(4), 215–227.

Calleo, D. P., & Rowland, B. M. (1973). *America and the world political economy: Atlantic dreams and national realities*. Bloomington, IN: Indiana University Press.

Cardoso, F. H. (1972). Dependency and development in Latin America. *New Left Review*, *74*(74), 83–95.

Clark, I. (2011). *Hegemony in international society*. Oxford: Oxford University Press.

Cox, M. (2002). September 11th and US hegemony—Or will the 21st century be American too? *International Studies Perspectives*, *3*(1), 53–70.

Cox, M. (2007). Is the United States in decline-again? An essay. *International Affairs*, *83*(4), 643–653.

Cox, R. (1977). Labor and hegemony. *International Organization*, *31*(3), 385–424.

Cox, R. (1981). Social forces, states, and world orders: Beyond international relations theory. *Millennium: Journal of International Studies*, *10*(2), 126–155.

Cox, R. (1987). *Production, power, and world order*. New York: Columbia University Press.

Cronin, B. (2001). The paradox of hegemony: America's ambiguous relations with the United Nations. *European Journal of International Relations*, *7*(1), 103–130.

Dabat, A., & Paulo, L. (2013). Declinación de Estados Unidos: Contexto histórico mundial. *Problemas del Desarrollo*, *44*(174), 61–88.

Danish, F. (2017). Classification and tabulation. In *Fundamentals of statistics – A brief insight* (pp. 28–51). Indira Nagar: OnlineGatha – The Endless Tale.

Destler, I. M. (2005). *American trade politics*. Washington, DC: Institute for International Economics.

Dewitt, D., & Kirton, J. (1983). *Canada as a principal power: A study in foreign policy and international relations*. Toronto, ON: John Wiley and Sons.

Dominguez, J. (1997). *Technopols: Ideas and leaders in freeing politics and markets in Latin America in the 1990s*. University Park, PA: Pennsylvania State University Press.

Donnelly, J. (2006). Sovereign inequalities and hierarchy in anarchy: American power and international society. *European Journal of International Relations, 12*(2), 139–170.

Donnelly, J. (2012). The elements of the structures of international systems. *International Organization, 66*(4), 609–643.

Donnelly, J. (2015). The discourse of anarchy in IR. *International Theory, 7*(3), 393–425.

Fernandes, M. P. (2015). Sobre o fim da hegemonia dos Estados Unidos: Uma análise conceitual. *Meridiano, 47,* 16(147), 3–10.

Friedman, R. B. (1990). On the concept of authority in political philosophy. In J. Raz (Ed.), *Authority* (pp. 56–91). New York: New York University Press.

Fukuyama, F. (1990). *The end of history?* Washington, DC: United States Institute of Peace.

Gill, S. (1986). Hegemony, consensus and Trilateralism. *Review of International Studies, 12*(3), 205–221.

Gilpin, R. (1981). *War and change in world politics*. Cambridge: Cambridge University Press.

Gilpin, R. (1987). *The political economy of international relations*. Princeton, NJ: Princeton University Press.

González, G. (2010). Un siglo de política exterior mexicana (1910–2010). Del nacionalismo revolucionario a la intemperie global. In M. A. Casar & G. González (Eds.), *México 2010, el juicio del siglo* (pp. 231–274). México: Taurus.

Graziano, M. (2013). *Consciousness and the Social Brain*. Oxford: Oxford University Press.

Greenberg, E. S. (1990). Reaganism as corporate liberalism: Implications for the American future. *Policy Studies Review, 10*(1), 103–125.

Hartlyn, J., Schoultz, L., & Varas, A. (1992). *The United States and Latin America in the 1990s: Beyond the cold war*. Chapel Hill, NC: University of North Carolina Press.

Hobson, J., & Sharman, J. (2005). The enduring place of hierarchy in world politics: Tracing the social logics of hierarchy and political change. *European Journal of International Relations, 11*(1), 63–98.

Hobson, J. M. (2014). The twin self-delusions of IR: Why hierarchy and not anarchy is the core concept of IR. *Journal of International Studies, 42*(3), 557–575.

Huntington, S. (1988). The U.S.: Decline or renewal? *Foreign Affairs, 67*(2), 76–96.

Ikenberry, G. J. (2005). Power and liberal order: America's postwar world order in transition. *International Relations of the Asia-Pacific, 5*(2), 133–152.

Ikenberry, G. J. (2011). *Liberal leviathan: The origins, crisis, and transformation of the American world order*. Princeton, NJ: Princeton University Press.

Ikenberry, J. G., Mastanduno, M., & Wohlforth, W. C. (2011). *International relations theory and the consequences of unipolarity*. Cambridge: Cambridge University Press.

International Herald Tribune (1999, February 5) To Paris, U.S. looks like a 'Hyperpower'. *New York Times.*

Kahler, M. (1980). America's foreign economic policy: Is the old-time religion good enough? *International Affairs (Royal Institute of International Affairs 1944-), 56*(3), 458–473.

Katzenstein, P. J., Keohane, R. O., & Krasner, S. D. (1998). International organization and the study of world politics. *International Organization, 52*(4), 645–685.

Kennedy, P. (1988). *Rise and fall of the great powers*. Lexington: DC Heath.

Keohane, R. O. (1984). *After hegemony: Cooperation and discord in the world political economy*. Princeton, NJ: Princeton University Press.

Kindleberger, C. P. (1981). Dominance and leadership in the international economy. *International Studies Quarterly, 25*(2), 242–254.

Kirshner, J. (2014). *American power after the financial crisis.* Ithaca, NY: Cornell University Press.

Knight, A. (2008). U.S. imperialism/hegemony and Latin American resistance. In F. Rose (Ed.), *Empire and dissent: The United States and Latin America.* Durham, NC: Duke University Press.

Krauthammer, C. (1990). The unipolar moment. *Foreign Affairs, 70*(1), 23–33.

Kurth, J. (2010). The United States as a civilizational leader. In P. J. Katzenstein (Ed.), *Civilizations in world politics: Plural and pluralist perspectives* (pp. 41–66). New York: Routledge.

Lake, D. (2009). Regional hierarchy: Authority and local international order. *Review of International Studies, 35,* 35–58.

Lanoszka, A. (2013). Beyond the consent and coercion: Using republican political theory to understand international hierarchies. *International Theory, 5*(3), 382–413.

Layne, C. (2009). The waning of U.S. hegemony-myth or reality? *International Security, 34*(1), 147–172.

Layne, C. (2012). This time it's real: The end of unipolarity and the Pax Americana. *International Studies Quarterly, 56*(1), 203–213.

Legler, T. (2013). Post-hegemonic regionalism and sovereignty in Latin America: Optimists, skeptics, and an emerging research agenda. *Contexto Internacional, 35*(2), 325–352.

Long, D. (1995). Conclusion: Inter-war idealism, liberal internationalism, and contemporary international theory. In D. Long & P. Wilson (Eds.), *Thinkers of the twenty years' crisis: Inter-war idealism reassessed* (pp. 302–328). Oxford: Clarendon.

Lowenthal, A. F. (1983). Ronald Reagan and Latin America: Coping with hegemony in decline. In K. Oye, R. J. Lieber, & D. Rothchild (Eds.), *Eagle defiant: United States foreign policy* (pp. 311–336). Boston, MA: Little, Brown and Company.

Marini, R. M. (1973). *Dialéctica de la dependencia.* Ciudad de México: Era.

Mattern, J. B., & Zarakol, A. (2016). Review essay: Hierarchies in world politics. *International Organization, 70*(3), 624–654.

Milner, H. V. (1991). The assumption of anarchy in international relations theory: A critique. *Review of International Studies, 17*(1), 67–85.

Nye, J. S. (1990). *Bound to lead: The changing nature of American power.* New York: Basic Books, Inc.

OEA. (2002). Acta de la cuarta sesión plenaria, Asamblea General, 4 de junio (AG/ACTA 380/02).

O'Keefe, T. A. (2018). *Bush II, Obama, and the decline of U.S. hegemony in the Western Hemisphere.* New York: Routledge.

Palma, G. (1978). Dependency: A formal theory of underdevelopment or a methodology for the analysis of concrete situations of underdevelopment. *World Development, 6*(7–8), 881–924.

Paulson, H. (2015). *Dealing with China: An insider unmasks the new economic superpower.* New York: Twelve.

Pempel, T. J. (1990). *Uncommon democracies: The one-party dominant regimes.* Ithaca, NY: Cornell University Press.

Poitras, G. E. (1990). *The ordeal of hegemony: The United States and Latin America.* Boulder, CO: Westview Press.

Prys, M. (2010). Hegemony, domination, detachment: Differences in regional powerhood. *International Studies Review, 12*(4), 479–504.

Quinn, A. (2011). The art of declining politely: Obama's prudent presidency and the waning of American power. *International Affairs, 87*(4), 803–824.

Rapkin, D., & Braaten, D. (2009). Conceptualising hegemonic legitimacy. *Review of International Studies, 35*(1), 113–149.

Reus-Smit, C. (1999). *The moral purpose of the state: Culture, social identity, and institutional rationality in international relations.* Princeton, NJ: Princeton University Press.

Reus-Smit, C. (2004). *American power and world order.* Cambridge: Polity Press.

Ricks, T. (2014, September 25). Who are the top international-relations specialists? Surprise! Scholars have a very different view than policymakers do. *Foreign Policy.*

Riggirozzi, P., & Tussie, D. (2012). The rise of post-hegemonic regionalism in Latin America. In *The Rise of Post-Hegemonic Regionalism* (pp. 1–16). Dordrecht: Springer.

Rodman, K. A. (1995). Sanctions at bay? Hegemonic decline, multinational corporations, and US economic sanctions since the pipeline case. *International Organization, 49*(1), 105–137.

Rosecrance, R. N. (1976). *America as an ordinary country: U.S. foreign policy and the future.* Ithaca, NY: Cornell University Press.

Ruggie, J. G. (1982). International regimes, transactions, and change: Embedded liberalism in the postwar economic order. *International Organization, 36*(2), 379–415.

Ruggie, J. G. (1992). Multilateralism: The anatomy of an institution. *International Organization, 46*(3), 561–598.

Russett, B. (1985). The mysterious case of vanishing hegemony; or, is Mark Twain really dead? *International Organization, 39*(2), 207–231.

Sartori, G. (1987). *The theory of democracy revisited (Vol. I).* Chatham, NJ: Chatham House Publishers.

Smith, P. H. (1999). *Talons of the eagle: Dynamics of U.S.-Latin American relations.* Oxford: Oxford University Press.

Smythe, E. (1980). International relations theory and the study of Canadian-American relations. *Journal of Political Science, 13*(1), 121–147.

Stepan, A. (1979). The United States and Latin America: Vital interests and the instruments of power. *Foreign Affairs, 58*(3), 659–692.

Strange, S. (1987). The persistent myth of lost hegemony. *International Organization, 41*(4), 551–574.

Strange, S. (1988). The future of the American empire. *Journal of International Affairs, 42*(1), 1–17.

Tokatlian, J. G. (2013, November 28). 'Bye bye Monroe, hello Troilo'. *El País.*

Triska, J. F. (1986). Introduction. In J. F. Triska (Ed.), *Dominant powers and subordinate states: The United States in Latin America and the Soviet Union in Eastern Europe* (pp. 1–23). Durham, NC: Duke University Press.

Walker, R. B. J. (1991). On the spatiotemporal conditions of democratic practice. *Alternatives: Global, Local, Political, 16*(2), 243–262.

Wallerstein, I. (2007). Precipitate decline: The advent of multipolarity. *Harvard International Review, 29*(1), 50–55.

Walt, S. (2011). The end of the American Era. *National Interest, 116,* 6–16.

Waltz, K. (1979). *Theory of international politics.* Reading, MA: Addison-Wesley.

Weber, M. (1978). *Economy and Society* (G. Roth and C. Wittich Eds.). Berkeley, CA: University of California Press.

Wendt, A. (1992). Anarchy is what states make of it: The social construction of power politics. *International Organization, 46*(2), 391–425.

Wesson, R. G. (1982). *United States influence in Latin America in the 1980s.* New York: Praeger Publishers.

Whitehead, L. (1986). Debt, diversitfication, and dependency: Latin America's international political relations. In K. J. Middlebrook & C. Rico (Eds.), *The United States and Latin America in the 1980s*. (pp. 87–130). Pittsburgh, PA: University of Pittsburgh Press.

Williamson, J. (1994). In search of a manual for technopols. In J. Williamson (Ed.), *The political economy of policy reform* (pp. 9–28). Washington, DC: Institute for International Economics.

Wilson, P. (1995). Introduction: The twenty years' crisis and the category of 'idealism' in international relations. In D. Long & P. Wilson (Eds.), *Thinkers of the twenty years' crisis: Inter-war idealism reassessed* (pp. 1–24). Oxford: Clarendon.

Wohlforth, W. C. (1999). The stability of a unipolar world. *International Security, 24*(1), 5–41.

Zakaria, F. (2008). The future of American power: How America can survive the rise of the rest. *Foreign Affairs, 87*(3), 18–43.

Zartman, I. W. (2009). *Imbalance of power: US hegemony and international order*. Boulder, CO: Lynne Rienner Publishers.

Zürn, M., Binder, M., & Ecker-Ehrhardt, M. (2012). International authority and its policization. *International Theory, 4*(1), 69–106.

Chapter 2

Hierarchy and Authority in Regional Orders

The Western Hemisphere

In this chapter I delve into the importance and purport of regional orders, focusing on the one that has been constructed in the Western Hemisphere. Significantly the New World's hierarchical arrangement came to reproduce the cultural, economic, political and social cleavages that existed in Europe, particularly the ones that existed between Spain and the United Kingdom. Early in its development, the United States became the hegemon of this largely dichotomous order. This chapter is divided into four sections. In the first one I elaborate on the significance of regional orders for world politics. In the second and third sections, I focus on the workings of hierarchical relations in the Western Hemisphere, considering the cases of Latin America and Canada, respectively. In the fourth and final section I succinctly recap the discussion.

1) Salience and Meaning of Regional Compacts for International Politics

Regional orderings are intrinsic to the modern state system.[1] A region can be said to consist "of two or more member states in geographical proximity ... characterized by regular interactions between them [and] perceived by both internal and external actors as a distinct regional space."[2] But as Peter Katzenstein has argued, regions also "reflect the power and purpose of states," and acquire "distinctive institutional forms."[3] Barry Buzan, for his part, has noted the "thicker" cultural fabric that exists in regional settings, compared to the global one.[4] Part of this "thickness" is the "diplomatic culture" Andrew Hurrell argues regions develop, which contributes to maintain a sense of we-ness among its members; for him, "regional diplomatic culture" refers to "a regional society of states which, although still often in conflict, conceived themselves to be bound by a common set of rules and shared in the workings of common institutions."[5]

The preceding attributes point to the existence of regional orders reminiscent of the kind Hedley Bull wrote about for the international society at large, as noted in the previous chapter. Regional societies are not only part and parcel of the wider system, but also "localizations" of it.[6] For as Mohammed Ayoob points out, "the ground rules of regional society must go beyond those of international society to give the concept its distinguishing mark as well as normative content."[7] In this way, both the hierarchical and authoritative nature of such subsystems possess features specific to the region in question.

Chief among the traits that distinguish regions, and particularly *hegemonic* regional orders, is the differentiated authority of its members. As noted before, the grammar of hierarchy varies with the cultural setting in question. Thus, hegemonic orders will to some extent operate under different ordering principles, assigning diverse rights and responsibilities to their members.[8] Even if in this gradated allocation of authority, one agent—the hegemon—plays a preponderant role, making its purpose and values dominant. The cement that holds this hierarchical order together is not an actor, but, as noted in the previous chapter, a social fact: legitimacy.[9] As Lake observes, "the legitimacy granted by regional states to a dominant state creates and shapes its authority."[10] Furthermore, in hierarchical regional orders hegemons not only lead their neighbors; they also impose limits on the relationships the latter can establish with other states.[11] The degree to which regional hegemonic orders fit into contractual models, as well as the extent to which they are benign or exploitative, is an empirical question; what matters is that the hierarchy at issue implies authority relations.[12] Let's now turn to consider how they have evolved in the region of interest here.

2) Workings of Hierarchical Relations in the Western Hemisphere: Latin America

The Western Hemisphere constituted itself into a separate regional order since the early 19th century.[13] Following Janice Mattern and Ayse Zarakol, we can distinguish three logics of hierarchy at work in the region since the early 19th century: the logic of trade-offs, as a solution to the problem of order; the logic of positionality, by means of which actors come to act and form interests depending on their position in the hierarchical order; and the logic of productivity, according to which actors are themselves constituted by the hierarchical order in which they are immersed.[14] I would argue that the first two logics have been dominant in this regional context; regardless of which logic has prevailed, however, it is clear that the Western Hemisphere has exhibited a particular kind of hierarchy. Let's briefly review the evolution of this regional system.

Significantly, the Western Hemisphere became a hegemonic order *before* the leading state—the United States of America—was unquestionably the strongest in terms of material capabilities. Thus, when in 1823 president James Monroe proclaimed the doctrine named after him, in effect doing what regional hegemons do—"take care of their own backyard"—the United States was some eight decades away from being able to actually enforce it; for instance, its Navy was smaller than the Chilean one.[15] This case is analogous to the Japanese case in the late 19th century when, after Tokyo's adoption of Western norms in both domestic and international affairs, it could be argued that it started "punching above its weight."[16] Tellingly, the Monroe Doctrine was welcomed by most Latin American leaders;[17] thus, for instance, liberator Simón Bolivar applauded it and Mexican president Guadalupe Victoria referred to it as "president Monroe's memorable promise."[18] This reaction to what was in fact the establishment of Washington's sphere of influence had to do with the admiration the first independent country of the New World inspired in a good portion of the Latin American elite. Not surprisingly, the United States became a political model for Latin America.[19]

This is not to suggest that the respect Latin American elites had of the United States amounted to feelings of amity, or even that this disposition was pervasive. After all, the New World was in more than one way a reenactment of the historic animosities (both religious and political) between Spain and the United Kingdom, a sort of "transplanted frontier"; hence "the great American dichotomy" Edmundo O'Gorman so eloquently wrote about.[20] The high regard in which the United States was held by liberal elites had more to do with recognition of its economic and political achievements than with affability. As Domingo Sarmiento, the Argentinian liberal intellectual and statesman wrote:

> The United States are something for which there is no previous model, a kind of folly which is repulsive at first sight, and frustrates any expectative by fighting against received wisdom, and nevertheless this unconceivable folly is grand and noble.[21]

Or, as the 19th century Brazilian educator José Veríssimo succinctly said of the United States: "I admire them but I don't esteem them."[22] Furthermore, the United States was far from being the model for a good portion of the Latin American elite: the so-called conservatives. For them, Spanish—and later French—culture and society were the example to follow.

Significantly, Washington remained the political model of the liberal factions even after its expansionist aims had become clear. Thus, for instance, despite the taking over of half of their country's territory in the 1846–1848 war, not even Mexican liberals changed their mind about the United States;[23] and later on, when the US government congratulated its Mexican counterpart on the passage of an important liberal piece of legislation, the president sent his foreign minister to read the letter in Congress—a telling sign of the importance of counting with the northern neighbor's blessing.[24]

In the United States, on the other hand, México in particular and Latin American in general were usually considered to be children in need of guidance. What Hobson has called "civilisational hierarchy" was at play here; Washington started to practice "imperial republicanism."[25] Thus, already in 1813 Thomas Jefferson wrote that "the vicinity of the New Spain to the United States and its associated intercourse might represent a school for the higher classes and example to the lower ones";[26] seven years later, secretary of state Henry Clay told Congress: "It is in our power to create a system of which we shall be the center, and in which all South America will act with us."[27]

The first decades of the 19th century were the time when Arthur Whitaker's "Western Hemisphere Idea" (WHI) was born. The meaning of the WHI, according to Whitaker, was "the proposition that the peoples of this Hemisphere stand in a special relationship to one another which sets them apart from the rest of the world."[28] This "separate system of interests" (Jefferson *dixit*) was of course led by the United States, and it enjoyed the acquiescence of the former penin-sular colonies, but it was also permeated by the resentment of the latter toward the former's expansionist ambitions and tutelary aims. The arrogant attitude of the rising hegemon was evinced, for instance, by the 1905 Roosevelt Corollary to the Monroe Doctrine (which claimed the role of hemispheric policeman for Washington), by Woodrow Wilson's 1913 statement to Congress asserting: "we are the friends of constitutional government in America; we are more than its friends, we are its champions ... I am going to teach the South American republics to elect good men," and by the fact the United States would not accept the nonintervention principle, so dear to its southern nations, until the 1936 Inter-American Conference for the Maintenance of Peace.[29] These and other signs and actions would only contribute to the ill-feelings of these coun-tries toward the United States.

Irrespective of the tensions running in the Americas, by the end of the second decade of the 20th century, Latin America was internationally recognized as a veritable sphere of influence of the United States. Thus, as noted, the European powers sanctioned the Monroe Doctrine at Versailles. The understanding that the Western Hemisphere possessed a distinct, hegemonic regional order was only reinforced at home and abroad by what transpired during World War II and the Cold War. Accordingly, at the 1945 Inter-American Conference on the Problems of War and Peace, held in México City, the participating states agreed to establish an inter-American collective security system once the war was over. More telling, though, was the zeal with which, a month after the Chapultepec meeting, Latin American states defended the recognition of regional systems at the United Nations Conference on International Organization, held in San Francisco. The Latin American effort, supported by the United States, was suc-cessful, as reflected in articles 52–54 of the UN Charter.[30]

Thus, the "separate system" Jefferson had envisioned for the Americas would materialize 135 years later, with the promulgation of the Bogotá Charter and the establishment of the Organization of American States (OAS) in 1948. Latin American states aimed not only at cooperating with, but also at contain-ing, the United States. This political compact was imbued by the republican legacy according to which "independent states are nevertheless connected, and not just by circumstance"[31] in a hierarchical realm where the leader must still justify its actions.[32] Furthermore, in the emerging Cold War context, Latin America was successful in creating, at least formally, a more democratic organi-zation than the UN, as manifested in the OAS Charter's recognition of formal equality for all member states.[33] As the Mexican representative to the regional body would put it in 1970:

> This is a peculiar organization, in which the most powerful nation of the earth, the United States and more than twenty that are not rich or powerful are grouped together. There is no doubt, however, that in spite of that, the Organization has gained a democratic spirit.[34]

The irreducible common denominator that republicanism represented in the hemisphere implied the extrapolation, to the continental level, of the principle according to which in any republic "coercion and concern for the common good dance on together."[35] That is, there was an implicit understanding regarding not only the ubiquitous presence of coercion in the relations among the states of the hemisphere (despite their formal equality), but also regarding the latent existence of common interests. These common interests were, of course, peace and security—but this composite understanding had to adapt to the Cold War context. As the latter was primarily an ideological battle between two superpowers (the United States and the Union of Soviet Socialist Republics), the OAS largely became a tool of Washington's self-proclaimed mission to contain Communism in the hemisphere;[36] its role in ostracizing Cuba in 1962, and in approving US interventionism in the Dominican Republic in 1965, are just two examples of this. The regional order was thus shot through and through by consent and coercion.

Around the time when the wider academic debate on the decline of US hegemony started, relations between the United States and its southern neighbors remained inscribed within the same hierarchical order, but also within the Cold War framework—regardless of Washington's alleged change in capabilities. A clear sign of the bipolar prisms through which the regional hegemon viewed hemispheric politics was provided by the United States' response to the rise, through democratic elections, of the left in Chile in 1970, as discussed at length in Chapter 8. Despite the United States' intervention in Chile and other Southern Cone countries during the decade, Washington seemed to be both out of touch with the rest of the hemisphere and losing control of it; thus, for instance, by the end of the decade, most countries had re-established diplomatic relations with Havana. This was the time when both the foreign policy and the academic debate in the region emphasized the need for "autonomy" vis-à-vis the regional hegemon.[37] There were also some heated arguments in the regional forum, which reached their apex in 1979, when a US initiative designed to prevent the arrival of the Sandinistas to power in Nicaragua was dismissed in favor of another that clearly favored the rebels.[38]

The overall relationship between Washington and Latin America only got worse during the 1980s. Thus, for the first time, the sub-continent as a whole confronted Washington over the Malvinas/Falklands War.[39] Reagan's anti-communist crusade in Central America particularly contributed to aggravate hemispheric relations. The emergence in the early 1980s of the Contadora Group, and later of the Support Group, and eventually of the Rio Group, all explicitly excluding the United States, and proposing ideas to solve the Central American imbroglio that were at odds with those emanating from Washington, was further evidence of the increasing futility of the OAS.

There was, however, a triple movement in the opposite direction: first, the wave of democratic transitions in Latin America; second, the greater emphasis on democracy in the OAS, which in 1985 amended its charter and gave the organization a new mission: the promotion of democracy; third, Washington moved "democracy promotion" center stage in its foreign policy. Although the sudden democratic commitment of the Reagan administration rang hollow among Latin American leaders, it did have real effects. Thus, Chile became a crucial test for the "democracy promotion" policy of the Reagan administration. In 1985, US Ambassador Harry Barnes had arrived to Santiago, making clear his sympathies to the Chilean democratic forces, and, the following year, Washington issued a statement noting that it opposed all forms of dictatorship, left or right.[40] This change in US attitude no doubt contributed to General Pinochet losing the 1988 plebiscite that brought the end of his regime.

By this time, the hemispheric conversation had changed substantially. With the end of the Cold War, Washington seemed to be in a similar situation to that in which it had found itself after World War II, but only better: with the vanishing of its economic, ideological and military counterpart (the USSR), the United States seemed to emerge, as noted, as the global hegemonic power. But the transformation in the hemispheric conversation had more to do with internal factors. The noted democratic transitions in the region altered the structure of political incentives regarding hemispheric collaboration to secure democracy. A renovated spirit imbued the OAS, which, for instance, played a central role in the Nicaraguan 1990 electoral process.

It is worth pointing out, though, that beyond the ups and downs of the hemispheric relations during the 1970s and 1980s, both the United States and the Latin American countries kept framing their discussion in terms consistent with the WHI—that is, the Americas as a "separate system of interests" that is nevertheless divided by a cultural, economic and political frontier. As Robert Wesson noted in the mid-1980s:

> The Latin Americans can and do appeal on legalistic and moral grounds, and call upon the United States to act not in accordance with its capacities but with its principles. They in effect ask the hegemonic power to restrain itself in the name of justice, legal order and humanitarianism to which it subscribes.[41]

Actually, the prevalence of statements in the regional forum pointing out to the hierarchical nature of the regional order—in the sense discussed in the first section— is noteworthy. Thus, for instance, on the issue of the Americas as being composed of two different cultures (along the lines of O'Gorman's "Great American Dichotomy"), in the 1970 General Assembly, Chilean representative Patricio Silva referred to the regional forum as one composed not of many countries, but of "two great collectivities: Latin American and the United States," while Bolivian representative Camacho Omiste acknowledged his "deep admiration for the North American people (sic), who have been able to build this civilization, which constitutes the highest expression of economic and technological power in history."[42] Venezuelan representative Gonzalo García, for his part, noted the obligation of the United States "toward the Latin American bloc" in terms of development aid.[43]

Similarly, at the 1971 General Assembly, Colombian representative Alfredo Vázquez observed that Latin America formed a "regional system" with the United States on security matters, and suggested that Latin America could learn from Washington.[44] At the 1977 General Assembly, as if obliging to his Latin American counterparts regarding the civilizational commonalities of the countries of the hemisphere, US representative Gale W. McGee mentioned the "more or less common heritage" the United States shared with its southern neighbors, in reference to the ideals of George Washington, whose birthday was being commemorated in that session.[45] Shared fundamental values notwithstanding, Venezuelan representative José Alberto Zambrano would later insist that "the OAS is not a regional organization, but rather an Organization that encompasses two regions: Latin America and the United States, which is a region by itself."[46] And, as his Bolivian counterpart a decade before, in the 1980 General Assembly Santa Lucía representative Barry Auguste referred to the special role of the United States in international affairs, while acknowledging that it was "one of the richest, most democratic and esteemed countries in the world."[47]

But the appreciation of the regional hegemon was often accompanied with rancor or resentment. Thus, at the 1983 General Assembly Colombian representative Rodrigo Lloreda lamented the "paternalist" post-war arrangement according to which hemispheric security rested in the United States alone, "as a kind of an extemporaneous continuation of the Monroe Doctrine."[48] Likewise, three years later, Guatemalan president Vinicio Cerezo noted at the General Assembly that the Americas are "the fruit of a common [European] historical process," and pointed out that Latin American states had established a political dialogue with the United States "to tell them that we respect their position ... but we want to be their partners and not the instruments of their international policy."[49] Toward the of end the Cold War, secretary of state George Shultz addressed the General Assembly to reiterate the special responsibility Washington had toward its neighborhood; thus, he noted his country's "obligation to offer our moral, political, and material support to those people already struggling to implant true democracy in their countries."[50]

The supposed decline of the United States as the West's hegemon, thus, did not seem to affect hemispheric relations much. Washington remained the by and large unquestioned regional hegemon, and the changes that transpired in the area had more to do with internal developments—particularly the wave of democratic transitions in the 1980s, than with any alteration of the relative material capabilities of the United States. Latin American recognition of Washington as a sort of *primus inter pares* would only continue during the decade following the end of the Cold War. The region's acknowledgement of US authority of course did not mean that its leaders considered their countries powerless vis-à-vis Washington; hegemony is not zero-sum—as many Latin American states successful efforts to influence the United States during the Cold War made clear.[51]

During the 1990s inter-American relations deepened and expanded. The expansion had to do with Canada becoming a member of the regional body. Ottawa's move was a most-applauded event by the Latin American states, since they perceived the newcomer as a potential ally that could contribute to balance Washington's presence in the organization.[52] As Costa Rican representative Rodrigo Madrigal, with a jibe for the United States, put it when welcoming Ottawa to the "American family," the new member possessed an "intelligent foreign policy ... without hegemonism or further intentions."[53]

But Canada also contributed to the deepening of the hemispheric agenda. The OAS embraced several of Ottawa's distinctive foreign policy concerns, such as democracy and human rights; not surprisingly, the new member became an active player on those matters. However, the deepening of the regional agenda also took place in a host of issues that had been of interest to Washington but had, for the most part, been taboo for the other states. Thus, in 1995 the OAS established the Hemispheric Security Committee and the Conference of Defense Ministers of the Americas, so that the top brass of the region could discuss topics relevant to the new security environment of the hemisphere: civil–military relationships, terrorism, and transnational organized crime among them.[54]

Nonetheless, the most conspicuous issue that contributed to the intensifying of hemispheric relations was the convergence, noted in the previous chapter, on the "Washington Consensus." A term coined in 1989 by John Williamson, it refers to a 10-item list of policy recommendations for countries that wanted to adopt the economic model promoted by the United States and other developed countries (it should be noted, though, that there was a lot of dissent within the consensus during the following years;[55] more on this in Chapter 4). Thus, at the June 1990 General Assembly, Chilean representative Enrique Silva called for OAS involvement not only in the hemisphere's trade liberalization agenda, but also in the promotion of private foreign investment in the region.[56] The emphasis on hemispheric economic integration had a lot to do, as Mexican representative Sergio González put it in the same event, with the "renewed pragmatism" of the of the Latin American countries.[57] Similarly, Venezuela's

Foreign Minister would point out that the region had made an "important turn" on economic affairs "as a matter of conviction or of financial necessity."[58]

Later that month, at the White House, president George Bush announced the "Enterprise for the Americas Initiative: An Opportunity for Trade, Investment, and Growth"; the move was a response to a request made by Latin American leaders four months earlier in Cartagena, Colombia. The Latin American heads of state present at the meeting that took place in that city had explicitly stated they were not interested in aid for their countries; what they wanted was access to the US market. As Venezuelan Foreign Minister Armando Durán put it in the 1991 General Assembly, president Bush's invitation constituted "the opportunity to solve the disconnect between the United States and Latin America," as well as "the possibility ... to promote the region's economic development."[59] The Initiative of the Americas was thus, as Joseph Tulchin put it, George Bush's "acknowledgment" of the prevailing mood in the region.[60] Keeping with the renewed interest in commercial affairs, a "Special Trade Committee" was established within the OAS in 1993.

Bringing together the political and economic commonalities in the hemisphere, in December 1994 president Clinton invited all "democratically-elected" leaders of the Western hemisphere to attend the First Summit of the Americas in Miami. The agenda included three main topics: democracy, economic integration, and sustainable development. For Colombia's Foreign Minister Rodrigo Pardo, the gathering,

> convened and directed in a timely fashion, by the President of the United States, undoubtedly left a schedule that is an invitation for optimism. The topics included, the chosen priorities, and the plans for action agreed upon are the best agenda for the management of hemispheric affairs.[61]

Tellingly, this was the first hemispheric conference attended by a US president since the 1967 OAS Punta del Este meeting. It was thus not that surprising that the US representative at the regional organization, Mark B. Feierstein, would remark the "unprecedented degree of consensus on how we can secure the future of the region" as well as the "convergence of values" among the states of the Americas.[62] The alleged convergence was revelatory of Washington's self-perception, for, as US Ambassador to the OAS had claimed, in the early 1990s,

> in this revolutionary new world, in this new democratic era, we and our partners alike need to understand that the values in which we believe are not those of the United States at all—they are American values, universal values which all of us strive to achieve.[63]

In any case, at least on economic matters there was some consensus; the Miami Summit's main objective became the creation of the Free Trade Area of the Americas (FTAA) by 2005.[64]

By this time, as suggested, the hemispheric organization had made big strides on political matters. Since the early 1990s, the OAS support for democracy had gained momentum; thus, for instance, in October 1990 the Unit for the Promotion of Democracy was created—headed first by Canadian John Graham and subsequently by Canadian Elizabeth Spehar—and a torrent of electoral monitoring missions to Latin American countries ensued. Furthermore, in June 1991 the regional organization adopted the Santiago Commitment and Resolution 1080; by means of these two instruments, the OAS substantially reinforced not only its pro-democracy doctrine, but also its muscle (the Secretary General was instructed to call the Permanent Council or the General Assembly in the event of an interruption of the democratic regime in one of its members). Additionally, the 1992 Washington Protocol established that a member state could be suspended if its democratically elected government was overthrown.

Seven years after the project for FTAA was launched, a political component was added to it. At the 2001 Quebec Summit of Heads of State of the Americas—at the request of some Latin American states—a "democracy clause" was inserted into the process. The Inter-American Democratic Charter (IADC) adopted later that year in Lima—on the same day the terrorist attacks in the United States took place—specified the criteria needed to collectively defend democratically elected regimes in the hemisphere. A liberal approach, consistent with the guidelines of the WHI, seemed to guide the politics and economics of the hemisphere. A week after both the promulgation of the IADC and the terrorist attacks, in presenting his country's condolences to Washington at a meeting of the OAS Permanent Council, Venezuela's representative Jorge Valero remarked:

> We come with the best intention to cooperate in a selfless and tight manner in order to reach an effective response to the aggression to a friendly country, the United States, a member state of our organization [the OAS]. This response is unanimous on the part of all the countries of the hemisphere, because we all feel we have been attacked.[65]

The terrorist attacks broadly coincided in time with the already mentioned discussion about the emergence of the BRICs, as well as with what seemed to be the consolidation of the European Union (with its recent expansion and introduction of the Euro), all of which rekindled the discussion of US decline. The new geopolitical reality became more conspicuous in the Western Hemisphere with the increased economic interest of China in the region, both as a supplier of raw materials (such as copper, oil and soy) and as an export market. Countries like Argentina, Brazil and Chile particularly benefited from their increased trade in commodities with China.[66] Venezuela, as a big oil producer, also profited handsomely from the higher price of oil in world markets, a circumstance that allowed it to play a more important role in hemispheric politics.

But global geopolitical shifts were, I would argue, not the most important drivers of the sea change that took place in inter-American politics in the first decade of the 21st century. The most proximate causes had to do with what happened in the Western Hemisphere itself: first, the ascendance to power of George W. Bush in the United States and, second, the referred turn to the left in several Latin American countries. As for the first factor, even if it was clear from early on in his administration that Bush Jr. intended to play the unilateral-ist card more prominently than his predecessors (as made evident, for instance, by his refusal to ratify the Kyoto Protocol), soon after the 9/11 terrorist attacks, that is, less than a year into the new administration, Washington's unilateralism had gained full speed. Not surprisingly, by and large, Latin America and Canada opposed the Bush administration on one of the issues that came to define it: the invasion of Iraq. Thus, for instance, the two Latin American countries (Chile and México) that happened to be in the Security Council at the time—both of which, incidentally, had a close and friendly attitude toward the United States—opposed Washington; another traditionally close partner—as well as security ally in NORAD and NATO—Canada, also opposed Washington on the matter.[67] Thus, partly as a result of its increased unilateralism in world affairs, Washington began to lose influence within the OAS. Indeed, as Peter Hakim noted, "Throughout the region, support for Washington's policies has diminished. Few Latin Americans, in or out of government, consider the United States to be a dependable partner."[68]

The other proximate cause of the shift in hemispheric relations, as noted, was a political shift in several Latin American Countries. Thus, for instance, what was to become the legacy of the hemisphere's shared interests and cooperation, the FTAA, saw its demise at the November 2005 Summit of the Americas in Mar del Plata. At the gathering, not only Venezuela's president, Hugo Chávez, but also its host, Argentinian president Néstor Kirchner, made known their opposition to the continental pact; meanwhile, Brazil was successfully playing the "regional card" to gain increased leverage, both at the hemispheric and global level.[69] By that time, the Bolivarian Alliance for the Peoples of Our America (ALBA), spearheaded by Cuba's Fidel Castro and Venezuela's Hugo Chávez had already been established (on December 2004), and would become a veritable front against what they considered Washington's imperialist policies.

Whereas the previous two developments constituted the driving forces of the increasingly divergent stances of Washington and the rest of the hemi-sphere, there have been also three developments that operated in the opposite direction since late in the last decade until 2016. The first one was the rap-prochement between Washington and the rest of the countries of the Western Hemisphere after the arrival of Barack Obama to the White House and the return of the United States to a more multilateralist, even collegial, approach.[70] The reestablishment of diplomatic relations with Cuba—for which the United States president received great praise by his hemispheric counterparts—epito-mized the change in Washington's attitude.

A second development that contributed to the partial amity of hemispheric relations was due to the split among Latin American countries that followed the establishment of ALBA; this rupture materialized in 2011 with the founding of an analogous group, the Alliance of the Pacific, among four more market-oriented, Washington-friendly countries: Chile, Colombia, México and Perú. It is worth noting that all of them but Colombia, plus Canada, joined the Obama administration in what was its most important geopolitical project: the Trans-Pacific Partnership. The division amongst Latin American countries has transpired even when they have attempted to act in tandem. Thus, for instance, the creation of the Community of Latin American and Caribbean States (CELAC), in 2010, made clear the different positions vis-à-vis the United States, which, along with Canada, is one of the two hemispheric states excluded from the new arrangement; whereas Nicaraguan president Daniel Ortega would note that with the new arrangement "We are sentencing the Monroe Doctrine to death," Colombian president José Manuel Santos would later make clear that "CELAC isn't being born to be against anyone."[71]

Finally, the third development that has operated to reverse the course on the tendency in inter-American relations in this decade has been the weakened position of the regional left (within ALBA or not), both due to exogenous factors, such as the crash in commodity prices that started in 2014, and endogenous ones, such as the coming to power of more moderate or right-wing regimes in countries such as Argentina and Brazil.

3) Workings of Hierarchical Relations in the Western Hemisphere: Canada

At the opposite end of the social and political schism between Washington and its southern neighbors, it is commonplace to note the close relationship between it and Ottawa. Part of the usual explanation for the cordial relation has to do with their cultural commonalities. The sharing of historical roots and features, such as language and religion, have no doubt contributed to the solid relationship these "twins separated at birth" enjoy. For, as Seymour Lipset has noted, the two countries "resemble each other more than either resembles any other nation."[72] However, in times past—kinship notwithstanding—things used to be radically different. As J.L. Granatstein and Norman Hillmer have pointed out, "North America's peaceful character, its penchant for arbitration over warfare, was largely a myth. There had been wars, rebellions, bloodshed, and strife aplenty as the relations between the two peoples sorted themselves out."[73]

From the founding of the United States until around the mid-19th century, the bilateral relationship could hardly be characterized as amicable. Initially, Washington considered Canada, then a British colony, a threat. Accordingly, it attempted to disengage its northern neighbor from the British Empire.[74] During the 1812 War it invaded Upper Canada and declared it occupied territory, and although the expansionist adventure did not prosper, annexation plans, such as those of the Irish-American Fenian, continued well after the war. Thus, six years after British North American soldiers burned down the White House, John Quincy Adams wrote about his country's "natural dominion in North America."[75]

Similarly, Canadians conceived of themselves not as a North American, much less as an American (in the sense of Western Hemispheric) nation; they saw themselves as belonging to the British Empire—if with their own specificities. As MP Paul Martin would later put it: "While a preference for the material benefits of inclusion within the US might well have been understandable during the nineteenth century, confederation was the alternative Canadians chose";[76] thus, their deeply engrained attachment to London remained. And this stance was reciprocated: still after confederation (in 1867), Washington often perceived Ottawa as an imperial extension. By the late 19th century, however, it had become obvious to the United States that Canada's future lay in North America and, accordingly, started treating it as an independent country.[77]

By this time, significantly, war was on its way out as an option in the bilateral relationship. Thus, in 1880, prime minister Sir John A. Macdonald noted:

> My opinion is, that from the present aspect of affairs, and from a gradual improvement in the feeling between the people of the United States and the people of Canada, that the danger of war is annually decreasing, so much so that it is in the highest degree improbable that there will ever be a war between England and the United States, except for causes altogether unconnected with Canada of which I cannot judge.[78]

By the early 20th century the transition in the mutual understanding of the northernmost Western Hemisphere's neighbors was in its preliminary phase. The peaceful bilateral record, which had been accompanied—and promoted—by a series of key confidence-building steps, such as increasing economic interaction and the demilitarization of the border, was starting to instill a sense of community between the two countries. This of course is not to suggest that all were good feelings between Ottawa and Washington; anti-Americanism, for instance, was still Canada's "state religion."[79] Indeed; the 1911 Canadian election was run on the supposed threat that a proposed trade agreement with its southern neighbor represented to the very existence of Canada. However, by this time, anti-American sentiment was more of an elite artifice to gain popularity than state policy. Furthermore, the developments leading to World War I, the conflict itself (with both countries fighting on the same side), and its aftermath made the shared security interests evident to both countries. As Theodore Roosevelt wrote in a personal letter in 1914:

> I cannot help hoping and believing that in the end nations will gradually get to the point that, for instance, Canada and the US have now attained,

where each nation, as a matter of course, treats the other with reasonable justice and friendliness and where war is unthinkable between them.[80]

The new understanding was further deepened during the interwar years. Thus, when Canada established its first diplomatic post abroad in 1926 (even though it was not to become a sovereign country until 1931), it did so in Washington. It is during that period that their security interests coalesced; that both countries developed similar grand strategies, and that Canada started to include, at least in some respects, the "other" the United States represented, as part of itself.[81] Thus, shortly before the outbreak of World War II, prime minister Mackenzie King commented that his country's relations with its neighbor were so intimate that for some Canadians they were "not foreign relations at all."[82]

Canada's more substantial redefinition of its identity and, therefore, of its security vis-à-vis its neighbor came about during World War II. It started in 1940, with the Ogdensburg Declaration, and was followed the next year by the Hyde Park Declaration, both pertaining meetings between prime minister Mackenzie King and president Franklin Roosevelt. The intent of these two simple documents would lead to the establishment of a complex network of military cooperation between the two countries, the operational foundation of which is the 1940 Permanent Joint Board on Defense.[83] But it was the cultivation of shared values, common interests, and even an embryonic common identity that allowed both countries to change the course of their history and eventually form what in the IR literature is called a Security Community.[84] It was precisely this transformation that made the emergence of the myth about the ever-friendly Canada–United States relationship possible.

By the end of World War II there was no doubt that Ottawa had cast its lot with Washington. This alignment had been facilitated by three related conditions: first, the fact that part of Canada's identity in world politics was still inextricably linked to the British Commonwealth, with which, for historical reasons, Washington had a close association; second, and relatedly, the nascent Anglo-American "special relationship"; and, third, the recent auspicious record in the bilateral (Canada–United States) relationship.[85] Hence, for Canada supporting her neighbor meant not only rallying behind it, but more broadly, upholding the principles and interests that held together the nascent Western bloc against its Soviet-led opponent. In the bipolar confrontation, as suggested before, Washington's post-war grand strategy had two components: containment of Communism and the establishment of an international liberal economic order.[86] Canada's situation was a fortunate one, for its ideals coincided with its interests.

Moreover, after World War II, Canada defined itself at the international level as a "middle power."[87] This meant placing the country's interests on par with those of the US-led bloc. Thus, by the late 1950s, when the bipolar nuclear confrontation was in full swing, the imperative for collective defense became even clearer to Canadian leaders. As prime minister John Diefenbaker put it, "the defence of North America has become a joint enterprise of both Canada and the United States;"[88] it was thus early during his leadership that the North American Air (later Aerospace) Defence Command (NORAD) was created.

Canada's intricate relationship with the U.S. in security matters has not really been a surprise. Its peculiar political economy (nearly 80 percent of its population lives within 100 miles of the border with the United States, in an otherwise sparsely populated, extensive territory) has made the establishment of tight economic and social ties with its southern neighbor a leitmotif throughout her history.[89] Furthermore, the perceived beneficial character of economic integration has arguably had spillover effects into the political component of the relationship. As former MP Paul Martin put it in 1971, "The fact that Canada has lived and prospered for more than a century ... is evidence to all countries of the basic decency of the United States' foreign policy."[90]

This sort of relationship has of course not gone uncontested in Canadian politics—an ideological battle that has continued and reflected the foundational ones that followed the separation of the "twins" in the late 18th century. As the saying goes, "Canada has had to choose between the State and the States."[91] Thus, prime minister Pierre Elliott Trudeau's pursuit of the "third option" in the early 1970s was clearly a reaction to the perceived disproportionate Washington-focus of his country's foreign relations, no matter how allegedly benign the treatment Canada received from the neighbor might have been. It was indeed around this time that the "special relationship" Canada maintained with its southern neighbor began to unravel.[92] As president Nixon put it in a 1972 speech to the Canadian Parliament: "It is time for us to recognize that we have very separate identities; that we have significant differences; and that nobody's interests are furthered when these realities are obscured."[93]

Trudeau's ultimately failed effort was telling; although he might have put it more explicitly than most of his predecessors, the attempt to escape from the overbearing embrace of the United States has been a constant of Canadian diplomacy. Here lies another reason for Canada's internationalist vocation—as instantiated in its already noted role as a middle power role and, perhaps more saliently, in its multilateralist practice. But more important for my argument here, multilateralism served as an instrument of self-assertion vis-à-vis the country's powerful neighbor. As former Foreign Affairs Minister Lloyd Axworthy would put it:

> Multilateralism has been at the heart of Canada's foreign policy, above all because we have sought to be in good company in our dealings with our great neighbour and because we have insisted that rules—the rule of law—mitigate the unilateral impulses of other 'large players.'[94]

Although it is clear that Canada had operated with a built-in tension—on the one hand, wanting to be close to the U.S. in order to be able to exert influence over it but, on the other, aiming to keep its distance in order to maintain its autonomy—by the time the Cold War was coming to an end it had become much closer to the United States. Thus, in 1985 prime minister Mulroney's government approached Washington to suggest negotiating a Free Trade Agreement, a proposal that came to fruition in 1988 (more on this in Chapter 5).

It was in the post-Cold War Washington Consensus environment that Ottawa, as noted before, "discovered" Latin America and joined the OAS. Furthermore, in 1990 Ottawa not only became a member of the regional organization, but also México's partner in the North America Free Trade Agreement (NAFTA) that went into effect in 1994 (more on this in Chapter 6).

Canadian security cooperation with its southern neighbor continued when the "unipolar moment" started, and throughout the 1990s.[95] Thus, it supported the United States over the three strikes against Iraq in 1991, 1996, and 1998, as well as the 1999 NATO-led bombing of Belgrade.[96] As the 1999 Canadian *Strategy 2020* read: "our most important ally now and for the future is the US where our strong relationship has long benefited both countries."[97]

During the aftermath of the 9/11 terrorist attacks, the bilateral relationship went through a testing period. Obliged by its interpretation of the bilateral compact, Canada immediately supported Washington's actions in Afghanistan; other than the U.S. and Great Britain, Canada was indeed the only country that defined its mission in the Asian country in terms of its national interest.[98] Furthermore, in December 2001 Ottawa signed a "Smart Border" agreement with Washington. However, as noted, in 2003 Canada was not willing to accompany its neighbor in the invasion of Iraq, as it was not persuaded by Washington's arguments about the Gulf country's relationship with the terrorist attacks. This was no doubt a momentous decision for Ottawa. There would be of course political costs to be paid for the affront to the Bush administration. But prime minister Jean Chrétien's stance enjoyed broad support at home.

What ensued was a difficult process of compromising (explicitly or implicitly) on some of the fronts that Washington had demanded. Especially since the departure of prime minister Chrétien in 2003, Ottawa took several political measures to mend its tense relationship with Washington.[99] Thus, it passed new anti-terrorism legislation, established the Public Safety and Emergence Preparedness department (which mirrors the US Department of Homeland Security's) in December 2003, and created CanCom (after the US North Com) in February 2006, among other measures. It would seem that, as Joel Sokolsky and Philippe Lagassé have observed, 9/11 "did not change but only exhibits more of the fundamental factors that have shaped [the Canada–US security relationship] since before the Second World War."[100]

Still on security matters, but extending to the economic front, in March 2005 prime minister Paul Martin, president Bush and president Fox announced the creation of the Security and Prosperity Partnership, intended to increase regional economic and security cooperation. This was certainly a modest move to advance the economic agenda among the North American partners;

it was, as the former Deputy Assistant Secretary of State Department director for North American affairs Roberta Jacobson put it, "an incrementalist approach," one that lacked "a big vision."[101] Thus, the security agenda was the one that kept progressing in the Ottawa–Washington relationship—even when apparently dealt with in conjunction with the economic one. Thus, for instance, in 2011 prime minister Harper and president Obama announced a plan called "Beyond the Border: A Shared Vision for Perimeter Security and Economic Competitiveness"; its main components referred again to the security agenda.[102] It was clear that "security has trumped economics in the United States;[103] Canada, for its part, was willing to go along, at least formally.

4) Summary

As discussed above, regional orders are part and parcel of the modern state system. Although different hierarchical orders might show different inner depths and divisions of authority, what they all share is what holds each of them together: legitimacy. In the case reviewed in this chapter, the legitimacy enjoyed by the United States among the rest of the hemispheric countries has been fundamental to make the regional order work. As noted, this has never meant consensus or blind following of US dictates, only sufficient recognition of Washington as a sort of *primus inter pares*—sovereign equals that formed a separate system of values and interests. This was the nature of the Western Hemisphere Idea.

Both to the north and to the south, Washington remained a largely legitimate leader around the time the debate on its hegemonic decline initiated. This state of affairs would extend until the end of the first sub-period of study in this work (1971–1989). During the second one (1990–2000), the United States' privileged position improved substantially; it was the time of the Washington Consensus. US ascendancy suffered during the first half of the last sub-period (2001–2016), in large part due to the pronounced unilateral turn or the Bush administration. The rise of the left in Latin America no doubt also contributed to the diminished US hegemony in the region. During the Obama years, though, the tendency reverted to some extent, as the Washington administration went back to its more multilateralist tradition, and the consolidation of market-friendly economies in the hemisphere, and the weakening of the left-wing governments, mainly in South America. Canada–United States relations, for their part, were still close if not friendly during the second half of this sub-period, as the administrations in Ottawa and Washington did not see eye to eye during most of it. Thus, both hierarchy and authority have been at work in the Western Hemisphere.

Notes

1　Hobson and Sharman 2005: 64.
2　Katzenstein 2005; Paasi 2009; Prys 2010: 485.

3   Katzenstein 2005: 2, 6.
4   Buzan 2010: 23.
5   Hurrell 1998: 535.
6   Acharya 2004.
7   Ayoob 1999: 248.
8   Lake 2007; Hobson and Sharman 2005: 93; Bukovansky et al. 2012.
9   Lake 2009: 57; Katzenstein 2005: 21; Prys 2010: 484.
10 Lake 2009: 57. See also Hurrell 2006: 16, Cox 2002: 67.
11 Donnelly 2006: 164, 156; cf. Wendt and Friedheim 1995: 697.
12 Hobson and Sharman 2005: 70. Contrast Lake 2009: 36.
13 In this section I draw on Santa-Cruz 2005a, Santa-Cruz 2005b, and Santa-Cruz 2015.
14 Mattern and Zarakol 2016: 634–643.
15 Prys 2008: 12; Williams 2015: 199; Nye 2015: 5.
16 Cf. Gong 1984: 179, 195; Murase 1976: 285; Storry 1979: 23; Hobson and Sharman
    2005: 87.
17 Rojas 2009: 233.
18 Corrales and Feinberg 1999: 4; Victoria 1826: 299.
19 O'Gorman 2003 [1958]: 156.
20 Sullivan 2005: 5; O'Gorman 1977: 5.
21 In Ocampo 2009: 131.
22 In Pratt 2004: 38.
23 Cosío Villegas 1997: 245–246; Krauze 2001.
24 Foster 1909: 49-50.
25 Hobson 2014: 574; Freed 2008.
26 Carreño 1951: 83.
27 In Reinhold, 1938: 351.
28 Whitaker 1954: 1.
29 Dent 1999: 266; Burr 1973: xxv.
30 Burr 1973: xxviii.
31 Onuf 1998: 4.
32 Ibid.: 7.
33 Farer 1988: 25.
34 OEA 1970.
35 Onuf 1998: 8.
36 Wilson and Dent 1995: 27.
37 Russell and Totatlian 2002: 167; Olaya 2007: 289; Schenoni and Escudé 2016: 1.
38 Muñoz 1990: 31.
39 Corrales and Feinberg 1999: 7; Wesson 1986: 149.
40 Fernández 1997.
41 Wesson 1986: 152.
42 OEA 1970.
43 Ibid.
44 OEA 1971.
45 OEA 1977.
46 OEA 1979.
47 OEA 1980.
48 OEA 1983.
49 OEA 1986a.
50 OEA 1986b.
51 Long 2015. Cf. Long 2013: 19; Scarfi and Tillman 2016.
52 Pellicer 1998: 21.
53 OEA 1989.

54   Klepak 2000:18.
55   Cf. Naim 2000.
56   OEA 1990a.
57   OEA 1990b.
58   OEA 1992.
59   OEA 1991.
60   Tulchin 1993: 60.
61   OEA 1995.
62   Ibid.
63   OEA 1992.
64   Moss 1994: i.
65   OEA 2001.
66   Wise 2017.
67   Bravo and Santa Cruz 2012.
68   Hakim 2006: 39.
69   Malamud 2011: 19; Merke 2015: 181–182.
70   Bagley and Defort 2015: 374.
71   Shifter 2012: 60.
72   Lipset 1990: 212.
73   In Haglund 2004: 23.
74   Stewart 1992: 53, 185.
75   Adams 1965: 36.
76   Martin 1971: 34.
77   Shore 1998: 336–337.
78   In Ibid.: 346.
79   Granatstein 2003: 2.
80   In Shore 1998: 354.
81   Martin 1971: 28–29; Nossal 2004: 505; Haglund 2004: 12.
82   Shore 1998: 352.
83   Murray 1994: 63–64.
84   Deutsch et al. 1966; Adler and Barnett 1998; Shore 1998.
85   Tupper and Bailey 1967: 41.
86   Stairs 2001: 43.
87   Chapnick 2005.
88   Murray 1994: 62.
89   Ibid.; Stewart 1992: 194.
90   Martin 1971, 25.
91   In Golob 2002: 11.
92   Bow 2009
93   In Granatstein and Bothwell 1990: 71.
94   In Roussel 2004, 24.
95   Cf.Collenette 1994; Crosby 1997: 49.
96   Vucetic 2006: 133; Hristoulas 2010: 126.
97   In Haglund 2004: 16.
98   Clarkson and Fitzgerald 2009: 12.
99   Nimijean 2006: 72.
100 Sokolsky and Lagassé 2005/2006: 17.
101 Roberta Jacobson, personal interview with author, Washington, D.C., 15 July 2008; Anderson and Sands 2007: 33.
102 Fry 2012: 883.
103 Jones 2011: npn.

References

Acharya, A. (2004). How ideas spread: Whose norms matter? Norm localization and institutional change in Asian regionalism. *International Organization, 58*(2), 239–275.

Adams, J. Q. (1965). *John Quincy Adams and American continental empire: Letters, papers and speechs* (W. LaFeber, Ed.). Chicago, IL: Quadrangle Books.

Adler, E., & Barnett, M. (1998). Security communities in theoretical perspective. In E. Adler and M. Barnett (Eds.), *Security communities* (pp. 3–28). Cambridge: Cambridge University Press.

Anderson, G., & Sands, C. (2007). *Negotiating North America: The security and prosperity partnership.* Washington, DC: Hudson Institute.

Ayoob, M. (1999). From regional system to regional society: Exploring key variables in the construction of regional order. *Australian Journal of International Affairs, 53*(3), 247–260.

Bagley, B. M., & Defort, M. (2015). *Decline of the United States hegemony? A challenge of ALBA and a new Latin American integration of the twenty-first century.* Lanham, MD: Lexington Books.

Bow, B. (2009). *The politics of linkage: Power, interdependence, and ideas in Canada-US relations.* Vancouver, BC: UBC Press.

Bravo, J., & Santa Cruz, A. (2012). Hegemonía pírrica: La influencia estadounidense sobre Canadá y México en el contexto de la Invasión a Iraq. *Foro Internacional, 52*(3), 557–583.

Bukovansky, M., Clark, I., Eckersley, R., Price, R., Reus-Smit, C., & Wheeler, N. (2012). *Special responsibilities: Global powers and American power.* Cambridge: Cambridge University Press.

Burr, R. (1973). *The dynamics of world power: A documentary history of United States foreign policy 1945–1973.* (A. M. J. Schlesinger, Ed.) (Vol. III). New York: Chelsea.

Buzan, B. (2010). Culture and international society. *International Affairs, 86*(1), 1–25.

Carreño, J. M. (1951). *La diplomacia Extraordinaria entre México y Estados Unidos, 1789–1947* (Vol. II). México: Editorial Jus.

Chapnick, A. (2005). *The middle power project: Canada and the founding of the United Nations.* Vancouver, BC: UBC Press.

Clarkson, S., & Fitzgerald, E. (2009). A special military relationship? Canada's role in constructing US military power. *Journal of Military and Strategic Studies, 12*(1), 1–24.

Collenette, D. (1994). *White paper on defence: Canada-United States cooperation* [White paper]. Retrieved from http://publications.gc.ca/collections/collection_2012/dn-nd/D3-6-1994-eng.pdf

Corrales, J., & Feinberg, R. (1999). Regimes of cooperation in the Western Hemisphere: Power, interests, and intellectual traditions. *International Studies Quarterly, 43*(1), 1–3.

Cosío Villegas, D. (1997). *Estados Unidos contra Porfirio Díaz.* México: Clío.

Cox, M. (2002). September 11th and US hegemony—Or will the 21st century be American too? *International Studies Perspectives, 3*(1), 53–70.

Crosby, A. D. (1997). A middle-power military in alliance: Canada and NORAD. *Journal of Peace Research, 34*(1), 37–52.

Dent, D. W. (1999). *The legacy of the Monroe doctrine: A reference guide to U.S. involvement in Latin American and the Caribbean.* Westport, CT: Greenwood Press.

Deutsch, K., et al. (1966). *International political communities.* Garden City, NY: Anchor Books.

Donnelly, J. (2006). Sovereign inequalities and hierarchy in anarchy: American power and international society. *European Journal of International Relations, 12*(2), 139–170.

Farer, T. J. (1988). *The grand strategy of the United States in Latin America.* New Brunswick, NJ: Transaction Books.

Fernández, S. (1997). *Mi lucha por la democracia.* Santiago: Editorial Los Andes.

Foster, J. W. (1909). *Diplomatic memoirs.* Boston, MA: Houghton Mifflin Co.

Freed, F. C. (2008). *Joel Poinsett and the Paradox of Imperial Republicanism: Chile, Mexico, and the Cherokee Nation, 1810–1841.* M.A. thesis, Department of History, University of Oregon, OR.

Fry, E. (2012). The Canada-US relationship one decade after 9/11. *International Journal, 67*(4), 879–893.

Golob, S. R. (2002). North America beyond NAFTA? Sovereignty, identity, and security in Canada-U.S. relations. *Canadian-American Public Policy, 52*(December), 1–44.

Gong, G. W. (1984). *The standard of civilization in international society.* Oxford: Claredon Press.

Granatstein, J. L. (2003). *The importance of being less earnest: Promoting Canada's national interests through tighter ties with the U.S.* Toronto, ON: C.D. Howe Institute.

Granatstein, J. L., & Bothwell, R. (1990). *Pirouette: Pierre Trudeau and Canadian foreign policy.* Toronto, ON: University of Toronto Press.

Haglund, D. G. (2004). The comparative "Continentalization" of security and defence policy in North America and Europe: Canadian multilateralism in a unipolar world? *Journal of Canadian Studies, 38*(2), 9–28.

Hakim, P. (2006). Is Washington losing Latin America? *Foreign Affairs, 85*(1), 39–53.

Hobson, J., & Sharman, J. (2005). The enduring place of hierarchy in world politics: Tracing the social logics of hierarchy and political change. *European Journal of International Relations, 11*(1), 63–98.

Hobson, J. M. (2014). The twin self-delusions of IR: Why hierarchy and not anarchy is the core concept of IR. *Journal of International Studies, 42*(3), 557–575.

Hristoulas, A. (2010). La política de seguridad canadiense: Pasado, presente y futuro. In R. Benitez Manaut (Ed.), *Seguridad y defensa en America del Norte: Nuevos dilemas geopoliticos* (pp. 103–151). Washington, DC: Woodrow Wilson International Center for Scholars FundaUngo.

Hurrell, A. (1998). Security in Latin America. *International Affairs, 74*(3), 529–546.

Hurrell, A. (2006). Hegemony, liberalism and global order: What space for would-be great powers? *International Affairs, 82*(1), 1–19.

Jones, D. T. (2001, November 01). Trading over the fence. *Policy Options Politiques.*

Katzenstein, P. J. (2005). *A world of regions: Asia and Europe in the American Imperium.* Ithaca, NY: Cornell University Press.

Klepak, H. (2000). Algunas Ideas Acerca De Las Primeras Reformas Al Sistema Interamericano De Seguridad. *Fasoc,* Año 15, no. 2, abril-junio, 14–25.

Krauze, E. (2001). Sumarísima historia del Antiyanquismo. *Letras Libres.*

Lake, D. (2007). Escape from the state of nature: Authority and hierarchy in world politics. *International Security, 32*(1), 47–79.

Lake, D. (2009). Regional hierarchy: Authority and local international order. *Review of International Studies, 35,* 35–58.

Lipset, S. M. (1990). *The values and institutions of the United States and Canada.* New York: Canadian American Committee.

Long, T. (2013). *Convincing the colossus: Latin American leaders face the United States.* Ph.D. dissertation, American University School of International Service, Washington, DC.

Long, T. (2015). *Latin America confronts the United States: Asymmetry and influence.* New York: Cambridge University Press.

Malamund, A. (2011). A leader without followers? The growing divergence between the regional and global performance of Brazilian foreign policy. *American Politics and Society*, *53*(3), 1–24.

Martin, P. (1971). The American impact on Canada. In J. Redekop (Ed.), *The star-spangled beaver* (pp. 25–35). Toronto, ON: Peter Martin Associates Limited.

Mattern, J. B., & Zarakol, A. (2016). Review essay: Hierarchies in world politics. *International Organization*, *70*(3), 624–654.

Merke, F. (2015). Neither balance nor bandwagon: South American international society meets Brazil's rising power. *International Politics*, *52*(2), 178–192.

Moss, A. H. J. (1994). Introduction: The summit of the Americas, 1994. *Journal of Interamerican Studies and World Affairs*, *36*(3), i–x.

Muñoz, H. (1990). The rise and decline of the inter-American system: A Latin American view. In R. J. Bloomfield & G. F. Treverton (Eds.), *Alternative to intervention: A new U.S.-Latin American security relationship* (pp. 27–37). Boulder, CO: Lynne Rienner.

Murase, S. (1976). The most-favored-nation treatment in Japan's treaty practice during the period 1854–1905. *The American Journal of International Law*, *70*(2), 273–297.

Murray, D. J. (1994). Canada. In D. J. Murray & P. R. Viotti (Eds.), *The defense policies of nations: A comparative study* (pp. 57–93). Baltimore, MD and London: The Johns Hopkins University Press.

Naim, M. (2000). Fads and fashion in economic reforms: Washington consensus or Washington confusion? *Third World Quarterly*, *21*(3), 505–528.

Nimijean, R. (2006). The politics of branding Canada: The international-domestic nexus and the rethinking of Canada's place in the world. *Revista Mexicana de Estudios Canadienses*, *11*, 67–85.

Nossal, K. R. (2004). Defending the "realm": Canadian strategic culture revisited. *International Journal*, *59*(3), 503–520.

Nye, J. S. (2015). *Is the American century over?* United States: Polity Press.

O'Gorman, E. (1977). La gran dicotomía americana: Angloamérica e Iberoamérica. *Vuelta*, *1*(10), 1–7.

O'Gorman, E. (2003 [1958]). *La invención de América*. México: FCE.

Ocampo, E. (2009). *De la Doctrina Monroe al Destino Manifiesto. Alvear en Estados Unidos*. Buenos Aires: Editorial Claridad.

OEA (1970). Acta de la segunda sesión plenaria, Asamblea General, 26 de junio (AG/ACTA 5).

OEA (1971). Acta de la segunda sesión plenaria, Asamblea General, 15 de abril (AG/ACTA 25).

OEA (1977). Acta de la sesión inagural, Asamblea General, 22 de febrero (AG/ACTA 92/77).

OEA (1979). Acta de la segunda sesión plenaria, Asamblea General, 23 de octubre (AG/ACTA 130/79).

OEA (1980). Acta de la segunda sesión plenaria, Asamblea General, 20 de noviembre (AG/ACTA 145/80).

OEA (1983). Acta de la sexta sesión plenaria, Asamblea General, 16 de noviembre (AG/ACTA 185/83).

OEA (1986a). Acta de la sesión inaugural, Asamblea General, 10 de noviembre (AG/ACTA 216/86).

OEA (1986b). Acta de la tercera sesión plenaria, Asamblea General, 11 de noviembre (AG/ACTA 219/86).

OEA (1989). Acta de la segunda sesión plenaria, Asamblea General, 13 de noviembre (AG/ACTA 256/89).

OEA (1990a). Acta de la xxx sesión plenaria, Asamblea General, 4 de junio (AG/ACTA xxx/xxx).

OEA (1990b). Acta de la quinta sesión plenaria, Asamblea General, 6 de junio (AG/ACTA 270/90).

OEA (1991). Acta de la xxx sesión plenaria, Asamblea General, 3 de junio (AG/ACTA xxx/xxx).

OEA (1992). Acta de la tercera sesión plenaria, Asamblea General, 19 de mayo (AG/ACTA 291/92).

OEA (1995). Acta de la quinta sesión plenaria, Asamblea General, 7 de junio (AG/ACTA 326/95).

OEA (2001). Acta de la session extraordinaria, Consejo Permanente, 19 de septiembre (CP/ACTA 1293/01).

Onuf, N. G. (1998). *The republican legacy in international thought.* Cambridge: Cambridge University Press.

Olaya, S. (2007). Autonomía y relaciones internacionales: un análisis de las propuestas desarrolladas en América Latina. *Desafíos, 17*(2), 283–238.

Paasi, A. (2009). The resurgence of 'Region' and 'Regional Identity': Theoretical perspectives and empirical observations on regional dynamics in Europe. *Review of International Studies, 35*(S1), 121–146.

Pellicer, O. (1998). La OEA a los 50 años; ¿hacia su fortalecimiento? *Revista Mexicana de Política Exterior, 54*, 19–36.

Pratt, M. L. (2004). Back yard views. In A. Ross & K. Ross (Eds.), *Anti-Americanism* (pp. 32–46). New York London: New York University Press.

Prys, M. (2008). *Developing a contextually relevant concept of regional hegemony: The case of South Africa, Zimbabwe and "Quiet Diplomacy".* GIGA Working Papers, 77. Hamburg: GIGA German Institute of Global and Area Studies.

Prys, M. (2010). Hegemony, domination, detachment: Differences in regional powerhood. *International Studies Review, 12*(4), 479–504.

Reinhold, F. L. (1938). New research on the first pan-American congress held at Panama in 1826. *The Hispanic American Historical Review, 18*(3), 342–363.

Rojas, R. (2009). *Las repúblicas de aire. Utopía y desencanto en la revolución de Hispanoamérica.* México: Taurus.

Roussel, S. (2004). *The North American democratic peace. Absence of war and security institution-building in Canada-US Relations, 1867–1958.* Montreal, QC: McGill–Queen's University Press.

Russell, R., & Tokatlian, J. G. (2002). De la autonomía antagónica a la autonomía relacional: una mirada teórica desde el Cono Sur. *Perfiles Latinoamericanos, 10*(21), 159–194.

Santa-Cruz, A. (2005a). *International election monitoring, sovereignty, and the Western Hemisphere Idea: The emergence of an international norm.* New York: Routledge.

Santa-Cruz, A. (2005b). Constitutional structures, sovereignty, and the emergence of norms: The case of international election monitoring. *International Organization, 59*(3), 663–693.

Santa-Cruz, A. (2015). Liberalism, constructivism and Latin American politics since the 1990s. In J. I. Domínguez & A. Covarrubias (Eds.), *Routledge handbook of Latin America in the world* (pp. 97–111). New York: Routledge.

Scarfi, J. P., & Tillman, A. R. (2016). *Cooperation and hegemony in US-Latin American relations: Revisiting the Western Hemisphere idea.* New York: Palgrave Macmillan.

Schenoni, L., & Escudé C. (2016). Peripheral realism revisited. *Revista Brasileria de Política Internacional, 59*(1), 1–18.

Shifter, M. (2012). The shifting landscape of Latin American regionalism. *Current History*, *111*(742), 56–61.

Shore, S. M. (1998). No fences make good neighbors: The development of the Canadian-US security community, 1871–1940. In E. Adler & M. Barnett (Eds.), *Security communities* (pp. 333–367). Cambridge: Cambridge University Press.

Sokolsky, J. J., & Lagassé, P. (2005/2006). Suspenders and a belt: Perimeter and border security in Canada-US relations. *Canadian Foreign Policy*, *12*(3), 15–29.

Stairs, D. (2001). Canada in the 1990's: Speak loudly and carry a bent twig. *Policy Options*, *22*(1), 43–49.

Stewart, G. T. (1992). *The American response to Canada since 1776*. East Lansing, MI: Michigan State University Press.

Storry, R. (1979). *Japan and the decline of the West in Asia 1894–1943*. London: The Macmillan Press Ltd.

Sullivan, H. W. (2005). The border that refused to go away: The Río Grande as replication of the Rhine-Danube frontier. In R. A. Galoppe & R. Weiner (Eds.), *Explorations on subjectivity, borders, and demarcation* (pp. 3–22). Lanham, MD: University Press of America.

Tulchin, J. (1993). La inicicativa para las américas: ¿Gesto vacio, astuta maniobra estrategica, o notable giro en las relaciones hemisfericas? In *America latina y la iniciativa para las* americas (pp. 53–79). Santiago: FLACSO.

Tupper, S. R., & Bailey, D. I. (1967). *One continent-two voices: The future of Canada/U.S. relations*. Toronto, ON: Clarke, Irwin & Company Limited.

Victoria, G. (1986 [1826]). *Guadalupe Victoria: Correspondencia diplomática*. México, D.F.: SRE.

Vucetic, S. (2006). Why did Canada sit out of the Iraq war? One constructivist analysis. *Canadian Foreign Policy*, *13*(1), 133–153.

Wendt, A., & Friedheim, D. (1995). Hierarchy under anarchy: Informal empire and the East German state. *International Organization*, *49*(4), 689–721.

Wesson, R. (1986). Summary and conclusions. In R. Wesson & H. Muñoz (Eds.), *Latin American views of U.S. policy*. New York: Praeger.

Whitaker, A. P. (1954). *The Western Hemisphere idea: Its rise and decline*. Ithaca, NY: Cornell University Press.

Williams, M. E. (2015). The United States and Latin America. In J. Domínguez & A. Covarrubias (Eds.), *Routledge handbook of Latin America in the world* (pp. 199–210). New York: Taylor and Francis.

Wilson, L. C., & Dent, D. W. (1995). The United States and the OAS. In D. W. Dent (Ed.), *U.S. – Latin American policymaking: A reference handbook* (pp. 25–44). Westport, CT: Greenwood Press.

Wise, C. (2017). After the China boom: What now for Latin American emerging economies? In M. Myers & C. Wise (Eds.), *The political economy of China-Latin America relations in the new millennium* (pp. 143–169). New York: Routledge.

Chapter 3

On Power

As the previous chapter made clear, hegemony entails power. The origin of the word [hegemony] itself refers to command, guidance or dominance exerted over others. Power is indeed a pervasive term, and not only in IR. As Harold Lasswell and Abraham Kaplan noted long ago: "The concept of power is perhaps the most fundamental in the whole of political science."[1] Similarly, within the discipline, Keohane has written that when dealing with the "Big Questions" of international politics, such as war, cooperation, and sovereignty, the notion of power is ever-present.[2] However, defining power has never been an easy task. Thus, for instance, Peter Bachrach and Morton Baratz noted long ago: "The concept of power remains elusive."[3] More recently, in a similar vein, Gilpin commented that its conception is "one of the most troublesome in the field of international relations and, more generally, political science."[4] Interestingly, despite its being for some an "essentially contested concept,"[5] the consensus on its [i.e., power] centrality in the discipline predates that of anarchy, as well as the popularity of the concept of hegemony.[6] Unfortunately, however, the term has by and large been abused and reduced. Abused because it has been treated as if its maximization was the states' sole purpose, and reduced because it has been oftentimes been made synonymous with military capabilities.[7]

It is worth noting that the above-noted difficulty of defining power, or its alleged essentially contested nature, does not necessarily stem from the incommensurability of the different approaches, such as Classical Realism, Neo-Realism, or World System Theory in IR; that is, the problem is not that theoretical understandings are "non-translatable."[8] While it is true that, as Guzzini has noted, concepts are "theory-dependent," in the sense that they derive their full meaning from the analytical approach in which they are embedded,[9] I would argue that they are not theory-dependent all the way down. That is, theoretical concepts sometimes work as building blocks that can be put to use in different analytical perspectives.[10]

Without aiming to settle the discussion on either the conception or the operationalization of power, this chapter reviews different understandings of it used in the discipline and advocates the adoption of a social-relational one since, it is argued, it allows both for a more nuanced grasp of the phenomenon and for a less reductionist operationalization of it. Furthermore, I would contend that such an understanding is one that can travel across approaches, which goes a long way in building bridges that may make theoretical dialogue in the discipline possible. The chapter is divided into five sections. The first one discusses the notion of power as an attribute; the second and third sections take on the understanding of power as a relation, with the former reviewing its "thin" variant and the latter the "thick" one. Section four deals with the operationalization issues that come about when doing power-centered empirical analysis. A final section summarizes the discussion.

1) Power as an Attribute

Let's thus start with what has become the most common understanding of power in the discipline: power as an attribute. Both in the academic realm as in the one of international political practice, it is common to find a materialist and asocial understanding of power. In the academic rendering, power is an attribute, property or thing that actors possess; it springs from the material resources agents own.[11] Power thus is the functional equivalent of money in a market economy: its possession readily translates into the achievement of the desired objectives in myriad markets. Similarly, one can easily find instances of a merely materialist understanding of power among international politics practitioners. Thus, for example, the inner circle of former US president George W. Bush held that the extent to which economic and military resources were concentrated in the United States automatically turned it into the most powerful country in the world. Illustrative in this regard is the 2002 US National Security Strategy, which began stating: "The United States possesses unprecedented—and unequaled—strength and *influence* in the world."[12]

Both in the academic literature and in the policy document just mentioned, power (or influence) appears as a thing. That is, the authors of both kinds of works accept as a given that the larger the aggregate combination of material capabilities of a state (be they weapons, financial resources, territories or even populations) the more power it will exert in the different spheres of world politics. The implicit assumption most approaches in the discipline make is that resources ultimately serve as a (potential) threat to coerce others to do what the resource-wielder wants.[13] Such understanding implies not only that different power resources are highly fungible, functioning across issue areas in the international agenda, but also that they operate in a similar fashion, regardless of whether the state in question is dealing with friends or foes.[14] In this approach capabilities are thus a heuristic, serving as a cognitive shortcut to make sense of the power relationships among states.

Joseph Nye has argued that the focus on capabilities makes the concept of power "concrete, measurable, and predictable," and that "policymakers do tend to focus on resources."[15] Practitioners may indeed use material resources as a proxy for power in their day-to-day practice, but the analyst, with the benefit of time and reflection can trace the process by which resources are actually effected—or not—as power. This is important, for material capabilities, even when considered in relative terms (i.e., as a universe distribution and, consequently, relationally), are politically inert;[16] capabilities require human volition, that is, purpose, so they can be put into use.

Interestingly, even approaches that emphasize non-material elements tend to think of them in terms of quantifiable resources. Take the case of "soft" power. For Nye, who coined the term, soft power refers to the capacity of "getting others to want the outcomes that you want".[17] But soft power is not just persuasion, "It is also the ability to attract," and "soft power resources are the assets that produce such attraction";[18] for him, the main assets are culture, political values and public policy. However, as Nye recognizes, "Attraction does not always determine others' preferences, but this gap between power measured as resources and power judged as the outcomes of behavior is not unique to soft power."[19] For the purposes of my discussion here, what is interesting about the concept of soft power is that its creator, as well as many of his followers, think of it as a thing—hence the reference to soft power as a "resource" or an "asset." Nye aimed to measure US "soft" power by the amount of film productions, patents or top universities it possessed.[20] *Pace* Nye, soft power is not susceptible to be "objectively measured."[21]

If power, as Guzzini has pointed out, is "dependent on the specific encounter of people with their values and preferences in their historical context,"[22] quantification of resources is not all that useful. This is not to deny that assets, be they "hard" or "soft," are relevant features when accounting for power relations in international politics; after all, there is still no record of a pauper or outcast state that is considered influential. The point is simply that the possession of resources of any kind by itself is not enough to account for a state to be considered powerful. Ownership of a thing says little about a social relationship, which is what power is about—even if we look at the distribution of the ownership of resources. When tallying possessions is not enough, one needs to take a more encompassing view of power, one that begins with the fundamentally relational nature of power.

2) Power as a Relation: Thin Account

Broadly speaking, one can take a relational view of power from two very different vantage points. The first one, in a sense closer to the one just reviewed, is a contractual approach. In this perspective, social interaction establishes a bargaining situation for actors; thus, the focus of the analyst is the strategic behavior that agents adopt in order to pursue their interests. The approach is relational not only because of the explicit quid pro quo that takes place in the interaction, but also because agents take the calculated actions and interests of the other agents into account when trying to maintain or maximize their power. If the purposeful component of the interaction is not heeded, and the focus remains purely on material resources, the analysis of the relational character of the power relationship is socially thin, as in game theoretical accounts.[23]

Still within a relatively thin conception of social interaction, focusing on the strategic component of power relations, the analysis can include meaning-imbued categories such as authority and legitimacy. David Lake is perhaps the author who has developed this approach to its fullest extent within IR. Although for him the foundations of authority are to be found in material exchange,[24] his perspective allows for ideational, non-material elements to be taken into account in a way that goes beyond the mere asset-tallying approach alluded to above. Lake's relational understanding of authority means that "the right to rule rests on a social contract in which the ruler provides a political order of value to the ruled, who in turn grant legitimacy to the ruler and comply with the restraints on their behavior necessary for the production of that order."[25]

What sets Lake's perspective apart from the previous ones is not only its resort to authority and legitimacy, but that even if it is conceived in transactional terms, the exchange itself is anchored in a normative component: a right. That is, in Lake's approach even strategic interaction—the focus of his analysis—rests on a logic that transcends it: a political one in which rights can be created, recognized, claimed, and fought about (Merriam-Webster's definition of right: "something that one may properly claim as due").[26] As Lake puts it:

> Authority is, simply stated, rightful rule. That is, an authoritative ruler has the right to command subordinates to perform certain actions and, because the commands are rightful, the ruled have a duty to comply. In this way, authority is a type of power over others.[27]

Significantly for Lake, authority does not stop at the water's edge, that is, it is not the monopoly of domestic politics, as mainstream understandings of IR maintain. For him, authority also takes place "between states, with dominant states exercising more or less authority over subordinate ones."[28]

Furthermore, for him, authority is a form of power that is more important than coercion—a concept that tends to be associated with approaches that privilege the material element of power—since it is usually with arms that violence ultimately takes place in interstate disputes (but note that the claim is *not* that authority is bereft of coercion).[29] Thus, for Lake, power in its authoritative manifestation refers to a situation in which "A commands B, but B still does something he would otherwise not do."[30] As Lake himself makes clear, he is drawing on Robert Dahl's understanding on power in his definition of authoritative power.

Importantly, however, Dahl's account of power is amenable to a second relational interpretation of power. This view is thicker in terms of social interaction, less materially oriented and strategy-confined than Lake's. It is therefore

worth exploring Dahl's thinking on the matter in order to trace what is arguably a more social version of relational power that, while also compatible to a
purely contractual approach, can better accommodate meaning-imbued categories—and not only authority but also others like norms and identities, which,
as it will be seen below, prove useful when taking a full-fledged interpretivist
understanding of power.

3) Power as a Relation: Thick Account

Although Dahl was not an IR scholar, his succinct conception of power is
acknowledged to be the most influential in the discipline,[31] and it might as well
be the most influential in political science in general.[32] Although his definition
of power evolved over the years, it remained focused on it being "a relation
among people," and particularly about the effect of one on another's behavior
or dispositions.[33] Thus, in his seminal 1957 piece, "The Concept of Power," he
conceived of it (along with "influence," since he used both terms interchange-
ably) in the following terms: "*A* has power over *B* to the extent that he can get
B to do something that *B* would not otherwise do."[34] Almost five decades later,
in the sixth (and last, 2003) edition of his (with Bruce Stinebrickner's) *Modern
Political Analysis*, a more elaborate formulation read:

> influence can be defined as *a relation among human actors such that the wants,
> desires, preferences, or intentions of one or more actors affect the actions, or predispo-
> sitions to act, of one or more actors in a direction consistent with—and not contrary
> to—the wants, preferences, or intentions of the influence-wielder(s).*[35]

Its ascendancy notwithstanding, Dahl's approach has had many critics. And
although Dahl was certainly not able to fully address all of the criticisms leveled
at his concise conception of power, one could argue that it is able to accommodate most of them. Thus, since my purpose here is not to offer an exhaustive
review of the many approaches to power that have existed, but rather to work
with a definition that can serve as an umbrella, following Baldwin's take in his
Power and International Relations, I focus on Dahl's understanding as the epitome
of a relational approach to power, while trying to illustrate how it can deal with
some of the criticisms leveled against it.

Dahl's understanding of power is eminently social not only, as suggested,
because it is relational (and not in the [statistical] distribution of capabilities
sense), but also because it goes beyond merely strategic behavior or transac-
tionally based authority. For Dahl's definition entails matters such as character, charisma, friendship, opportunities, persuasion, rules and social standing.[36]
Significantly though, for Dahl, such bases of power, as well as more tangible
ones like money or weapons, do not produce power by themselves. In this he
concurs with Hans Morgenthau, who, when elaborating "A Political Theory
of Foreign Aid" argued that

it is not aid as such or its beneficial results that creates political loyalties on the part of the recipient, but the positive relationship that the mind of the recipient establishes between the aid and its beneficial results, on the one hand, and the political philosophy, the political system, and the political objectives of the giver, on the other.[37]

Hence, along the same lines, for Dahl, unlike for those who tend to identify the possession of material capabilities with power, the sources of power are "inert, passive."[38] This highlights the inherently relational character of power in Dahl's understanding. On this he was closely following Lasswell and Kaplan, for whom power "is defined relationally, not as a simple property."[39] That is why, for Dahl, power cannot be an attribute or a thing—that is, a property concept.[40]

There are two corollaries from the previous discussion: 1) that the instantiation of power is contingent on the power-resources wielder's intentions and skills and, 2) that the effect of such instantiation on the target's interests or preferences is indeterminate.[41] The two previous points are crucial to the discussion here, as they do away with both the common materialist fixation in the discipline and the assumption that power relations are zero-sum. That is, if a well-endowed potential power-wielder lacks the motivation or the skill to adroitly deploy her resources she will, in effect, not be a powerful actor on the matter at hand; analogously, if power-wielder A successfully utilizes her power resources in her relationship with B, that does not mean that the latter will be worse-off as a result of it—it simply means that B is doing something it would have not otherwise done, and that this is an effect of A's power.

Dahl's thoroughly social and inclusive definition of power is certainly an improvement over the previous narrower, more rationally and materially focused approaches. It is worth noting, however, that Dahl's cardinal virtue seems to have been his capacity to synthesize and articulate what others had already suggested, while emphasizing the importance of comparability (more on this later). Indeed. Dahl acknowledges his debt to Harold Lasswell who, among other things, has written about the relational and persuasive aspects of power, and favorably cites Max Weber, whose definition of power ("the probability that one actor within a social relationship will be in a position to carry out his own will despite resistance, regardless of the basis on which this probably rests"[42]), bears some resemblance to his own. Furthermore, Weber's notion of domination—a kind of power imbued with authority—cited in the 1957 article, is also eminently social, a key point in both Dahl's seminal piece, as well as in his subsequent iterations of the concept of power.

As for Dahl's emphasis on power comparability, it is worth noting that his contribution in this regard was not limited to methodological or operational matters, although these were both plentiful and consequential, but it also had ontological implications. That is, Dahl conceived of power as contextual, multidimensional, and polymorphic—features that reveal a non-essentialist understanding of the concept.

Once again, he is not unique in thinking of power in these complex terms; others before and after him have advanced similar ideas. Thus, for instance, on the contextual side, in 1960 Talcott Parsons noted that power need not be distributive, as Weber's conception emphasized, but also collective, that is, positive-sum[43]—a possibility that, as suggested, Dahl's approach allows for. Similarly, in their 1962 "Two Faces of Power" article, Bachrach and Baratz took issue with the pluralist approach in general and Dahl's in particular because they "concentrate their attention, not upon the sources of power, but its exercise."[44] For them, "power may be, and often is, exercised by confining the scope of decision-making";[45] that is, the problem was Dahl's apparent exclusion of agenda control. However, agenda control is compatible with Dahl's approach. There is nothing in it that precludes consideration of "the values and biases that are built into the political system" so that the analysis inquires into the "mobilization of bias" of the case at hand.[46] Indeed, Bachrach and Baratz recognize that Dahl writes about the existence of "a kind of false consensus," as well as of an "adherence to the norms and goals of the elite by broad sections of a community" (although they claim that he nevertheless "largely misses our point.")[47]

More recently, Rebecca Adler-Nissen and Vincent Pouliot have argued that power can be generated by social relations themselves; for them "power also emerges from the interaction *per se*."[48] Although they claim that this instantiation of power is a frequent omission in power approaches, including the relational one, it is worth noting that it is not precluded by Dahl's—even if it is certainly not the most common instance of it in his evolving conceptualization of power. Adler-Nissen and Pouliot's emphasis on practice and the recognition of competence are closely related to concepts such as authority and respect, which play a central role in Dahl's conception of power, as well as in those of the authors he was drawing on—particularly Lasswell and Kaplan.[49] As they wrote, "What is affected and on what basis are variables whose specific content in a given situation can be determined only by inquiry into the actual practices of the actors in that situation."[50]

Relatedly, on the multidimensional side of Dahl's approach, although the actors' intentions are a fundamental part of it, the unintentional effects of the actions of *A* over *B* are not necessarily excluded by it. While Dahl's emphasis on the relational aspect of power, and particularly his initial focus on behavior, lead him to stress the intentional component of action (Dahl's was, after all, operating within the behaviorist tradition[51]), there is no reason why the wider context in which the relationship is embedded, which itself could have unintended effects on power relations, would be at odds with his approach.[52] Thus, Steven Luke's "third face" of power (e.g., ideological power) regarding the roots of the agents' motivations is not antithetical to Dahl's understanding. Similarly, Michael Mann's distinction between "authoritative power" (intentional and vertical power) and "diffused power" (power that does not require command) is also compatible with the wider Dahlian conception of power.[53]

As for the polymorphic side of Dahl's approach: it is clear that, as suggested, for him the bases of power are multiple and, therefore, so are its potential instantiations. Thus, Michael Mann's four substantive sources of power, to wit, economic, ideological, military, and political, are all amenable to Dahl's understanding of power. For instance, the nature of subsistence-related activities, which encompass both "authoritative" and "diffused" power, make it possible for economic power to find expression within Dahl's framework.[54] By the same token, the contents of the above-mentioned concept of soft power, as noted, are actually an integral part of Dahl's (and his predecessors) understanding of power as a relationship. Thus, in his discussion of the power the US president might have over Congress, Dahl mentions the former's "charisma" and "charm"—no doubt a form of soft power.[55]

Ontologically, therefore, for Dahl, power has no essence. Just like for the Spanish philosopher José Ortega y Gasset people have no nature but history, it could be said that for Dahl power has no nature but diverse relational manifestations.[56] Most manifestations of power take place in hierarchical environments, ones in which authority is generally a constitutive element. In the international realm, to go back to the discussion regarding the power the United States has exercised in world affairs during the last five decades or so, it should be clear that its hierarchical character has not had a single source or manifestation. As Lasswell and Kaplan noted, "The forms of power are interdependent: a certain amount of several forms of power is a necessary condition for a great amount of any form."[57] The challenge for the analyst, as Michael Barnett and Raymond Duvall suggest, is

> to imagine how different forms interact to sharpen empirical analysis. Different forms of power have different domains of application to the extent that they illuminate different ways in which social relations affect and effect the ability of actors to control their fates.[58]

In this task, I would argue, the Dahlian perspective is particularly useful, for it should allow us to operationalize the term and, subsequently, make meaningful comparisons.

4) Translating and Unpacking Power

As noted before, for Dahl, the issue of power comparability was crucial, and he made important contributions in this regard. Let's briefly look at some of them that are relevant for this work. In order to be able to compare the exercise of power either across simultaneous instances or diachronically, one needs to precisely specify power. This requires two methodological moves: first, to operationalize the abstract concept of power so that it fits the case at hand and, second, to disaggregate the component parts of it. Regarding the first move, the challenge is to work with a notion that, as Dahl put it in his seminal paper "will undoubtedly modify [the] pure meaning" of the more abstract concept of power while remaining truthful to it.[59] The same rationale applies to related concepts such as hegemony; while the analyst needs to work with a concrete definition of it for specific research purposes, it must do justice to the authoritative relationship the concept connotes. It is therefore necessary to narrow the wider concept to a particular dimension. Just like the dimension chosen, the operational term used will be one of many possible, whose election should be guided both by the research question at hand as well as by the available data.[60] At this point it should be clear that, strictly speaking, we are not dealing, or "measuring," the abstract concept, but rather a mere proxy of it. The assumption is that power manifests vicariously through the specified criterion. The crux of the matter is, as Baldwin has suggested, that in the translation from the abstract concept of power to its operationalization one should be able to clearly state "who is influencing who with respect to what"[61]—which leads us to the second methodological move: the unbundling of the concept of power.

As Dahl noted when formulating his basic dictum ("A has power over B to the extent that he can get B to do something that B would not otherwise do"): "To specify the actors in a power relation— A has power over B—is not very interesting, informative, or even accurate."[62] To make a statement about power relations more meaningful we need to at least specify the base, domain, scope and means involved. The base refers to the resources—not necessarily material, as noted before—the power wielder can use in her relationship with her target.[63] A's power domain, in turn, is composed by the actors, in the hypothetical example cited, B, influenced by her, while the scope makes reference to the issues ("in such and such particulars" as Lasswell and Kaplan put it[64]) over which A can exercise her power. As Dahl notes, "Any statement about influence that does not clearly indicate the domain and scope it refers to verges on being meaningless."[65] Lastly, the means of power refers to the instruments A might use to actualize her power base. There are of course other matters to consider when analyzing power relations, such as the variable importance A might attribute to specific issues (depending on the historical moments or the relative costs of pursuing them), or the role the emergent ingenuity of actors plays in uncertain contexts, but these are more contingent than definitional matters.

However, there is one other definitional consideration that underlies the elements of power disaggregated in the previous paragraph: the distinction between property and relational concepts. This differentiation is paramount to understand Dahl's approach to power. Thus, for him, somewhat counterintuitively, "power resource" or "power base" is a relational concept; this is so because it acquires its meaning in context—in the context, that is, of power relations. It is worth pointing out, however, that noting the importance of the social setting for the salience of resources is not exclusive to political analysis—and that it is not a novelty. Thus, economist Frank Knight wrote in his 1921 *Risk and Uncertainty* (based on his 1916 dissertation):

It seems that what we call a 'resource' is such, not on its own account, but solely because of the uses to which it can be put, and its quantitative aspect, how much resource there is, is still more evidently determinable only in terms of the use.[66]

It should be clear why, in this understanding, "power resource" is a relational concept (an understanding, incidentally, that sits well with an interpretivist approach, insofar as in it emphasizes context and purport).

In contrast, the means used by A to exercise her power, such as a specific policy, is a property concept, insofar as it is an instrument created by the power wielder in order to influence her target. Now, the means chosen by A will be related to both its conception of self and the purposes it pursues—that is, to its identity. Thus, for instance, the policies designed and implemented by different industrialized states in the 1970s oil crisis, as analyzed in Peter Katzenstein's *Between Power and Plenty*, were to a large extent determined by the policy networks (i.e., the pattern of state–society relations) that existed in each of them—that is, they were the result of the states' identities. Recalling the above-mentioned motto, "politics is politics is politics," it is worth noting that not only foreign economic policy, but policy in general bears the imprint of state identity. Hence, as the wellspring of policy instruments, state identity could be considered—somewhat counter-intuitively—a property concept (bracketing international interaction).[67]

The definitional distinction between relational and property concepts is important because it makes clear that power relations are a process—not an inanimate, determinist structure or an agentive trait or possession. Thus, for instance, conceiving of resources in relational terms and of means in property ones allows the analyst to keep A's efforts and effects separate; a specific policy, say public diplomacy, may or may not achieve its intended objectives. Just as in the case of legitimacy, the outcome of a power attempt is a gradation. That is, it is not something that can or should be expressed in dichotomous terms; in the same way that legitimacy is a continuum, in the sense that, for instance, a hegemonic power can be legitimate to other states to varying degrees, the influence A can achieve over B on a particular occasion is not at all or nothing matter. Furthermore, since power is relational, its analysis should shed light not only about A or the interaction itself, but also about B;[68] that is, since B is not a passive object, its means and resources should also be part of the equation.[69] In the next chapter I discuss a framework for thinking about how power relations transpire in the international political economy.

5) Summary

As discussed above, even though the study of power is pervasive both in political science in general and IR in particular, there is no consensual definition of the term. Conventional approaches treat power as an attribute, as a possession to be employed. This perspective more often than not entails a materialist and an asocial understanding of power. Alternatively, power can be considered as a relationship. On this broad take, power can be approached in contractual, mostly strategic terms; this is a thin relational perspective. A thicker one is that which sees power as involving more than strategy and interests; it privileges instead meaning, legitimacy and social interaction. Dahl's influential account of power focuses precisely on the relations among people, and particularly on the effects such intercourse produces on the behavior and dispositions of the agents involved. Although Dahl's concept focused first on the behavioral effects of power, its ulterior specification made clear that it was also applicable to the other two "faces" of power: agenda-setting and ideology.

Crucially, for Dahl, power has no essence. It is contextual, multidimensional, and polymorphic; therefore, its deployment and effects are contingent. Moreover, the broader Dahlian approach to power is also useful, as it emphasizes the need to specify it and operationalize it; while the former requires its unpacking (e.g., in base, scope, domain, means) the latter implies choosing a proxy that, while not being the abstract concept of power anymore—therefore altering its meaning—it does not betray it either. Particularly helpful in the disaggregating of power is Dahl's distinction between property and relational concepts. As noted, for him power resources should be thought of as being an instance of relational concepts, as they acquire meaning in context. Conversely, the means utilized by the power wielder in a relationship are occurrences of property concepts, as they are instruments created by it to influence her target. I argued above that when studying power relations in the international arena, identity can be considered a property concept—a property concept from which other, more specific ones, such as economic statecraft policies, to some extent emanate. The relevance of considering state identity as a property concept is that it underscores both the congruity that should exist between it and the means chosen, and that the target state experiences it as a social fact. Furthermore, as noted, the distinction between relational and property concepts is significant because it helps to keep influence efforts separate from their potential effects, thus evincing that power relations should be considered a contingent social process.

Notes

1   Lasswell and Kaplan 1950: 75.
2   In Keohane 2008: 709.
3   Bachrach and Baratz 1962: 947.
4   Gilpin 1981: 13.
5   Gallie 1955–1966; Barnett and Duvall 2005: 41; Collier et al. 2006.
6   Baldwin 2016: 96–100.
7   Ibid.: 89, 106, 109.
8   Wight 2002: 31.
9   Guzzini 2013: 235.

10 Cf. Baldwin, 2016: 60; Sil and Katzenstein 2010.
11 Wohlforth 1999; Brooks and Wohlforth 2002.
12 USNSS 2002, 1; Italics mine.
13 In Lake 2013: 56.
14 Wendt 1999: 301; Shambaugh 1999: 11.
15 Nye 1990: 26; Nye 2011: 240.
16 Adler-Nissen and Pouliot 2014: 891; Wendt and Friedheim 1995: 692.
17 Nye 2004: 5.
18 Ibid.: 6.
19 Ibid.: 6.
20 Nye 1990: 26.
21 Nye 2004: 34.
22 Guzzini 2013: 5.
23 Morrow 1994; Snidal 1985; Fearon 1994; cf. Wendt 1994: 390.
24 Lake 2009: xi.
25 Ibid.: 3
26 Cf. Ashley 1983.
27 Lake 2009: 8.
28 Lake 2013: 61.
29 Lake 2009: ix; 8, 21.
30 Ibid.: 21.
31 Barnett and Duvall 2005: 49.
32 Stinebrickner 2015.
33 Dahl 1957: 203.
34 Ibid.: 202–203.
35 Dahl and Stinebrickner 2003: 17; Italics original.
36 Dahl 1957: 203; Dahl and Stinebrickner 2003: 34, 49.
37 Morgenthau 1962: 308–309.
38 Dahl 1957: 203.
39 Lasswell and Kaplan 1950: 75.
40 Oppenheim 1981.
41 Baldwin 2016: 36; Morgenthau 1962.
42 Weber 1947: 152.
43 Parsons 1960: 221.
44 Bachrach and Baratz 1962: 948.
45 Ibid.: 948.
46 Bachrach and Baratz 1962: 950, 952; cf. Baldwin 2016: 17.
47 Bachrach and Baratz 1962: 949.
48 Adler-Nissen and Pouliot 2014: 893.
49 Ibid.: 893–894; Lasswell and Kaplan 1950: 87. On practice theory and relationism see McCourt 2016 and Nexon et al. 2017.
50 Lasswell and Kaplan 1950: 92.
51 Cf. Lukes 1974.
52 Baldwin 2016: 75; see also Lasswell 1935: 20, 21, 309.
53 Mann 1986: 8.
54 Ibid.; see also Lasswell and Kaplan 1950: 90.
55 Dahl 1957: 203; see also Lasswell 1935: 309; Lasswell and Kaplan 1950: 84.
56 Ortega y Gasset 1942: 63.
57 Lasswell and Kaplan 1950: 92.
58 Barnett and Duvall 2005: 68.
59 Dahl 1957: 214.
60 Ibid.: 202, 214.

61 Baldwin 2016: 76.
62 Dahl 1957: 203.
63 Ibid.: 203.
64 Lasswell and Kaplan 1950: 76
65 Dahl 1976: 33
66 In Baldwin 2016: 54; cf. Sartori 1987: 142.
67 Cf. Wendt 1999: 367.
68 Cf. Baldwin 2016: 50, 55; cf. Kirshner 1997: 33; Mastanduno, 1999: 306.
69 Morgenthau 1962.

References

Adler-Nissen, R., & Pouliot, V. (2014). Power in practice: Negotiating the international intervention in Libya. *European Journal of International Relation*, *20*(4), 889–911.

Ashley, R. K. (1983). Three modes of economism. *International Studies Quarterly*, *27*(4), 463–496.

Bachrach, P., & Baratz, M. S. (1962). Two faces of power. *The American Political Science Review*, *56*(4), 947–952.

Baldwin, D. A. (2016). *Power and international relations: A conceptual approach*. Princeton, NJ: Princeton University Press.

Barnett, M., & Duvall, R. (2005). Power in international politics. *International Organization*, *59*(1), 39–75.

Brooks, S., & Wohlforth, W. (2002). American primacy in perspective. *Foreign Affairs*, *81*(4), 20–33.

Collier, D., Hidalgo, F. D., & Maciuceanu, A. O. (2006). Essentially contested concepts: Debates and applications. *Journal of Political Ideologies*, *11*(3), 211–246.

Dahl, R. A. (1957). The concept of power. *Behavioral Science*, *2*(3), 201–215.

Dahl, R. A. (1976). *Modern political analysis* (3rd ed.). Upper Saddle River, NJ: Prentice Hall.

Dahl, R. A., & Stinebrickner, B. (2003). *Modern political analysis* (6th ed.). Upper Saddle River, NJ: Prentice Hall.

Fearon, J. D. (1994). Signaling versus the balance of power and interest. *Journal of Conflict Resolution*, *38*(2), 236–269.

Gallie, W. (1955–1996). Essentially contested concepts. *Proceedings of the Aristotelian Society*, *56*, 167–198.

Gilpin, R. (1981). *War and change in world politics*. New York: Cambridge University Press.

Guzzini, S. (2013). *Power, realism and constructivism*. New York: Routledge.

Katzenstein, P. J. (1978). *Between power and plenty: Foreign economic policies of advanced industrial states*. Madison, WI: University of Wisconsin Press.

Keohane, R. O. (2008) Big questions in the study of world politics. In C. Reus-Smit & D. Snidal (Eds.), *The Oxford handbook of international relations* (pp. 708–715). New York: Oxford University Press.

Kirshner, J. (1997). The microfoundations of economic sanctions. *Security Studies*, *6*(3), 32–64.

Lake, D. (2009). *Hierarchy in international relations*. Ithaca, NY: Cornell University Press.

Lake, D. (2013). Authority, coercion, and power in international relations. In M. Finnemore & J. Goldstein (Eds.), *Back to the basics, state power in a contemporary world* (pp. 55–77). New York: Oxford University Press.

Lasswell, H. D. (1935). *World politics and personal insecurity*. New York: Free Press.

Lasswell, H. D., & Kaplan, A. (1950). *Power and society: A framework for political inquiry*. New Haven, CT: Yale University Press.

Lukes, S. (1974). *Power: A radical view*. London: Macmillan.

Mann, M. (1986). *The sources of social power, Vol. I: A history of power from the beginning to 1760 AD*. New York: Cambridge University Press.

Mastanduno, M. (1999). Economic statecraft, interdependence, and national security: Agendas for research. *Security Studies, 9*(1–2), 288–316.

McCourt, D. M. (2016). Practice theory and relationalism as the new constructivism. *Internatinal Studies Quarterly, 60*(3), 475–485.

Morgenthau, H. (1962). A political theory of foreign aid. *The American Political Science Review, 56*(2), 301–309.

Morrow, J. D. (1994). *Game theory for political scientists*. Princeton, NJ: Princeton University Press.

Nexon, D. et al. (2017). *Seizing constructivist ground? Practice and relational theories*. International Studies Quarterly Online Symposium.

Nye, J. S. (1990). *Bound to lead: The changing nature of American power*. New York: Basic Books Inc.

Nye, J. S. (2004). *Soft power: The means to success in world politics*. New York: Public Affairs.

Nye, J. S. (2011). *The future of power*. New York: Public Affairs.

Oppenheim, F. (1981). *Political concepts: A reconstruction*. Oxford: Basil Blackwell.

Ortega y Gasset, J. (1942). *Historia como sistema*. Madrid: Revista de Occidente.

Parsons, T. (1960). *Structure and process in modern societies*. New York: Free Press.

Sartori, G. (1987). *The theory of democracy revisited (Vol. I)*. Chatham, NJ: Chatham House Publishers.

Shambaugh, G. E. (1999). *States, firms, and power: Successful sanctions in United States foreign policy*. Albany, NY: SUNY Press.

Sil, R., & Katzenstein, P. J. (2010). *Analytical eclecticism in the study of world politics*. New York: Palgrave Macmillan.

Snidal, D. (1985). Coordination versus Prisoners' Dilemma: Implications for international cooperation and regimes. *The American Political Science Review, 79*(4), 923–941.

Stinebrickner, B. (2015). Robert A. Dahl and the essentials of modern political analysis: Politics, influence, power, and polyarchy. *Journal of Political Power, 8*(2), 189–207.

USNSS (September 2002). *The national security strategy of the United States of America*. Washington, DC: U.S. Government Printing Office.

Weber, M. (1947). *The theory of social and economic organization* (A. M. Henderson & T. Parsons, Trans.). New York: Free Press.

Wendt, A. (1994). Collective identity formation and the international state. *American Political Science Review, 88*(2), 384–396.

Wendt, A. (1999). *Social theory of international politics*. Cambridge: Cambridge University Press.

Wendt, A., & Friedheim, D. (1995). Hierarchy under anarchy: Informal empire and the East German State. *International Organization, 49*(4), 689–721.

Wight, C. (2002). Philosophy of social science and international relations. In W. Carlsnaes, T. Risse & B. A. Simmons (Eds.), *Handbook of international relations* (pp. 23–51). London: Sage Publications.

Wohlforth, W. C. (1999). The stability of a unipolar world. *International Security, 24*(1), 5–41.

Chapter 4

Thick Economic Statecraft and the Political Economy of US Power

The economy is an arena of power relations. Just like the case of authority discussed before, economics does not stop at the water's edge either. Furthermore, like politics more broadly, the economy is embedded in a thick tapestry of social relations.[1] As Edward Carr noted on the eve of World War II in *The Twenty Years Crisis*, "Economic forces are in fact political forces. [...] The science of economics presupposes a given political order, and cannot be profitably studied in isolation from politics."[2] Similarly, in the aftermath of the armed struggle, in *National Power and the Structure of Foreign Trade*, Albert O. Hirschman noted the way international commerce can be used for political purposes, particularly when an economically powerful country withholds economic intercourse with a weak one.[3]

The close connection between economics and politics notwithstanding, the two disciplines parted company and tended to study their subject matters in isolation circa the publication of the two works just mentioned; this problem has been particularly acute in International Relations. One of the reasons for this estrangement had to do with the widespread belief, at least in Western politics and academia, that the liberal economic system had its own laws, and that it should not be contaminated by political considerations. Matters of political economy in general, or economic statecraft in particular, tended to be ignored in the IR literature.[4]

Thus, in 1970, Susan Strange lamented the predominance of purely economic analysis of the international economy, to the detriment of the "political analysis" such a topic requires.[5] It was precisely the disconnect in the study of economic and political affairs at the international level that led to the renaissance of International Political Economy later in the same decade.[6] The bringing together of economic and political matters in general, and in the international realm in particular, has provided many valuable insights, not the least of which is the uncovering of the power effects the interaction of politics and economics produces—an insight especially germane for this work. Although still analytically different, politics and economics, particularly at their intersection, can be considered from a political economy approach as arenas of power production and contention. Accordingly, matters that before the revival of IPE were dismissed in IR, on grounds that they were only of marginal relevance to the core aspects of the discipline, such as security, have been fruitfully studied as the formerly rigid disciplinary boundaries have partially blurred.

Hence, IR's research agenda has been expanded to issues previously neglected because of their economic character, such as foreign aid, foreign investment, raw materials and trade.[7] Furthermore, the partial fading of disciplinary boundaries has also enriched the way the issues themselves are framed. Thus, for instance, foreign economic policy is no longer seen as responding only to the imperatives of comparative advantage, the international division of labor, or resource endowment, but also as a medium that both serves the broader goals of a country and corresponds to its identity.[8] It is thanks to this new understanding that international economic relations have come to be considered a legitimate matter in what used to be the preserve of "high politics," that is, issues directly related to what was considered to be "the struggle for power" in international affairs, such as war.[9]

In this chapter, I connect the previous discussion on the concept of power to its exercise in the International Political Economy with the objective of displaying a sphere where diverse theoretical understandings of power can partially converge. Such convergence should allow us to find common ground among those perspectives and thus help in obtaining a more focused discussion on the matter of how US power has waxed and waned during the last five decades in the Western Hemisphere. The chapter is divided into six sections: the first focuses on economic statecraft as an academic field, making the case for what I call "thick" economic statecraft; the second reviews the political and power dimensions of US economic statecraft, whereas the third deals with the practice of US economic statecraft in general. Section 4 focuses on the evolution, since the 1970s, of the paradigmatic instance of US economic statecraft: trade policy, broadly defined. The fifth section is devoted to the operationalization of the concept of power in the economic realm, as understood by a thick economic statecraft approach; in the sixth and final section I present a summary of the discussion.

1) Thickening Economic Statecraft

Economic relations have long been used for broader political purposes. Around 432 BC, Athens passed a decree bringing to a halt trade with Megara for what it considered disloyal political actions on the part of the port city.[10] Already in the modern state system, but before the United States was established as an independent country, the colonists resorted to several trade measures in order to protest British rule and gain independence.[11] This repertoire of intercourse with other political units is oftentimes called "economic statecraft." For Stephen Collins, economic statecraft "encompasses all applications of material sanctions and material assistance to alter the behavior of foreign states."[12] More specifically, David Baldwin, the foremost expert on the matter, has defined economic statecraft as "influence attempts relying primarily on resources which have a reasonable semblance of a market price in terms of money."[13] He distinguishes three constituent parts of economic statecraft: "1. Type of policy instrument used in the influence attempt, i.e., economic. 2. Domain of the influence attempt, i.e., other international actor(s). 3. Scope of the influence attempt, i.e., some dimension(s) of the target(s)' behavior (including beliefs, attitudes, opinions, expectations, emotions, and/or propensities to act)."[14] In addition to sanctions and assistance, to which Collins and other authors reduce economic statecraft,[15] Baldwin also includes economic warfare as one of its main clusters.[16]

However, Baldwin conceives of economic statecraft as "a normal, routine, everyday, ordinary, commonplace activity."[17] I consider this significant because it points to the quotidian nature of power relations in the economic realm. That is, although Baldwin by and large focuses on "instruments" or "techniques"[18] such as economic sanctions or foreign aid, which are used sporadically, the fact that he thinks of economic statecraft as an everyday activity broadens the concept to more regular practices. That is why Baldwin recognizes that even though free trade policies "may not be obvious economic techniques of statecraft (...) they can be and have been important ones."[19]

Baldwin is explicit in that economic activities are part and parcel of "an overarching set of values and priorities" of the country that undertakes them, and that they are intended to serve the "higher goals of the polity."[20] While he privileges the study of the instruments of economic statecraft because they are what distinguishes this kind of statecraft,[21] and therefore focuses on this practice "as a form of bargaining behavior,"[22] for him economic statecraft is always a political act.[23] Furthermore, the political act in question is not unidirectional nor exclusively material. That is, Baldwin posits that A's actions are intended to exert an effect or response on B's part—thus creating a loop or feedback mechanism—and that the purpose of the influence attempt might have to do with nonmaterial issues, such as reputation or respect.[24]

Extending the concept of economic statecraft beyond the myriad instruments falling within its punitive (e.g., sanctions, trade embargoes, tariffs, currency manipulation) or positive (aid, trade preferences, grants, technical assistance) facets places it beyond a merely strategic or bargaining framework (a-là Lake, per previous chapter). In a purely strategic understanding, politics is reduced to what Richard Ashley calls "logical economism," which for him refers to "the reduction of the practical interpretive framework of political action to the framework of economic action: the reduction of the logic of politics to the logic of economy."[25] In contrast, a broader conception of economic statecraft, let's call it "thick statecraft," opens the possibility to transcend socially thin accounts of interaction, ones in which actors are assumed to relate to others only instrumentally (considering their transactions as mere quid pro quo, while pursuing the largest payoff). This wider understanding rightly restores, Ashley suggests, "the logic of politics as the starting-point and framework of political analysis."[26] Furthermore, in doing so, this broader conception places economic statecraft squarely within classical political economy approaches in general, and more particularly within the more recent literature on Economic Diplomacy, Foreign Economic Policy (FEP) and International Political Economy (IPE).

Baldwin's rather implicit thick strand of economic statecraft is analogous to what Ashley called "practical" realism, in contradistinction to "technical" realism in IR theory; for Ashley, "Practical realism's approach is interpretive" and "it must express its concepts, norms and knowledge claims in terms of the very language it interprets."[27] Reminiscent of Dahl's and Baldwin's insistence on the importance of using concepts close to ordinary language when talking about power relations and economic statecraft, respectively, Ashley asserts that in practical realism the terms used must correspond to "the classical diplomatic language of traditional statesmanship."[28] In a similar fashion, I argue that Baldwin's concept of statecraft—which represents the most thorough and thoughtful work on the matter—is at its best if understood in a wider manner than the one he often emphasizes. That is, his deep understanding of the problem in question seems to be constrained by his focus on instruments or techniques (however, it should be noted that at times Baldwin is also quite open to take into account wider, less technical issues, such as the values and broad policies on the international economic realm, as noted above).

Baldwin's penchant for policy instruments or techniques comes from his conviction that economic statecraft is characterized by the "'peculiar nature of its means'" (Baldwin is alluding to Carl von Clausewitz's conception of war).[29] Therefore, for him, economic statecraft as a field of study should be defined in terms of them—not in terms of intended effects or processes (by which policy was made), as other approaches dealing with international economic relations do. Interestingly, however, he concedes that two related perspectives are quite close to his own understanding of economic statecraft. Thus, for instance, Baldwin writes that "'foreign economic policy' is sometimes used in much the same way as 'economic statecraft' is used here," and that "economic diplomacy is sometimes used in much the same sense that 'economic statecraft' is used here."[30] However, he finds fault with them because, in the case of foreign economic policy, it oftentimes "says nothing about the *means* to be used, thus leaving open the possibility that noneconomic techniques, such as threats or violence, could be considered foreign economic policy ,"[31] and, in the case of economic diplomacy, because "it broadens the concept of 'diplomacy' so much that it makes it difficult to think in terms of diplomatic alternatives to economic techniques."[32]

Thus, keeping in mind the reasons his approach departs from the way those two are generally dealt with—reasons that certainly give more focus to his own perspective—but emphasizing the common ground he found with them, I intend to "thicken" Baldwin's. I do so by bringing back to it deeply embedded factors other perspectives reveal more clearly than Baldwin's often does. Thus, for instance, for Charles S. Maier, a sound political economy perspective "interrogates economic doctrines to disclose their sociological and political premises".[33] This idea might actually be implicit in Baldwin's work; for instance, in his point that the "peculiar nature" of the means used relate to "foreign policy goals"—as these goals constitute ideas about what the interests of the state are, about its conception of what its political economy and its role in world affairs ought to be.[34] In order to try to do justice to Baldwin's well-articulated perspective, I keep what I noted before I consider the core (for both substantive and methodological issues; more on the latter below) of his approach: the focus on means. I think Baldwin's reason to concentrate on it is a solid one, methodologically speaking: means are property concepts, that is, "features" that belong to the power wielder, thus allowing the analyst (and the practitioner) to differentiate between influence attempts and outcomes—something that should prove useful when inquiring into power relations in the international economic sphere.

This move, however, presents a methodological challenge: to reconcile the broader, less technical concepts alternative approaches entertain with the specific "instruments" Baldwin concentrates on. Let's take the case of state identity. Even if the other perspectives generally do not use it explicitly, it is quite amenable to them. Peter Katzenstein's seminal work *Small States in World Markets*, which contrasts the domestic structures of liberal and statist countries, for instance, is quite compatible to the later literature on state identity.[35] Similarly, Egon Rohrlich's work on economic culture and foreign economic policy, which puts cognition, norms, perceptions and value systems at the center of analysis, is also amenable to what the IR literature on identity has to say.[36] Identity, however, is not usually thought of as an instrument, a means or a technique. It is usually conceived of as something that works at a different level of analysis; let's consider it briefly.

Identity is a social category. It contains two dimensions in corporate actors, which vary with time: its content and the degree to which it is contested. The purpose of the collectivity, its worldview, which implies a certain degree of solidarity—however illusory and contested—among the members of society, is part of the first dimension.[37] The second refers to the extent to which the content of the identity is accepted by the members of the group.[38] Whereas the contentious nature of identity points to its fluidity, its substantive component directs us in the opposite direction: its (relative) permanence. However, if identity is to be useful as a practical and analytical concept, the resultant of this tension should contain a certain bias for continuity; for if identity were completely unstable there would be no point in talking about it, either as a belief or as a concept.[39]

Hence, being a relatively stable structure, once established identity creates interests and limits the range of choice—not "everything goes" with a given identity.[40] To say that identity stands analytically apart from interests and that on many occasions precedes them is not to postulate a clear-cut division between them, nor to privilege an ethereal concept over a more "concrete" one. On the one hand, the relationship between identity and interests is a recursive one.[41] Interests frequently impinge on an actor's identity; thus, for instance, the interests pursued through foreign economic policy can serve to cement the state's identity.[42] Furthermore, corporate actors such as states possess some "pre-social" interests—that is, interests that are not constructed in the interaction with other states, such as survival—that not only can be said to be independent from identity, but also have an effect on it.[43] On the other hand, the fact that identity (like power) might be a "contested concept" does not mean that interest is not—and in that sense it is not the case that the former is "fussy" and the latter precise. In international politics, for instance, national interests do not just stand out there or are simply derived from each state's position in the distribution of capabilities; their definition always entails political contestation.[44]

Moreover, identity is neither transparent nor an objective social fact. Hence, the language to articulate the discourse on state identity is often used strategically by players; as a category of practice, agents often use it instrumentally for their political advantage. However, regardless of the sincerity of the claims advanced, such instrumentality tells something about the importance of identity; that is, actors react to such utterances and engage in battles over them because identity matters to them.[45]

The role of identity in both international politics and International Political Economy has actually long been recognized in the literature—even if, as implied, this has happened at times with other names. Thus, Hans Morgenthau considered "cultural identity" to be part of the national interest states should protect, and the process by which identity is partially formed in the international system is certainly part of the realist tradition.[46] Similarly, Kal Holsti's notion "national role conceptions" is similar to that of identity, as far as they are said to limit the policy makers' range of choice by becoming part of the country's political culture.[47] Even neo-realists who infer a state's strategic culture from its relative capabilities are in some way talking about identity.[48] As noted, both Katzenstein's and Rohrlich's work on domestic structures and economic culture, respectively, sit well with the concept of state identity.[49]

Significantly, identity is anchored in history.[50] As in the case of the sense of community of interests and purpose, the construction of national histories is a deeply political process. Founding myths and historical watersheds intermingle and vie for political salience in this undertaking, in which collective memory plays a fundamental role. Without collective memory, both the solidarity anchored in the past and the notion of a common future that imbues the state with a sense of purpose would not coalesce to form the identity any collectivity needs to function.[51] For instance, liberal capitalism, one of the founding myths of the US political economy, has served as a defining feature of the US identity in international affairs.[52]

I am not suggesting that only one overarching state identity exists; identities often vary according to both the issue area in question and its dominant cultural or political traditions (more on this below). So, for example, a state can instantiate its identity as "non-aligned" in some contexts and as a "trading" state in others.[53] However, not all identities carry the same weight nor have the same endurance—there are some that have a greater prominence and resilience than others. Furthermore, identities do not do all the explanatory work in social interaction; thus, an approach that privileges identities and problematizes the origins of interests can readily accept that once interests are established, actors might simply pursue them, with identity factors receding to the background.[54]

As the previous paragraphs have argued, identity impinges on the policies a state adopts. The methodological question, as noted above, is to accommodate this more abstract concept to the more specific ones Baldwin focuses on, as identity is not generally thought of as an instrument. But can it be considered a property concept? Yes, if one brackets A's (i.e., the power wielder's) international interaction (more on this later).[55] Let's thus pose the question differently: should one ignore a property concept, in the case at hand, identity, that affects the means used, just because it is not an instrument itself? I would respond in the negative, since ignoring it would create some sort of endogeneity or omitted variable bias.[56]

Let's consider an analogy from domestic economic policy (or, indeed, simply from domestic politics: "a rose is a rose is a rose … ") to illustrate how the state's identity or, more precisely in this case, the government's or decision-maker's identity, ideology, or worldview affects the instruments chosen. In 1953, Argentinian president Juan Domingo Perón wrote to his Chilean counterpart Carlos Ibañez that he should

> Give the people, especially to the workers, all that is possible. When it seems to you that already you are giving them too much, give them more. You will see the results. Everybody will try to scare you with the specter of economic collapse. But all of this is a lie. There is nothing more elastic than the economy which everyone fears so much because no one understands it.[57]

Although it could be argued that the alleged mysterious nature of the economy was just plain ignorance on the Argentinian president's part, I think it was actually related to Perón's political economy conception, as well as to what he considered appropriate a state led by his left-leaning Justicialist party should do; these ideational matters therefore greatly affected the economic policies, that is, the means, his government implemented. In this reading, then, Baldwin's instruments or techniques could be more accurately thought of as "intervening variables," in the sense stated in Chapter 1 (as a "variable that explains a relation or provides a causal link between other variables") but also as "a 'contingency', which is added on to a basic causal variable"—in my case state identity.[58] Identity thus delimits the repertoire of policy instruments.[59]

The kind of thick economic statecraft I am advocating follows on the tradition of classical political economists such as Karl Marx, John Stuart Mill, David

Ricardo and Adam Smith who, putting the interaction between politics and economics front and center, recognized the primacy of politics, conceived of the polity in societal (as opposed to atomistic) terms, and focused on the role played by production and exchange in the nation's evolution.[60] It is worth noting that thick economic statecraft, like the classical approach to political economy, is akin to the social relational understanding of power reviewed before.[61]

Thick economic statecraft is also compatible with economic diplomacy. Like the conventional treatment of economic statecraft, economic diplomacy is commonly understood to deal with positive and negative incentives, although it explicitly excludes frankly hostile ones, such as blockades, as they are considered to be beyond the diplomatic pale (therefore falling within warfare).[62] Thick economic statecraft resemblance to economic diplomacy comes from the latter's holistic conception of its subject matter;[63] diplomacy is understood as the art of communication, dialogue and legitimacy-building amongst states.[64] In this, economic diplomacy is actually not that far from thick economic statecraft, for "statecraft," according to Merriam-Webster, is about "the art of conducting state affairs." Art in turn is defined as "skill acquired by experience, study, or observation." The same source notes that whereas art and skill "mean the faculty of executing well what one has devised," art "implies a personal, unanalyzable creative power." Thick economic statecraft is therefore amenable to the wider understanding of diplomatic practice the field of economic diplomacy entails.

The methodological commitment that comes with this understanding of statecraft, as well as the one that the use of the term diplomacy carries, can hardly be analyzed in mere positivist fashion, or pretending economic statecraft is only about strategic interaction. Thus, for instance, a country's projection of power and values abroad, such as the embedded liberalism that followed World War II is considered in the literature an instance of economic diplomacy—and one that, significantly, had not as its only purpose the attainment of economic benefits.[65] The term statecraft is thus actually quite close to the art of diplomacy and government in ordinary usage. Katen E. Young in the *Washington Post*, for instance, makes statecraft synonymous with "visions of governance,"[66] an idea that resembles the Spanish translation of the term (*arte de gobernar*, art of ruling[67] or, simply, *política*, politics[68] [similarly, the French translation of statecraft is *habilité politique*, political ability,[69] and the German rendering *Staatskunst*, closer to the English term, also remits to politics]).[70] This is no mere semantic disquisition, as for both Dahl and Baldwin it is important that analytical concepts should maintain some resemblance to ordinary language.[71]

Likewise, thick economic statecraft's affinity with FEP is evident not only in that both focus on the economic component, but also in that they deal with foreign policy—that is, with the state's planned and implemented attempts to influence the international realm, in light of its interests and values.[72] Thick economic statecraft would thus be consistent with the more prominent role some FEP accounts give to social mores. As noted, Baldwin hints that national values are an important element in the making of economic statecraft. Similarly, in the FEP literature, Dobson conceives of economic statecraft as a practice that reflects the state's "individual traditions, characteristics and circumstances."[73] A thick economic statecraft account can benefit from FEP's careful consideration of the ideational frameworks from which both broad policy scripts and specific instruments of statecraft emerge.[74]

In a similar fashion, thick economic statecraft is also close to IPE, in that while both acknowledge the analytical separability of politics and economics, they explicitly focus on the generative effect their practical interaction produces. Thus, for instance, Peter Katzenstein's mentioned 1978 *Between Power and Plenty* put forward not only the interaction between the domestic and international realms—and therefore the already noted false dichotomy between them—but also the way the interaction of political and economic factors within industrialized states produced differentiated responses to a common external shock. Similarly, Baldwin maintains that "beliefs that the economy and the polity can and should be insulated from one another ... hinder thinking about economic statecraft."[75]

Furthermore, another distinctive contribution of IPE which fits well with the literature on economic statecraft is the blurring of IR's already mentioned customary divide between high and low politics—the former referring to issues such as security and the latter to those such as trade.[76] This blurring is also in synch with Baldwin's thicker account of economic statecraft, as when he writes: "To the extent that the distinction between 'high' and 'low' politics implies that foreign economic policy is either unimportant or outside the scope of foreign policy in general, it discourages inquiry about economic statecraft."[77]

I think the thicker understanding of economic statecraft I advocate, while remaining faithful to Baldwin's articulate, illuminating and thorough approach, benefits from more openly incorporating insights from related traditions.

2) US Economic Statecraft: Politics and Power

The field of US economic diplomacy, economic statecraft—thick or thin—or foreign economic policy has become a wide and influential one within IR in general and IPE in particular.[78] Part of the reason lies in the fact that, as suggested, economic statecraft seems to be intrinsic to the United States. Thus, not only the colonists resorted to this practice in order to gain independence, but continued to do so on a regular fashion—with "dollar diplomacy" being a prominent instance of it. But no doubt a larger part of the rationale for the consolidation of US economic diplomacy, foreign economic policy or economic statecraft as an academic field, has to do with the role the country acquired in the international system after World War II. As an observer of the nascent era put it,

> The fact is that today much of our foreign policy centers around economic matters, and economic and commercial policies are of prime importance in

all of our international negotiations. The United States is now the greatest single economic force on earth and the kind of foreign economic policy we follow now and in the next few years will inevitably determine in large measure the policies to be followed by the rest of the world.[79]

Stanley Hoffman's quip about IR being an "American social science" could perhaps be extended to the study of economic statecraft.[80]

This is not to suggest, as some did in the case of US dominance in IR, that the field is subservient to US interests or that its scholars are the handmaidens of American statesmen.[81] After all, as noted, economic statecraft predated the emergence of the United States as a major player in international affairs, and practices such as dollar diplomacy faced plenty of homegrown criticism.[82] Furthermore, the first consistent and coordinated efforts at economic statecraft emerged before the U.S. became a global hegemonic power in the 1930s.[83]

What is not in question is the increased US attention to and capacity in engaging in economic statecraft after World War II.[84] Significantly—as noted by Thomas Blaisdell and Eugene Braderman above—the "kind" of foreign economic policy to be pursued by the rising hegemonic power would prove crucial to the emerging *liberal* international order. This was not a settled or preordained matter. Just as there were within the United States multiple political culture traditions (e.g., liberalism and republicanism) competing to become dominant, there were also contending foreign policy traditions, such as the Hamiltonian, Jacksonian and Wilsonian, each with a corresponding conception of economic statecraft.[85] As Walter Russell Mead has noted, "each generation of Americans has struggled to define the national interest and the national values, and to relate the two concepts in an overall foreign policy strategy."[86]

Furthermore, each tradition produces its own narrative. Thus, for instance, the political culture tradition that Roger Smith calls "ascriptive Americanist," maintained that non-white people in the United States were inferior to whites and therefore should not be regarded as full citizens.[87] Similarly, the proponents of economic liberalism constructed a narrative in which protectionists are portrayed as egotistic, mean people, opposed to the liberal's penchant to pursue the general welfare.[88] Thus, the tradition that prevailed in the post-war era was the liberal one which, extrapolated to the international level, has been described as "embedded liberalism," as noted before.[89] As Stephen Krasner put it in the late 1970s, "For two and a half decades after the Second World War Lockean liberalism was the key to American foreign policy."[90] More fundamentally, as suggested before, political culture, foreign policy and economic statecraft traditions are part and parcel of a corresponding identity; state identity plays an important role in the definition of state interests, and arguably also of the kind of economic statecraft practiced.[91] Now, the United States had certainly not had a unique identity since its founding —hence the importance of the kind of foreign economic policy Washington adopted in the aftermath of World War II.

One of the key elements in the construction of the post-war international order was the trade regime. In promoting free trade, Washington was not only pursuing its economic interests, but also its political ones. This was made clear, for instance, in the selective use of trade policy with other countries, where the treatment they received depended on whether the counterpart was considered an ally or an enemy (more on US trade policy in Section 4).[92] As secretary of state Dean Acheson put it in the late 1940s, "we are willing to help people who believe the way we do, to continue to live the way they want to live."[93] US foreign economic policy goals worked in tandem with its broader foreign policy ends, a state of affairs that remained during various decades.[94]

Thus, in the keeping with US practices and the then-fashionable modernization theory, Washington presented itself as a paragon in its relations with less developed countries, advocating and supporting development models that matched its economic, ideological and political interests.[95] Although the region's responses to American tutelage were variegated, for several decades the United States maintained its foreign economic policy in general, and toward Latin American in particular, consistent.[96] Certainly, new ideas and practices of several Latin American countries—as when in the late 1960s nationalization of foreign assets became a common practice in the region—brought the political element of economic relations to the forefront of Washington's international agenda.[97] Thus, as Nixon's National Security Advisor and secretary of state Henry Kissinger would remark regarding what would seem to be a merely economic disagreement with the government of Chile in the early 1970s: "Our concern with Allende was based on national security, not economics. Nationalization of American-owned property was not the issue."[98]

But it was not only Chile. Things started to change in Washington's approach to economic statecraft around that time, when talk about the decline of US hegemony became widespread, as noted in the first chapter. A protracted process of "disembedding liberalism," which would culminate in the 1990s, started in the 1970s.[99] Thus, in 1971, president Nixon proclaimed his New Economic Policy, which included a substantial modification of the Bretton Woods Agreements—particularly as they related to the convertibility of the U.S. dollar for gold—as well as major amendment of its trade policy (by imposing a 10% tariff surcharge). The meaning of the policy change did not go unnoticed. As Stephen Cohen has written, it constituted a "monumental shift in U.S. economic philosophy ... What was once the unquestioned priority of cultivating a global environment consistent with U.S. values was pushed aside."[100] From then on, and particularly since the 1980s, US foreign economic policy became less predictable and preeminent, with parochial interests and overtly ideological factors stepping in.[101] Thus, as a Latin American Economic System's document noted early on in the Reagan years (1981–1989), the "treatment of international economic issues was largely influenced by its foreign policy priorities, which concentrated on recovering a dominant position in U.S. relations with the Soviet Union and establishing decisive U.S. leadership among its allies."[102] As secretary of state Alexander Haig put it, "in the formulation of economic policy, in the allocation of our resources, in decisions on international economic issues, a major determinant will be the need to protect and advance our security."[103]

With the Cold War over, things went back to some extent to their more traditional track in the following decade, particularly during the Clinton years (1993–2001). The standard version of US international economic liberalism returned, but it underwent important amendments. The new script, neoliberalism, as its critics called it, went well beyond the Bretton Woods orthodoxy, including matters such as financial deregulation and capital account liberalization.[104] To get an idea of the degree to which the emerging orthodoxy departed from the previous one, it is worth recalling that a fundamental element of the post-war economic liberal order was the financial sector. According to John Maynard Keynes, one of the main architects of the embedded liberalism compromise, the non-liberalization of the capital account, was the key factor in making the domestic side of the post-war equation work. That is, capital controls were the *sine qua non* for the effective management of national economies. As Keynes put it, "the whole management of the domestic economy depends upon being free to have the appropriate rate of interest without reference to the rates prevailing elsewhere in the world. Capital control is a corollary to this."[105] In the late 1990s, the IMF suggested changing the Articles of Agreement in order to make capital account liberalization one of the purposes of the IMF, and the World Bank adopted a similar position on the matter.[106]

This economic zeitgeist, which coincided with the "unipolar moment," informed Washington's economic statecraft. Thus, for instance, treasury secretary Larry Summers statement: "The United States' economic policy should and will be based on the idea that promoting integration and prosperity around the world is enormously in our national interest because of the stability it brings in a world that is still a dangerous place."[107] It is worth noting that the connection between economics and politics, particularly security, was not absent in the rationale for promoting said agenda; as Summers pointed out, "mistakes in international economic policy can have grave security consequences."[108] Despite the changes undergone by American diplomacy during the George W. Bush administrations, the economic component of it did not suffer major alterations.[109]

The commitment to international liberalism was, not surprisingly, reaffirmed during Barack Obama's eight years in office. For his first secretary of state, Hillary Clinton, "economic statecraft [was] at the heart of our foreign policy agenda," because it served to "harness the forces and use the tools of global economics to strengthen our diplomacy and presence abroad"; hence, as she noted, the importance free trade in the international economy. But for her, and presumably for the Obama administration, economic statecraft is something deeper than prosperity and international relations—at bottom, it is about values and power. As she put it, "we are not only in a political and economic competition, we are in a competition for ideas. If people don't believe that democracy and free-market [sic] deliver, then they will be looking elsewhere for models ... we happen to believe that our model is not only the best for us, we think that this embodies universal principles ... that make it the best model for any country."[110] That is why economic statecraft is not only about politics or economics, nor about bargaining or policy instruments; it is also about power.

3) The Practice of Economic Statecraft

The exercise of US power through economic statecraft, though, is not as simple or neat as the previous narrative might suggest. That is, in addition to the conceptual problem of reification, the practice of economic statecraft is more messy than the discourse about it often suggests. Let's briefly consider, by way of illustration, the organizational challenges the enactment US economic statecraft faces. Both the hydra-headed nature of the matter—which affects myriad social groups—and the bureaucratic politics that go with the interaction of the many agencies involved in it, make managing foreign economic policy a daunting task.[111] Thus, for instance, Blaisdell and Braderman noted in the late 1940s that two mechanisms had been put in place to deal with the coordination challenge: "close consultation on a staff to staff basis between the State Department and individual agencies on international matters that lie within the special competence of a particular agency ... [and] through the interdepartmental committee mechanism."[112] As they elaborated,

> An idea of the vast scope of this work can be gained from an examination of the subjects with which this committee and its subcommittees have been concerned. The following are just a few examples—economic policy toward China, customs procedure, foreign patent protection, foreign travel, inter-American economic affairs, international commodity problems, private monopolies and cartels, and state trading.[113]

As a study from the mid-1950s noted:

> Foreign economic policy can, at best, be brought into manageable 'chunks' of related functions ... But, it is apparently impossible to give a comprehensive span of policy and administrative control—such as would be involved in the unification of all foreign economic policy—to any person short of the President.[114]

In the meantime, the "vast scope" of agencies involved in US economic statecraft of the 1940s had increased to over 60 by the 1970s, the time when the debate over the decline of US hegemony became more salient.[115]

Further complicating the design and implementation of economic statecraft is the diversity of US objectives and policies. As befits a hegemonic power, during the post-war period Washington usually adopted a global perspective of its foreign economic policy.[116] However, there have been strategic and practical limitations to an overall approach. Take the case of international trade; as noted, free trade policy has been selective, depending on the country, and also on the context.[117] Hence, even if Washington had had an overall, clearly designed objective on any foreign economic policy matter, it would have hardly be implemented uniformly across regions or countries—much less across time.

There have been attempts, though, to impose some control on this unruly subject. President Eisenhower created the Council on Foreign Economic Policy, placing it within the Executive Office of the President; the new office, however, proved ineffective, with its members rarely convening. The Council passed away with the departure of Eisenhower from office. President Kennedy returned to the State Department the responsibility for economic statecraft; however, the creation under his administration of the Agency for International Development (semi-autonomous) and of the Special Trade Representative undermined State's control over foreign economic policy. President Nixon, for his part, established the Council on International Economic Policy, again within the Executive Office of the President, two years after his arrival to the White House, in 1971. As its predecessor, the Council turned out to be inoperative, expiring in 1977, during the Carter administration.[118]

It was also under Carter that Congress strengthened the by-then statutory Special Trade Representative by turning it into the Office of the United States Trade Representative, assigning to it some responsibilities taken from the State Department.[119] During his second term, Reagan created the Economic Policy Council, under his powerful treasury secretary James Baker; Bush Sr. kept it, but it became weaker and less effective.[120] A major innovation came in 1993, when president Bill Clinton established the National Economic Council; among its stated objectives was "to coordinate the economic policy-making process with respect to domestic and international economic issues."[121] Significantly, the new office was analogous to the National Security Council, with the heads of both councils participating in the other; it originally contained representatives from 15 agencies, and more were added later.[122] The significance of the new coordinating body has been proven by the fact that both Bush Jr. and Obama maintained it.

The complex story of the bureaucratic organization dealing with the economic relations of the United States with the rest of the world provides a clue to the many actors and factors that intervene in the practice of economic statecraft. Take the case of Washington's foreign economic policy toward Latin America; most of the time, the myriad issues affecting the region have been dealt with in an extremely decentralized manner, one in which the economic and political interests of diverse domestic interest groups figure prominently.[123] As R. Harrison Wagner noted in 1970,

The process by which United States economic policies towards Latin America were formulated seems to have been characterized by the same fragmentation of power and difficulty of achieving a set of political goals insulated from the demands of private groups that characterize the rest of American Politics.[124]

Furthermore, traditionally there has not been a policy tailored for the region; rather, the wider policy has been applied to Latin America.[125] (Incidentally, the same goes for Canada. In the mid-1960s, a US ambassador to Canada noted that over 20 government agencies dealt with Canada separately; a successor of his made a similar observation in the 1980s.[126] As Edelgard Mahant and Graeme S. Mount have observed, "There is no single American Canada policy ...")[127] Only when the matter at hand, for some reason, becomes critical, the Department of State or the Treasury get actively involved.[128]

But it is not only the intricacies of bureaucratic politics and the difficulties of maintaining a coherent global position across regions that makes the design and implementation of foreign economic policy challenging; the consistency over time on particular subject matters is also fraught with conflicts and disagreements. Take the case of trade policy.

4) Evolution of US Trade Policy

Trade policy, as noted, was the foundation of the US-led, post-war international liberal order (the actually existing international liberal order was, of course, more messy than its stylized depiction suggests). Following Thomas Schelling, I use a broad definition of trade so as to include other, not strictly commercial matters, such as investment. I do this in part because a narrow conception of trade oftentimes does not shed much light on broader economic relations, and because it is frequently indeterminate; for instance, in a study of 25 cases between 1960 and 1978, John Odell found that Washington won only 12 of them.[129] Trade policy by itself frequently tells us more about the balance of power between myriad social forces in the United States than about the actual outcome of interstate bargaining on the matter. Furthermore, a broad understanding of trade is warranted since, as Schelling put it, it is "what most international relations are about"; trade policies, he notes "can antagonize governments, generate resentments in populations, hurt economies, influence the tenure of governments, even provoke hostilities".[130] I thus take trade policy to be not only representative of the larger US thick economic statecraft but also consequential for the ebb and flow of US power. I thus use this particular policy instrument as an instantiation of the US economic identity, and in that sense, as a property concept that other countries, particularly those of the Western Hemisphere, have faced as a social fact.

After three introductory paragraphs on the period that led up to the one this work deals with (1971–2016), I divide this brief overview of US trade policy in three parts, each corresponding to a sub-period (1971–1989, 1990–2000 and 2001–2016); I relate each of them to a kind of economic identity as it regards international trade. *To reiterate: even if trade policy is considered exemplary of the broader foreign economic policy, it will be necessary to contextualize it within the wider US discourse on economic matters in order to more accurately link it to the thick economic statecraft practiced during the period in question and also, to Washington's broad economic identity (in a loose sense) at the time.*

As can be surmised from the previous pages, free trade is frequently not well-liked at the domestic level by all social sectors. As James Madison noted in *Federalist* 10:

> Shall domestic manufactures be encouraged, and in what degree, by restrictions on foreign manufactures? are questions which would be differently decided by the landed and the manufacturing classes, and probably by neither with a sole regard to justice and the public good.[131]

This kind of controversy was present in the country that would emerge as the undisputed leader of the capitalist world in the 1940s. If the United States was able to set the course in these matters internationally during that decade and the two that followed, it was because Congress deferred to the president's authority. Thus, since 1934, with the passage of the Reciprocal Trade Agreements Act, Washington privileged the "reciprocity" objective of trade policy, that is, the achievement of reciprocal trade agreements that lower trade impediments, as the main objective of US trade policy (the two other "R's," for "revenue" and "restriction" were the priority in previous eras, the former from the creation of the federal government until the Civil War, and the latter from the Civil War to the Great Depression).[132] In this milieu, the trading regime, epitomized by the General Agreement on Tariffs and Trade (GATT), worked well—as the substantial advances in lowering tariffs made by the Kennedy round (1963–1967) made clear. There was no doubt Washington was the protagonist in the play.[133]

But things started to change during the late 1960s and early 1970s—on several fronts. For starters, the Keynesian perspective that had informed US domestic and foreign economic policy started to dwindle in Washington's commanding heights.[134] Moreover, around that time an overvalued dollar made US exports less attractive in international markets, the cohesion among GATT's members weakened—particularly with the emergence of new players—and non-tariff barriers became more salient.[135] These international factors, in turn, further impacted the politics of trade within the United States. Adversely affected producers lobbied their representatives, who in turn questioned in harder terms the executive's preference for free trade. All this was occurring of course at the time when the already alluded perception of both US abuse of its economic preponderance and, paradoxically, its economic decline, was widespread. It was not all that surprising, then, that in 1969 the International Monetary Fund created the Special Drawing Rights, as a way of providing the international financial system non-US dollar-based liquidity, and that a decade later the European Economic Community (EEC) created the European Monetary System; tellingly, Washington was not able to carry the day the way it used to during the Tokyo Round that concluded in 1979.[136]

During the 25 years that followed the end of World War II, the United States thus largely maintained a liberal identity on economic matters; this was instantiated, for instance, in its pro free trade policies.[137] This does not mean, of course, that Washington did not take on other identities as a hegemonic power. Indeed, allied states such as Germany and Japan were able to create "trading state" identities for themselves thanks precisely to the US dominant position in the security sphere.[138] As I noted before, state identity is both malleable and contested. Thus, the United States went from being a protectionist state in the 19th century to a trade-liberalizing one in the second half of the 20th century.

1971–1989: Contentious Politics, Protectionist Lurches, and Dented Pro-Trade Identity

Continuing the trend in economic ideas initiated in the mid-1960s, during this sub-period the more market-oriented approach continued to gain terrain not only during the Nixon years, but also during those of president Carter, when both deregulation and monetarist policies were introduced. Of course, the more radical change on these matters came during the Reagan administrations, when supply side economics was added to more orthodox monetarist ideas, constituting what came to be known as "Reaganomics."[139]

The 1970s and 1980s were also bound to bring significant changes to the world trading system. Economic nationalism was on the rise, worldwide.[140] Furthermore, as John S. Odell put it, "the fate of the liberal trade doctrine during the 1970s and 1980s in the United States (…) appeared to lose some ground."[141] Thus, as noted, on 15 August 1971 came the "Nixon shock"; three years later, Congress passed the Trade Act which, in Section 301, authorized the president to take retaliatory actions against countries deemed to be imposing any of a wide range of trade restrictions to US exports.

In addition, the Trade Act of 1974 also instituted other protective mechanisms for US exporters, such as countervailing duties and anti-dumping measures, as well as assistance for workers displaced by foreign trade; the legislation, however, also provided the president with authorization to take part in the Tokyo Round and to negotiate other international trade agreements under what came to be known as "fast-track" procedures. Moreover, the Trade Act of 1974 set the guidelines for a Generalized System of Preferences (GSP) for Third World countries—something that would be relevant for US economic relations with Latin American countries. Although the tone of US trade policy changed in the years that followed, particularly during the Reagan years, the menacing new tools at the president's disposal, particularly Section 301, were used rather sporadically (a handful of cases in the following decade), as was the use of import relief.[142]

Thus, a lustrum after the Nixon Shock it had become clear that the blow inflicted by it and posterior US measures to the international trading system had not been fatal. On the contrary; both the global trade regime and US policy seemed reinvigorated, as the successful competition of the Tokyo Round— which substantially reduced non-trade barriers to trade—demonstrated. The 1979 Trade Agreements Act certainly included some administrative and bureaucratic changes intended to make trade remedy law more effective (transferring its enforcement from the Treasury to the Commerce Department), but they did not seriously affect the volume of world trade.

In the mid-1980s, Congress authorized the president to negotiate a free trade agreement with Israel and Canada, and renewed the above-mentioned GSP. The Trade and Tariff Act of 1984 was indeed a mostly pro-trade bill. The revaluation of the dollar around that time would again make US trade policy more contentious. Legislators at times pushed for openly protectionist legislation, as exporters again lost competitiveness and the country's trade deficit worsened (reaching $112.5 billion (customs value) in 1984, up from $25.5 billion in 1980).[143] The administration acted in consequence, increasing the relief it provided to affected producers. However, after the Reagan administration orchestrated the 1985 Plaza Accords to weaken the dollar, US exports recuperated and the trade deficit began to shrink three years later (by early 1986, the U.S. still ran deficits with most of its trading partners).[144] But not all US trade recovery came from the exchange rate regime; it also came from what came to be known as managed trade, such as the U.S.–Japan Auto Agreement; this kind of arrangement was more often than not the result of not-so-veiled threats to countries that in Washington's opinion were incurring in unfair trade practices.[145]

Moreover, in 1988 president Reagan signed the Omnibus Trade and Competitiveness Act, a major trade bill which, as its name suggests, deals with a myriad issues; among the most consequential was no doubt the strengthening of the mixed creature that the statutory USTR was, as well as the sharpening of Section 301, making it more aggressive against what the legislators considered unfair actions on the part of US trading partners. The Omnibus Act, however, was not mostly a protectionist, Congress-controlling-trade piece of legislation;[146] it granted the executive fast-track authority. Thus, US trade policy during the 1970–1989 sub-period, for all its difficulties, did not represent a major departure from the post-war trade regime Washington had led.[147] Accordingly, the dominant discourse on broader economic matters toward the end of this 1971–1989 period was one that extolled the "magic of the marketplace,"[148] both at home and abroad. The more contentious nature of trade (in the United States as well as worldwide), and particularly some of the trade policy implemented during this period certainly dented the country's pro-trade identity, but it was not shattered. Washington was still the leader of the global trading system.

1990–2000: Primacy, Convergence, and Partial Restoration of Pro-Trade Identity

The collapse of the Soviet Union and its bloc had a profound impact on economic discourse; it produced a worldwide convergence on the United States' prevalent ideas. But the convergence actually started to take place about a lustrum before, in the Western Hemisphere—and particularly in Latin America. In the aftermath of the debt crisis, in the early and mid-1980s, countries in the region started to adopt free market policies, both for internal (realization that the previous development model did not work anymore) and external (pressure from Washington and international financial institutions) reasons. It was thus no coincidence that in 1989 John Williamson, as noted in Chapter 2, coined the term "Washington Consensus" to refer to, on the one hand, the policy recommendations the Colossus of the North was promoting in the region but, on the other, also to economic reforms that were already "being pursued in Latin America".[149] Significantly, as Williamson notes, the expression Washington Consensus "was in principle geographically and historically specific".[150] Thus, even before Central and Eastern European countries rushed en masse to adopt market-oriented reforms, most of Latin America was quite experienced in matters such as deregulation, fiscal discipline, import liberalization, opening to foreign direct investment and privatization.

Furthermore, although the Washington Consensus was minted in the aftermath of the Reagan years—it was indeed an exercise in distilling the economic thought that would likely survive the 40th president's economic policies[151]—it would survive during the next three administrations of this period (mostly during that of Bush Sr.); the persistence and durability of US discursive hegemony on this matter is indeed noticeable.[152] Incidentally, the term would become largely distorted in its neoliberal guise, particularly in Latin America—with Washington's blessing.[153] Among the policies not included in the original consensus (but that would become central to its neoliberal distortion) was complete capital account liberalization.[154]

Regarding US trade policy, in 1991, Congress granted fast track authority to president George H. W. Bush to negotiate the Uruguay Round and a trade agreement with México. By the early post-Cold War period, Washington was thus in a position—both ideological and material—to push for further trade liberalization; a task in which it would largely succeed in the years to come. Two salient illustrations of Washington's triumphs in the first half of the 1990s were the North American Free Trade Agreement, which went into effect on 1 January 1994 (more on this in Chapter 5), and the conclusion of the Uruguay Round on 15 April 1994, which led to the creation of the World Trade Organization (WTO; effective January 1995). Among its achievements, the Uruguay Round was able to more effectively deal with areas that were previously practically out of the GATT's purview, such as agriculture; introduce new issues, such as intellectual property, and reinforce dispute settlement mechanisms—all among a record number of signatory parties. The Clinton administration early trade achievements were indeed impressive. As Fred Bergsten, former Assistant Secretary for International Affairs at the Treasury Department and former Assistant for International Economic Affairs at the National Security Council, would put it,

> President Bill Clinton's first two years in office in fact represented the zenith of post-war U.S. trade policy while reaffirming the traditional bipartisanship of that policy by concluding major deals that had been launched by the first Bush and Reagan administrations.'[155]

Furthermore, in December 1994, at the already mentioned (in Chapter 2) Summit of the Americas in Miami, 34 signatory countries agreed to create the Free Trade Area of the Americas (FTAA) by 2005. US primacy, however, did not automatically translate into it being able to dictate the new trading rules: practically at the same time that Washington was successfully assembling an impressive international coalition to fight Iraq in Operation Desert Storm (December 1990), Uruguay Round negotiations were breaking down. But by the end of the lustrum, trade-related matters had been worked out as well, mostly in line with United States' preferences.

1994, however, seemed to be the apex of US trade liberalization. That same year, in what in hindsight appears as a sign of things that were to come, president Clinton failed to obtain fast-track authority from Congress; three years later, he failed again. By that time, particularly due to the contentious NAFTA debate, issues that by and large had been ignored in the post-war trade liberalization agenda had become prominent in the US trade debate: the environment and labor standards. The Seattle riots that accompanied the 1999 WTO ministerial conference were a vivid illustration of the new terms of the debate.

A major anomaly in the new trade milieu was the approval of normal trade relations with China in 2000, and the ensuing entry (in 2001) of the Asian country into the WTO (negotiations for the United States–Chile Free Trade Agreement were launched also in 2000, but this was, obviously, less significant in global terms). Thus, most of the interregnum (i.e., the decade following the end of the Cold War) was a somewhat difficult period for US leadership in free trade. For starters, the Clinton administrations were not as ideologically committed as the previous one to the cause of trade liberalization; additionally, they faced resurgent protectionist pressures, both from public opinion and Congress. The diminished support and increased difficulties were reflected in adoption of a more pragmatic strategy to enhance free trade: the abandonment of the traditional multilateralist venue, in favor of bilateral and minilateral arrangements.[156] On the broader economic discourse, the United States seemed to replace the classical liberal thought, as embodied in the post-war embedded liberalism consensus, for one that put the traditional doctrine on steroids. Hence, blindly extrapolating to international financial markets the virtues of free trade, Washington pushed for, as noted above, capital account liberalization; on this matter—powerful evidence to the contrary notwithstanding—the United States' still promoted the "magic of the marketplace." In general terms, in the twilight of the 20th century, the United States was able to partially restore its identity as the main architect of the free trade regime—although one that was certainly more disperse and less coherent that the one that existed during the two and a half decades that followed World War II.

2001–2016: Competitive Liberalization and Trade-Hub Identity

George W. Bush's administration succeeded in obtaining trade promotion authority (as fast-track authority was rebranded) in 2002. Equipped with it, it went ahead and concluded free trade agreements with Chile, Singapore, Australia, Morocco and several Central American countries in the following years. Furthermore, the Bush Jr. administration started free trade negotiations with several countries, among them Bolivia, Ecuador, Colombia, Panamá and Perú. In the meantime, the negotiations leading to the already mentioned FTAA stalled and then died in the mid-2000s. Thus, the Bush administration's "competitive liberalization" trade strategy promoted by USTR Zoellick as a means to foster multilateral free trade ended up turning into an end in itself—and probably having more trade-diversion than trade-creation effects at the global level.[157] The Bush administration participated in the 2001 launching of the WTO's Doha Round, but the negotiations moved slowly until they stalled in 2008.

Precisely in that year, a US-based financial crisis that would reach global proportions and lead to the Great Recession of the 2010s exploded. Whereas Europe resorted to extreme fiscal austerity, the United States under Obama adopted a less contractionist approach and was able to recover faster (by 2010, the United States had reached its pre-crisis GDP, although unemployment level recovered until 2016; in the Euro area employment has not recovered, and GDP reached its pre-crisis level in 2014).[158] In the meantime, for both political and economic reasons, the Obama administration started its "Pivot to Asia" policy—a turn that partially resulted in a diminished engagement with the Western Hemisphere.[159]

Part of the renewed attention to Asia was Washington's involvement and leading role, starting in 2010, in the Trans-Pacific Partnership, or TPP, as the budding 12-nation free trade accord was usually called (a process the Bush administration had already initiated when it announced its intention to join the trans-pacific negotiations); significantly, China was no part of it. The importance of the agreement, though, was more strategic than economic.[160]

As secretary of defense Ash Carter would say: "In terms of our rebalance in the broadest sense, passing TPP is as important to me as another aircraft carrier."[161] Four Western Hemispheric countries joined the United States in the trans-Pacific project: Canada, México, Perú and Chile, which in general meant strengthening their economic and political ties to Washington and, for the first two in particular, a back-door to renegotiating their 1992 agreement with the United States, as areas that had been excluded or did not exist (e.g., e-commerce) at the time of NAFTA were included in the TPP negotiations.[162] As a Canadian analyst put it, "Is TPP a re-negotiation of NAFTA? Technically, no—practically, yes. It will be NAFTA on steroids for the Asia-Pacific."[163] TPP negotiations concluded successfully in February 2016 [before it was ratified, though, one of the first actions of president Donald Trump was to withdraw his country from it].

Although during the Obama years the free trade agreements with Colombia and Panamá, started during the Bush administration, were concluded, Latin America was not, as suggested, an economic priority for Washington. Politically, the reestablishment of diplomatic relations with Cuba was a big coup for US policy toward the Americas. Part of the stated rationale for the daring move was, indeed, that it would "enhance the standing of our own country in the hemisphere."[164] In general terms, however, president Obama followed the same trade policy pursued by his predecessor.[165] The distinguishing trait of this period on the commercial front was perhaps the more pronounced departure from post-war multilateralism, and the emphasis on the attempt to make the United States the hub of the international trade system. On the broader approach to economic affairs, Washington's blind faith on "the magic of the marketplace," particularly on financial affairs, diminished, no doubt as result of the 2008 crisis.

Even if, overall, the 1971–2016 period shows remarkable continuity in US identity as instantiated in its economic discourse and, more specifically, on its trade policy broadly defined (per Schelling), there were minor but not negligible differences over the three sub-periods regarding the contents and contestation of the appropriate US role in world economic affairs, as well as concerning the corresponding trade strategies. That is, the shared understanding of the US body polity about the objectives of its international economic intercourse was not the same in 1971 than in, say, 2001. This should not come as a big surprise, since during the 45-year period covered here the world's, the hemisphere's and the United States' political economy all underwent substantial transformations.

To reiterate, trade-related identity and its associated trade policy are considered property concepts in this work, with the latter being of course more tangible and fungible than the former. A priori, however, the leverage that US trade policy can deliver is indeterminate—it depends on the context in which it is deployed. A crucial part of this context is, of course, the identity and policy of the target country—but since the focus of this work is on the US side, the other is of secondary importance, and will be brought in appositely in each specific case (more on this below). Now, the indeterminacy of policy could not be otherwise: policy is simply an instrument used to realize an objective. As noted before, being cognizant of an influence attempt is not synonymous with knowing what the outcome of such effort will be. That is why policy is a property concept. But not all property concepts are tools. Thus, as ventured above, state identity (e.g., trade identity), might also be considered a property concept, but this does not mean that it is just an instrument: it cannot be manipulated with the same ease.[166] But more on methodological matters in the next section.

5) Operationalizing Power in Thick Economic Statecraft

Interestingly, the literature on US economic statecraft toward the Western Hemisphere has tended to focus on critical cases, ignoring for the most part the bread and butter of US foreign economic policy toward the region: quotidian issues such as aid, investment, the promotion of economic ideas and trade.[167] This bias contributes to the reification problem pointed out above, as the extraordinary centralized nature in the management of the critical issues in question seems to be the normal state of affairs. Thus, the selection of extreme values obviously distorts the picture that emerges of the multifaceted relationship between the United States and the countries of the hemisphere; paraphrasing US Justice Holmes: it might be that great cases make bad theory.

In looking at economic statecraft as a practice through which Washington has exercised power in the Western Hemisphere from 1971 to 2016, it is important to put forward some general guidelines. As suggested above, I consider both the broad discourse on international economic matters, as well as specific policy initiatives vis-à-vis particular countries or a set of countries of the region to be covered here as influence attempts on Washington's part. That is, as I noted in the previous section, I treat both discourse and policy as property concepts. US instruments would therefore include general foreign economic policy doctrine and/or pronouncements, as well as those directed specifically towards the hemisphere, or the particular sub-region or country in question.

Thus, Washington's potential influence on the hemisphere has to do not only with the changes in specific actions or behaviors of the target countries, but also with their identities, doctrines or dispositions regarding economic matters, especially when they relate to either the bilateral (country in question—the United States) or the international realm. As noted, though, this work's focus is not the target states' identities and policies, but US thick economic statecraft. In this manner, I think I can better elucidate whether or not—and on what occasions—Washington has been able to get others to do what it would like.

The focus on the next four chapters will then be on property concepts pertaining to the economic realm, to the exclusion of others concerned with issues such as democracy and security, but in the understanding that any economic attempt is a political act, and that it need not be confined to economic matters on its effects. That is, the common denominator of the attempts considered will be their bearing on material or financial resources. In this manner, I hope I can—to a reasonable extent—separate US intentions from results in the practice of its economic statecraft.[168]

Thus, whereas the domain (or target) of US influence attempts will be the hemispheric countries and hemispheric regions included in this work, to wit (as noted in the introduction), Canada, México, Central America and South America, the scope will be the economic realm, as instantiated, for instance, in those states' approaches to economic integration, development models and trade policy, as they relate to the United States' dominant tradition in the sphere of (thick) economic statecraft.[169] The bases of power, on the other hand, will not be confined to the coercive power that ensues from the material resources at Washington's disposal. As noted in the previous chapter, there are multiple bases of power, and they do not all need be material; they are more broadly related to the authority, hierarchy and respect components of the power relationship the United States has had with the rest of the Americas.

6) Summary

The economy is a domain of power relations. Embedded in a thick political and social fabric, the economy knows no territorial boundaries. It is thus not surprising that international economic relations have been long used by nation states for political purposes. That this practice is frequently referred to by the composite term "economic statecraft" points to the eminently political nature of the endeavor, as the second word of the concept refers to the art of ruling, as noted. That is why, contrary to conventional academic usage, economic statecraft cannot be confined to a set of means per se (e.g., economic sanctions or foreign aid); such thin conception of economic statecraft prevents the analyst from going beyond both an understanding of power as an attribute and a notion of power that, while relational, limits interaction to its contractual, strategic component.

In order to get a fuller account, one that incorporates the deeper understanding of power as social relations that necessarily involve matters of legitimacy, meaning and norms, it is necessary to draw on other perspectives, such as Classical Political Economy, Economic Diplomacy, the literature on Foreign Economic Policy and International Political Economy. As noted, David Baldwin's approach offers a solid starting point, as he implicitly includes some of these issues, and also because he is very clear on both the political nature of economic statecraft and its quotidian nature. Furthermore, Baldwin's relational understanding of power (drawing on Dahl), as well as his analytical distinction between influence attempts and outcomes, facilitates the operationalization of his approach. But Baldwin's take on economic statecraft still needs broadening.

The theoretical broadening advanced above enables the embedding into economic statecraft of a richer understanding of diplomacy, of consideration of social mores, and of the concept of state identity, which to some extent functions as the wellspring of specific policy instruments. That is why one could argue that a state's trade policy (broadly defined, as above) is necessarily related to its identity as an actor in the International Political Economy. I thus contend that for analytical purposes, state identity can be thought of as a property concept created by the power wielder (thus bracketing the international-interaction component that goes into its construction, which is problematic, but for the purposes of this work, I think, justified) and which the target state faces as a social fact.

As noted, economic statecraft is intrinsic to the United States. As the country became hegemonic in the aftermath of World War II, the character of its foreign economic policy acquired new salience. For it was not pre-ordained that Washington would lead in the creation of the international order that came to be known as "embedded liberalism," of which the free trade regime was a central component. In pursuing this type of economic statecraft, the United States was acting out of enlightened self-interests in both the economic and the political realms, but it was also reflecting a deeply ingrained political tradition that has historically been part of its identity.

United States' practice of economic statecraft is of course not as neat as any analytical account—be it Economic Diplomacy or International Political Economy, to take two examples—might make it appear; theoretical approaches only provide stylized facts. Actually existing economic statecraft is much messier, as the narrative above illustrated. In the US case, not only multiple government agencies and private actors impinge on it, but the different economic endowments of other countries and, perhaps more importantly, the type of political relationship maintained with them, have prevented Washington from designing and undertaking coherent and consistent economic statecraft.

The exercise of US power through its foreign economic policy toward Latin America served above as a good illustration of this challenge. The brief overview of the three periods (1971–1989, 1990–2000, 2001–2016) in which United States' trade policy (broadly defined) since the debate on its decline started, attest to this difficulty. But the three periods also testify to the relatively malleable character of Washington's identity as a key actor in the International Political Economy, and to the concomitant changes its commercial policy has suffered. Thus, although in general terms a liberal attitude toward international commerce prevailed during the three sub-periods, there were moments in which trade practice became more explicitly protectionist, or simply contradicted the official discourse on the matter.

The extent to which US discourse on trade policy was shared by other countries of the hemisphere, however, is relevant in assessing the degree to which Washington has been able to exercise power in the region through its economic statecraft. That is, if discourse is thought of as a property concept, it can be seen as an instrument deployed in US influence attempts, in its efforts to affect other countries' dispositions regarding economic affairs. This two-way interaction on foreign economic policy should shed some light regarding authority, hierarchy and respect in the Western Hemisphere.

Notes

1   Polanyi 1944.
2   Carr 1964 [1939]: 116–117.
3   Hirschman 1980 [1945].
4   Cohen 1990: 263; Dobson 2002: 5.
5   Strange 1970: 308.
6   Caporaso and Levine 1992; Krasner 1996; Tooze 1989; Gill and Law 1988: 3–4.
7   For example, Krasner 1978; Gourevitch 1986; Oye 1992; Alt et al. 1996; Lumsdaine 1993.
8   Baldwin 1985: 65; Dobbin 1994: 10; Dobson 2002: 8.
9   Mastanduno 1999: 315.
10   Chan and Drury 2000: 1.
11   Kunz 1994: 453–454.
12   Collins 2009: 368.
13   Baldwin 1985: 13–14.
14   Ibid.: 32.
15   For example, Blanchard et al. 1999: 3; Drezner 2011.
16   Baldwin 1985: 55.
17   Ibid.: 61.
18   Ibid.: 12; cf. Odell 1990: 140, cites Baldwin 1985 as an instance of a work focusing on "trade sanctions."
19   Baldwin 1985: 46.
20   Ibid.: 65.
21   Ibid.: 65.
22   Ibid.: 96.
23   Ibid.: 32-33.
24   Ibid.: 99, 135, 336; cf. Kirshner 1997: 33; Mastanduno, 1999: 306.
25   Ashley 1983: 472.
26   Ibid.: 484.
27   Ashley 1981: 221, 213.
28   Ibid.: 214.
29   Baldwin 1985: 65.
30   Ibid.: 35.
31   Ibid.: 33.
32   Ibid.: 35.
33   Maier 1987: 4.
34   Baldwin 1985: 115-6.
35   Katzenstein 1985; cf. Jepperson, Wendt and Katzenstein 1996.
36   Rohrlich 1987.
37   Waever in McSweeney 1999: 70; Brubaker and Cooper 2000: 7.
38   Abdelal et al. 2006: 696.
39   Knight 2007: 193.
40   Katzenstein 1996: 30.
41   McSweeney 1999: 168.
42   Nossal 2010; Hynek and Thomsen 2006.

43   Wendt 1999: 233.
44   Chafetz, Spirats and Frankel 1998: 16; Klotz and Lynch 2007: 87.
45   Brubaker and Cooper 2000; Abdelal et al. 2006: 700; Rousseau 2006: 14.
46   McSweeney 1999: 34; Guillaume 2010: 20.
47   Holsti 1970: 298.
48   Haglund 2009: 348.
49   Katzenstein 1985; see also Katezenstein 1978; Rohrlich 1987.
50   Kratochwill 2008: 455.
51   Abdelal et al. 2006, 699.
52   Hofstadter 1989 [1948]; Hartz 1983 [1955]; Lipset 1996; Kurth 2009: 9; Walt 2017.
53   Holsti 1970; Jepperson, Wendt and Katzenstein 1996.
54   Hopf 2002: 16; Hurd 2008: 310; Legro 2009: 40.
55   Cf. Wendt 1999, Kowert 2007.
56   Cf. McCloskey and Ziliak 1996; McCloskey 1998.
57   In Hirschman 1979: 65.
58   Hobson 2000: 11. Cf. Krasner 1983a and Krasner 1983b; Johnston 1996: 227; Rose
     1998: 151; Wohlforth (1994/5): 109.
59   Cf. Johnston 1995: 37.
60   Caporaso and Levine 1992: 25–26, 52–53; Baldwin 1985: 32, 85.
61   Baldwin 1985: 4.
62   Kunz 1994: 451–452.
63   Turvey 2014; Drezner 2019.
64   Buzan 2004: 143; Watson 2005 [1982]; cf. Baldwin 1985: 115–116.
65   Kunz 1994: 456.
66   Young 2017.
67   es.oxforddictionaries.com and wordreference.com; linguee.com
68   translategoogle.com
69   The first one in wordreference.com and larousse.fr; the second one in translategoogle.
     com.
70   de-langenscheidt.com and wordreference.com
71   Dahl 1957: 207; Baldwin 2016: 74.
72   Baldwin 1985: 16; Ikenberry, Lake, and Mastanduno 1988: 1; Mastanduno, 1999: 299.
     Cf. Cohen 2000: 3–4.
73   Dobson 2002: 8; see also Dobbin 1994.
74   Cf. Adler 1987; Sikkink 1991; Hall 1989; Hall 1997; Biersteker 1995; Woods 1995;
     Kahler 1990; Goldstein 1989.
75   Baldwin 1985: 59.
76   Kohli et al. 1995: 10; Krasner 1996: 109; Tooze 1989: 381–382.
77   Baldwin 1985: 61.
78   Ikenberry, Lake, and Mastanduno 1988: 1.
79   Blaisdell and Braderman 1948: 37.
80   Hoffmann 1977.
81   Cf. Krippendorf 1987.
82   Leets 2016 [1912]; Nearing and Freeman 1925.
83   Blaisdell and Braderman 1948: 39; Cohen 2000: 17.
84   Rogowsky 2014: 1.
85   Hartz 1983 [1955]; Smith 1993; Mead 2002; Smith 1994.
86   Mead 1994/1995: 13.
87   Smith 1993: 563.
88   Mayer 2009: 21.
89   Ruggie 1982; Destler 2005: 21.
90   Krasner 1978: 347.

91   Jepperson, Wendt and Katzenstein 1996; Hopf 2002; Kowert 2007.
92   Baldwin 1985: 207–208, 210.
93   In Brands 2008: 246.
94   Cohen 2000: 19.
95   Cf. Rostow 1990 [1960]; Hirschmann 1980 [1945]; cf. Cox 1987: 108, 266; Cottam 1994: 23; Escobar 1995.
96   Brands 2008: 246, 248, 256; Blake and Walters 1976: 4.
97   Bitar 1984: 9.
98   Kissinger 1979: 656.
99   Blyth 2002.
100 Cohen 2000: 20.
101 Rich 1997: 94–95; Destler 2005: 104.
102 SELA 1984: 41.
103 U.S. House of Representatives 1981.
104 Bhagwati 1998; Stiglitz 1998.
105 In Simmons 1999: 38.
106 Noble and Ravenhill 2000: 16; Grabel 1996: 1772.
107 U.S. Department of the Treasury 1997.
108 Ibid.
109 Daalder and Lindsay 2003: 31.
110 Clinton 2011a.
111 Blaisdell and Braderman 1948: 38.
112 Ibid.: 41–42.
113 Ibid.: 42.
114 Wagner 1970: 81.
115 Destler 1980: 9.
116 Cohen and Meltzer 1982: 7; Bitar1984: 15.
117 SELA 1984: 112.
118 Destler 1980: 9–10.
119 Destler 2005: 103, 114, 118.
120 Orszag, Orszag and Tyson 2002: 989.
121 In Dolan and Rosati 2006: 102.
122 Ibid.: 103; Orszag, Orszag and Tyson 2002: 992.
123 Dent 1995: XX, XXIII.
124 Wagner 1970: 82.
125 Odell 1980: 217.
126 Mahant and Mount 1999: 6.
127 Ibid.: 199.
128 Cohen and Meltzer 1982: 5; SELA 1984: 112.
129 Odell 1980: 226.
130 Schelling 1971.
131 In Irwin 2017: 1.
132 Ibid.: 2.
133 Baldwin 1991: 365.
134 Salant in Hall 1989: 30.
135 Destler 2005: 53–54.
136 Baldwin 1991: 367–368.
137 Krasner 1985: 70; Gilpin 1987: 190.
138 Berger 1996; Katzenstein 1996.
139 Dietrich 2014: 69–70; Williamson 1990: npn.
140 Gilpin 1987: 192.
141 Odell 1990: 164.

142   Destler 2005: 124, 144.
143   Ibid.: 46.
144   Gilpin 1987: 194.
145   Schoppa 1993.
146   Ibid.: 357, note 7.
147   Destler 2005: 104.
148   Reagan 1984.
149   Williamson 2000: 254.
150   Ibid.: 254.
151   Ibid.: 254.
152   Agüero 2010; Betta 2016; Toscano 2009. Cf. Keeley 1990.
153   Dietrich 2014: 70; Kurth 2009: 1; Williamson 2000: 252.
154   Williamson 2000: 257. Cf. Cypher 1998: 47; Stiglitz 2002: 74, 92; Harvey 2005: 13.
155   Bergsten 2002: 88.
156   Aggarwal 2009: 2; Feinberg 2003: 1019.
157   Aggarwal 2009; Feinberg 2003; Quiliconi and Wise 2009.
158   BEA 2019; OECD 2016; OECD 2019; World Bank 2019.
159   Allen 2009; Clinton 2011b.
160   Krugman 2014; Rachman 2015.
161   Garamone 2015.
162   Fergusson et al. 2015.
163   Clark 2012.
164   Kerry et al. 2014.
165   Schneider 2013; Manyin et al. 2012: 21.
166   Alexandrov 2003: 42.
167   Dent 1995: XXII.
168   Baldwin 1985: 24, 39–40.
169   Ibid.: 16-17; Lake 2009: 74–75.

References

Abdelal, R., Herrera, Y. M., Johnston, A., & McDermott, R. (2006). Identity as a variable. *Perspectives on Politics*, 4(4), 695–711.

Adler, E. (1987). *The power of ideology: The quest for technological autonomy in Argentina and Brazil*. Berkeley, CA: University of California Press.

Aggarwal, V. (2009). Reluctance to lead: U.S. trade policy in flux. *Business and Politics*, 11(3), 1–21.

Agüero, J. O. (2010). Michel Foucault y la gubernamentalidad financier: Reflexiones sobre la crisis financiera internacional. *Revista Vision de Futuro*, 14(2), 207–220.

Alexandrov, M. (2003). The concept of state identity in international relations: A theoretical analysis. *Journal of International Development and Cooperation*, 10(1), 33–46.

Allen, M. (2009, November 13) America's first pacific president. *Politico*.

Alt, J., Frieden, J., Gilligan, M., Rodrik, D., & Rogowski, R. (1996). The political economy of international trade: Enduring puzzles and an agenda for inquiry. *Comparative Political Studies*, 29(6), 689–717.

Ashley, R. (1981). Political realism and human interest. *International Studies Quarterly*, 25(2), 204–237.

Ashley, R. (1983). Three modes of economism. *International Studies Quarterly*, 27(4), 463–496.

Baldwin, D. A. (1985). *Economic statecraft*. Princeton, NJ: Princeton University Press.

Baldwin, D. A. (2016). *Power and international relations: A conceptual approach*. Princeton, NJ: Princeton University Press.

Baldwin, R. (1991). The new protectionism: A response to shifts in national economic power. In J. A. Frieden & D. A. Lake (Eds.), *International political economy: Perspectives on global power and wealth* (pp. 362–375). New York: St. Martin's Press.

BEA (2019). Gross Domestic Product [GDPA]. FRED. Retrieved from https://fred.stlouisfed.org/series/GDPA

Berger, T. (1996). Norms, identity, and national security in Germany and Japan. In P. J. Katzenstein (Ed.), *The culture of national security: Norms and identity in world politics* (pp. 317–356). New York: Columbia University Press.

Bergsten, C. F. (2002). A renaissance for U.S. trade policy? *Foreign Affairs, 81*(6), 86–98.

Betta, M. (2016). Governmentality and the economy: A Foucauldian perspective. In *Ethicmentality – Ethics in Capitalist Economy, Business, and Society* (pp. 25–41). Dordrecht: Springer.

Bhagwati, J. (1998). The capital myth: The difference between trade in widgets and dollars. *Foreign Affairs, 77*(3), 7–12.

Biersteker, T. J. (1995). The "Triumph" of liberal economic ideas in the developing world. In B. Stallings (Ed.), *Global change, regional response: The new international context of development* (pp. 174–196). Cambridge: Cambridge University Press.

Bitar, S. (1984). United States-Latin American relations: Shifts in economic power and implications for the future. *Journal of Interamerican Studies and World Affairs, 26*(1), 3–31.

Blaisdell, T. C., & Braderman, E. M. (1948). Economic organization of the United States for international economic policy. In S. E. Harris (Ed.), *Foreign economic policy for the United States* (pp. 37–54). Cambridge, MA: Harvard University Press.

Blake, D. H., & Walters, R. S. (1976). *The politics of global economic relations*. Upper Saddle River, NJ: Prentice Hall.

Blanchard, J. M. F., Mansfield, E. D., & Ripsman, N. M. (1999). The political economy of national security: Economic statecraft, interdependence, and international conflict. *Security Studies, 9*(1–2), 1–14.

Blyth, M. (2002). *Great transformations: Economic ideas and institutional change in the twentieth century*. New York: Cambridge University Press.

Brands, H. (2008). Economic development and the contours of US foreign policy: The Nixon administration's approach to Latin America, 1969–1974. *Peace & Change, 33*(2), 243–273.

Brubaker, R., & Cooper, F. (2000). Beyond "Identity". *Theory and Society, 29*(1), 1–47.

Buzan, B. (2004). *From international to world society? English school theory and the social structure of globalisation*. Cambridge: Cambridge University Press.

Caporaso, J. A., & Levine, D. P. (1992). *Theories of political economy*. Cambridge: Cambridge University Press.

Carr, E. (1964 [1939]). *The twenty years' crisis, 1919–1939: An introduction to the study of international relations*. New York: Harper & Row Publishers.

Chafetz, G., Spirtas, M., & Frankel, B. (1998). Introduction: Tracing the influence of identity on foreign policy. *Security Studies, 8*(2–3), 7–22.

Chan, S., & Drury, A. (2000). *Sanctions as economic statecraft: Theory and practice*. New York: Palgrave.

Clark, P. (2012, January 10). Is the Trans Pacific Partnership a re-writing of NAFTA? *iPolitics*.

Clinton, H. R. (2011a). Secretary Clinton Remarks on Economics and Foreign Policy [Transcript]. Retrieved from https://www.c-span.org/video/?302086-1/secretary-clinton-remarks-economics-foreign-policy

Clinton, H.R. (2011b, October 11). America's pacific century. *Foreign Policy*.

Cohen, B. (1990). The political economy of international trade. *International Organization*, *44*(2), 261–281.

Cohen, S. D. (2000). *The making of United States international economic policy: Principles, problems, and proposals for reform*. Westport, CT: Praeger.

Cohen, S. D., & Meltzer, R. I. (1982). *United States international economic policy in action: Diversity of decision making*. New York: Praeger.

Collins, S. (2009). Can America finance freedom? Assessing U.S. democracy promotion via economic statecraft. *Foreign Policy Analysis*, *5*, 367–389.

Cottam, M. L. (1994). *Images and intervention: U.S. Policies in Latin America*. Pittsburgh, PA: University of Pittsburgh Press.

Cox, R. (1987) *Production, power, and world order: Social forces in the making of history*. New York: Columbia University Press.

Cypher, J. M. (1998). The slow death of the Washington consensus on Latin America. *Latin American Perspectives*, *25*(6), 47–51.

Daalder, I., & Lindsay, J. (2003). *America unbound: The Bush revolution in foreign policy*. Washington, DC: Brookings Institution Press.

Dahl, R. A. (1957). The concept of power. *Behavioral Science*, *2*(3), 201–215.

Dent, D. (1995). Introduction: U.S.-Latin American policymaking. In D. W. Dent (Ed.), *US-Latin American policymaking: A reference handbook* (pp. xiii–xxxi). Westport, CT: Greenwood Press.

Destler, I. M. (1980). *Making foreign economic policy*. Washington, DC: Brookings Institution Press.

Destler, I. M. (2005). *American trade politics*. Washington, DC: Institute for International Economics.

Dietrich, C. (2014). The U.S. economy since World War II: Unprecedented growth, inflation, and stagnation. In R. Wright & T. Zeiler (Eds.), *Guide to U.S. economic policy* (pp. 61–74). Thousand Oaks, CA: CQ Press.

Dobbin, F. (1994). *Forging industrial policy: The United States, Britain, and France in the railway age*. New York: Cambridge University Press.

Dobson, A. (2002). *U.S. economic statecraft for survival 1933–1991: Of sanctions embargoes and economic warfare*. New York: Routledge.

Dolan, C., & Rosati, J. (2006). U.S. foreign economic policy and the significance of the national economic council. *International Studies Perspectives*, *7*(2), 102–123.

Drezner, D. W. (2011). Sanctions sometimes smart: Targeted sanctions in theory and practice. *International Studies Review*, *13*(1), 96–118.

Drezner, D. W. (2019). Economic Statecraft in the Age of Trump. *Washington Quarterly*, *42*(3), 7–24.

Escobar, A. (1995). *Encountering development: The making and unmaking of the third world*. Princeton, NJ: Princeton University Press.

Feinberg, R. (2003). The political economy of the United States' free trade agreements. *The World Economy*, *26*(7), 1019–1040.

Fergusson, I. F., McMinimy, M. A., & Williams, B. R. (2015). *The Trans-Pacific Partnership (TPP) negotiations and issues for congress* (Report No. R42694). Washington, DC: Congressional Research Service.

Garamone, J. (2015, April 6). Carter discusses U.S. rebalance to Asia-Pacific region. *DoD News*.

Gill, S. and Law, D. (1988) *The Global Political Economy: Perspectives, Problems, and Policies.* Baltimore, MD: The Johns Hopkins University Press

Gilpin, R. (1987). *The political economy of international relations.* Princeton, NJ: Princeton University Press.

Goldstein, J. (1989). The impact of ideas on trade policy: The origins of U.S. agricultural and manufacturing policies. *International Organization, 43*(1), 31–71.

Gourevitch, P. (1986). *Politics in hard times: Comparative responses to international economic crises.* Ithaca, NY: Cornell University Press.

Grabel, I. (1996). Marketing the third world: The contradictions of porfolio investment in the global economy. *World Development, 24*(11), 1761–1776.

Guillaume, X. (2010). *International relations and identity: A dialogical approach.* New York: Routledge.

Haglund, D. (2009). And the beat goes on: "Identity" and Canadian foreign policy. In R. Bothwell (Ed.), *Canada among nations 2008: 100 years of Canadian foreign policy.* Montreal, QC: McGill–Queens University Press.

Hall, P. A. (1989). *The political power of economic ideas: Keynesianism across nations.* Princeton, NJ: Princeton University Press.

Hall, P. A. (1997). The role of interests, institutions, and ideas in the comparative political economy of the industrialized nations. In M. I. Lichbach & A. S. Zuckerman (Eds.), *Comparative politics: Rationality, culture, and structure* (pp. 174–207). Cambridge: Cambridge University Press.

Hartz, L. (1983 [1955]). *The liberal tradition in America.* San Diego, CA: Harvest/HBJ.

Harvey, D. (2005). *A brief history of Neoliberalism.* New York: Oxford University Press.

Hirschman, A. O. (1979). The turn to authoritarianism in Latin America and the search for its economic determinants. In D. Collier (Ed.), *The new authoritarianism* (pp. 61–98). Princeton, NJ: Princeton University Press.

Hirschman, A. O. (1980 [1945]). *National power and the structure of foreign trade.* Berkeley, CA: University of California Press.

Hobson, J. M. (2000). *The state and international relations.* Cambridge: Cambridge University Press.

Hoffmann, S. (1977). An American social science: International relations. *Daedalus, 106*(3), 41–60.

Hofstadter, R. (1989 [1948]). *The American political tradition and the men who made it.* New York: Vintage.

Holsti, K. (1970). National role conceptions in the study of foreign policy. *International Studies Quarterly, 14*(3), 233–309.

Hopf, T. (2002). *Social construction of international politics: Identities & foreign policies, Moscow, 1955 and 1999.* Ithaca, NY: Cornell University Press.

Hurd, I. (2008). Constructivism. In C. Reus-Smit & D. Snidal (Eds.), *The Oxford handbook of international relations* (pp. 298–317). New York: Oxford University Press.

Hynek, N., & Thomsen, R. C. (2006). Keeping the peace and national unity. *International Journal, 61*(4), 845–858.

Ikenberry, G. J., Lake, D. A., & Mastanduno, M. (1988). Introduction: Approaches to explaining American foreign economic policy. *International Organization, 42*(1), 1–14.

Irwin, D. (2017). *Clashing over commerce: A history of US trade policy.* Chicago, IL: University of Chicago Press.

Jepperson, R., Wendt, A., & Katzenstein, P. J. (1996). Norms, identity, and culture in national security. In P. J. Katzenstein (Ed.), *The culture of national security: Norms and identity in world politics* (pp. 33–75). New York: Columbia University Press.

Johnston, A. I. (1995). *Cultural realism: Strategic culture and grand strategy in Chinese history.* Princeton, NJ: Princeton University Press.

Johnston, A. I. (1996). Cultural realism and strategy in Maoist China. In P. J. Katzenstein (Ed.), *The Culture of national security: Norms and identity in world politics* (pp. 216–268). New York: Columbia University Press.

Kahler, M. (1990). Orthodoxy and its alternatives: Explaining approaches to stabilization and adjustment. In J. M. Nelson (Ed.), *Economic crisis and policy choice: The politics of adjustment in the third world* (pp. 33–61). Princeton, NJ: Princeton University Press.

Katzenstein, P. J. (1978). *Between power and plenty: Foreign economic policies of advanced industrial states.* Madison, WI: University of Wisconsin Press.

Katzenstein, P. J. (1985). *Small states in world markets: Industrial policy in Europe.* Ithaca, NY: Cornell University Press.

Katzenstein, P. J. (1996). *Cultural norms and national security: Police and military in postwar Japan.* Ithaca, NY: Cornell University Press.

Keeley, J. F. (1990). Toward a Foucauldian analysis of international regimes. *International Organization, 44*(1), 83–105.

Kerry, J., Pritzker, P., & Lew, J. (2014, December 20). Kerry, Pritzker, Lew: President Obama's new Cuba policy looks forward, not back. *Miami Herald.*

Kirshner, J. (1997). The microfundations of economic sanctions. *Security Studies, 6*(3), 32–64.

Kissinger, H. (1979). *The White House years.* Boston, MA: Little Brown and Company.

Klotz, A., & Lynch, C. (2007). *Strategies for research in constructivist international relations.* New York: M.E. Sharpe.

Knight, A. (2007). Mexican national identity. In S. Deans-Smith & E. Van Young (Eds.), *Mexican soundings: Essays in honour of David A. Brading.* London: University of London, Institute for the Study of the Americas.

Kohli, A., Evans, P., Katzenstein, P. J., Przeworski, A., Rudolph, S. H., Scott, J. C., & Skocpol, T. (1995). The role of theory in comparative politics: A symposium. *World Politics, 48*(1), 1–49.

Kowert, P. (2007). National identity: Inside and out. *Security Studies, 2*(3), 1–34.

Krasner, S. (1985). *Structural conflict: The third world against global liberalism.* Berkley, CA: University of California Press.

Krasner, S. D. (1978). *Defending the national interest: Raw materials investments and U.S. foreign policy.* Princeton, NJ: Princeton University Press.

Krasner, S. D. (1983a). Structural causes and regime consequences: Regimes as intervening variables. In S. D. Krasner (Ed.), *International regimes* (pp. 1–21). Ithaca, NY: Cornell University Press.

Krasner, S. D. (1983b). Regimes and the limits of realism: Regimes as autonomous variables. In S. D. Krasner (Ed.), *International regimes* (pp. 355–368). Ithaca, NY: Cornell University Press.

Krasner, S. D. (1996). The accomplishments of international political economy. In S. Smith (Ed.), *International theory: Positivism and beyond.* Cambridge: Cambridge University Press.

Kratochwill, F. (2008). Sociological approaches. In C. Reus-Smit & D. Snidal (Eds.), *The Oxford handbook of international relations* (pp. 444–461). New York: Oxford University Press.

Krippendorf, E. (1987). The dominance of American approaches in international relations. *Millenium: Journal of International Studies, 16*(2), 207–214.

Krugman, P. (2014, February 27). No big deal. *New York Times.*

Kunz, D. B. (1994). When money counts and doesn't: Economic power and diplomatic objectives. *Diplomatic History, 18*(4), 451–462.

Kurth, J. (2009). *What are we fighting for? Western civilization, American identity, and U.S. foreign policy.* Philadelphia, PA: Foreign Policy Research Institute.

Lake, D. (2009). *Hierarchy in international relations.* Ithaca, NY: Cornell University Press.

Leets, J. (2016 [1912]). *United States and Latin America; dollar diplomacy.* Wentworth Press.

Legro, J. (2009). The plasticity of identity under anarchy. *European Journal of International Relations, 15*(1), 37–65.

Lipset, S. M. (1996). *American exceptionalism. A double-edged sword.* New York: W.W. Norton & Company.

Lumsdaine, D. (1993). *Moral vision in international politics: The foreign aid regime, 1949–1989.* Princeton, NJ: Princeton University Press.

Mahant, E., & Mount, G. S. (1999). *Invisible and inaudible in Washington: American policies toward Canada.* Vancouver, BC: UBC Press.

Maier, C. S. (1987). *In search of stability: Explorations in historical political economy.* Cambridge: Cambridge University Press.

Manyin, M., Daggett, S., Dolven, B., Lawrence, S. V., Martin, M. F., O'Rourke, R., & Vaughn, B. (2012). *Pivot in the Pacific? The Obama Administration's "Rebalancing" Toward Asia* (Report No. R42448). Washington, DC: Congressional Research Service.

Mastanduno, M. (1999). Economic statecraft, interdependence, and national security: Agendas for research. *Security Studies, 9*(1–2), 288–316.

Mayer, F. W. (2009). *Narrative and the construction of interests: Implication for the politics of trade.* Paper presented at the American Political Science Meetings, Toronto.

McCloskey, D., & Ziliak, S. (1996). The standard error of regressions. *Journal of Economic Literature, 34*(1), 97–114.

McCloskey, D. N. (1998). Burgeois virtue and the history of P and S. *Journal of Economic History, 58*(2), 297–317.

McSweeney, B. (1999). *Security, identity and interests: A sociology of international relations.* Cambridge: Cambridge University Press.

Mead, W. R. (1994/1995). Lucid stars: The American foreign policy tradition. *World Policy Journal, 11*(4), 1–17.

Mead, W. R. (2002). *Special providence: American foreign policy and how it changed the world.* New York: Routledge.

Nearing, S., & Freeman, J. (1925). *Dollar diplomacy: A study in American imperialism.* New York: B.W. Huebsch and the Viking Press.

Noble, G. W., & Ravenhill, J. (2000). Causes and consequences of the Asian financial crisis. In G. W. Noble & J. Ravenhill (Eds.), *The Asian financial crisis and the architecture of global finance* (pp. 1–35). Cambridge: Cambridge University Press.

Nossal, K. R. (2010). 'Middlepowerhood' and 'Middlepowermanship'. In N. Hynek & D. Bosold (Eds.), *Canada's foreign and security policy: Soft and hard strategies of a middle power Canadian foreign policy* (pp. 20–34). Toronto, ON: Oxford University Press.

Odell, J. S. (1980). Latin American trade negotiations with the United States. *International Organization, 34*(2), 207–228.

Odell, J. S. (1990). Understanding international trade policies: An emerging synthesis. *World Politics, 43*(1), 139–167.

OECD (2016). Unemployment rate: Aged 15–64: All persons for the United States [LRUN64TTUSA156S]. FRED. Retrieved from https://fred.stlouisfed.org/series/LRUN64TTUSA156S

OECD (2019). Unemployment rate: Total: All persons for the Euro Area [LRHUTTTTEZA156S]. FRED. Retrieved from https://fred.stlouisfed.org/series/LRHUTTTTEZA156S

Orszag, J. M., Orszag, P. R., & Tyson, L. D. (2002). The role of institutions in the White House. In J. A. Frankel & P. R. Orszag (Eds.), *American economic policy in the 1990s* (pp. 983–1026). Cambridge, MA: Massachusetts Institute of Technology.

Oye, K. (1992). *Economic discrimination and political exchange: World political economy in the 1930s and 1980s.* Princeton, NJ: Princeton University Press.

Polanyi, K. (1944). *The great transformation: The political and economic origins of our time.* Boston, MA: Beacon Press.

Quiliconi, C., & Wise, C. (2009) The US as a bilateral player: The impetus for asymmetric free trade agreements. In M. Solís, B. Stallings & S. N. Katada (Eds.), *Competitive regionalism.* London: Palgrave Macmillan.

Rachman, G. (2015, May 18). Obama's Pacific trade deal will not tame China. *Financial Times.*

Reagan, R. (1984, September 29) Radio address to the Nation on United States-Soviet relations. Retrieved from https://www.presidency.ucsb.edu/documents/radio-address -the-nation-united-states-soviet-relations

Rich, P. G. (1997). Latin America and present US trade policy. *World Economy, 20*(1), 87–101.

Rogowsky, R. A. (2014). The revival of economic statecraft. *Journal of Political Sciences & Public Affairs, 2*(1), 1–2.

Rohrlich, P. (1987). Economic culture and foreign policy: The cognitive analysis of economic policy making. *International Organizations, 41*(1), 61–92.

Rose, G. (1998). Neoclassical realism and theories of foreign policy. *World Politics, 51*(1), 144–172.

Rostow, W. W. (1990 [1960]). *The stages of economic growth: A non-communist manifesto.* New York: Cambridge University Press.

Rousseau, D. (2006). *Identifying threats and threatening identities: The social construction of realism and liberalism.* Stanford, CA: Stanford University Press.

Ruggie, J. G. (1982). International regimes, transactions, and change: Embedded liberalism in the postwar economic order. *International Organization, 36*(2), 379–415.

Schelling, T. (1971). National security considerations affecting trade policy. In *United States international economic policy in an interdependent world* (pp. 723–737). Washington, DC: U.S. Government Printing Office.

Schneider, H. (2013, March 8). From a skeptical beginning, Obama has set a global round of trade talks in motion. *Washington Post.*

Schoppa, L. (1993). Two-level games and bargaining outcomes: Why gaiatsu succeeds in Japan in some cases but not others. *International Organization, 47*(3), 353–386.

SELA (1984). *Latin American-U.S. economic relations, 1982–1983.* New York: Westview Press.

Sikkink, K. (1991). *Ideas and institutions: Developmentalism in Brazil and Argentina.* Ithaca, NY: Cornell University Press.

Simmons, B. A. (1999). The internationalization of capital. In H. Kitschelt, P. Lange, G. Marks & J. D. Stephens (Eds.), *Continuity and change in contemporary capitalism* (pp. 36–69). Cambridge: Cambridge University Press.

Smith, R. M. (1993). Beyond Tocqueville, Myrdal, and Hartz: The multiple traditions in America. *The American Political Science Review, 87*(3), 549–566.

Smith, T. (1994). *America's mission: The United States and the worldwide struggle for democracy in the twentieth century.* Princeton, NJ: Princeton University Press.

Stiglitz, J. (1998). Must financial crises be this frequent and this painful? In *McKay Lecture*. Pittsburgh, PA. University of Pittsburgh.

Stiglitz, J. (2002). *Globalization and its discontents*. New York: W.W. Norton & Company Inc.

Strange, S. (1970). International economics and international relations: A case of mutual neglect. *International Affairs (Royal Institute of International Affairs 1944-)*, *46*(2), 304–315.

Tooze, R. (1989). International political economy and international relations: From 'Enfant Terrible' to child prodigy, or just a cuckoo in the nest? In H. C. Dyer & L. Mangasarian (Eds.), The Study *of International relations: The state of the art* (pp. 380–383). New York: Palgrave Macmillan.

Toscano, D. (2009). Crítica de la gubernamentalidad neoliberal: ¿Un giro hacia técnicas de autocolonización en América Latina? *Logos: Revista de Lingüística, Filosofía y Literatura*, *19*(1), 72–86.

Turvey, R. A. (2014). Economic diplomacy and security: Linkages, trends and changes. *International Journal of Diplomacy and Economy*, *2*(1/2), 4–22.

U.S. Department of the Treasury (1997). *America's role in global economic integration lawrence summers deputy secretary of the treasury Brookings conference on "Integrating National Economies: The Next Step"*. Press Release, January 9.

U.S. House of Representantives (1981). *Foreign assistance legislation for fiscal year 1982*. Hearing before the Committee on Foreign Affairs, March 13, 18, 19 and 23. Washington, DC: U.S. Government Printing Office.

Wagner, R. H. (1970). *United States policy toward Latin America. A study in domestic and international politics*. Stanford, CA: Stanford University Press.

Walt, S. (2017, September 21). Great powers are defined by their great wars. *Foreign Policy*.

Watson, A. (2005 [1982]). *Diplomacy: The dialogue between states*. Florence: Taylor and Francis e-library.

Wendt, A. (1999). *Social theory of international politics*. Cambridge: Cambridge University Press.

Williamson, J. (1990). What Washington means by policy reform. In J. Williamson (Ed.), *Latin American adjustment: How much has happened?* Washington, DC: Peterson Institute for International Economics.

Williamson, J. (2000). What should the world bank think about the Washington consensus? *World Bank Research Observer*, *15*(2), 251–264.

Wohlforth, W. C. (1994/1995). Realism and the end of the cold war. *International Security*, *19*(3), 91–129.

Woods, N. (1995). Economic ideas and international relations: Beyond rational neglect. *International Studies Quarterly*, *39*(2), 161–180.

World Bank (2019). Gross domestic product for the European Union [NYGDPMKTPCDEUU]. FRED. Retrieved from https://fred.stlouisfed.org/series/NYGDPMKTPCDEUU

Young, K. E. (2017, August 23). How Egypt wound up in the center of a Gulf Cooperation Council dispute on Qatar. *Washington Post*.

Chapter 5

United States' Economic Statecraft toward Canada

As noted in Chapter 2, Ottawa has had an intricate relationship with Washington in security affairs—and the same goes for its economic intercourse with its neighbor. For several decades (at least since 1948), Canada has been the United States' main trading partner—a connection that only grew both psychologically and in economic terms after the United Kingdom joined the European Economic Community (EEC) in 1973.[1] Paradoxically, this broadly coincides with the start of a period of both approaching and distancing between the two northernmost states of the Western Hemisphere.

The early 1970s was also the time, as noted in Chapter 1, when the debate on the decline of US hegemony became salient in both international politics and IR. The 1971 Nixon Shock or, more formally, New Economic Program, is particularly germane here, as it was not only related to the US self-perception of decadence (the president himself suggested his country was getting into a period of "decadence," making the analogy to the downfall of Greece and Rome) and was used as foil in the academic debate, but also because the Nixon Shock was a landmark in Canada–United States political and economic relations.[2] The measures announced by the president, particularly the 10% surcharge mentioned before, directly affected Ottawa, as it had an $800 million trade surplus with Washington;[3] but the effect was not only monetary, it was also psychological: Canadians were taken aback by the United States' lack of consultation and/or exemption—they resented the fact that Washington treated them just like it would treat any other country. As I will discuss below, US (thick) economic statecraft under the Nixon administration greatly contributed to Canada's search for alternatives to its ever-closer relationship to its southern neighbor, which in turn prompted the United States to take further actions on the foreign economic policy front.

The period symbolically inaugurated by the Nixon Shock (and the UK entrance into the EEC, for what it came to symbolize for the Ottawa–London relationship) comes to a close, for the purposes of this work, with the end of the Obama administration (which, incidentally, broadly coincides with the June 2016 UK's decision to leave the European Union); as noted before, I divide this long stretch on the examination of the ebb and flow of US hegemony into three sub-periods (1971–1989; 1990–2000; 2001–2016). As noticed, these three phases, being defined in terms of the debate over Washington's international power position, are "superimposed" on both the evolving US identity and, ultimately, on its concomitant—and even more fluid—foreign economic policies; this becomes clear if one compares the administrations at the two end-points of the whole period (Nixon's and Obama's), but it is also evident when one looks at the presidencies within each sub-period (e.g., Carter vs. Reagan).

This caveat is even more apropos when thinking about the character and foreign economic policy of the target countries, in this chapter, Canada; think of the contrast between Pierre Elliot Trudeau's government and Stephen Harper's (although the disparity is certainly less sharp when comparing the endpoints, that is, between the governments of Trudeau Sr. and Trudeau Jr.). However, there is arguably some continuity in both the identity and economic statecraft of the countries in question; take, for instance, Ottawa's more statist and pro-regulation approach to economic policy than Washington's during the whole 46-year period, as operationalized by the discourse and policies carried out by successive administrations.

Despite the mostly benevolent character of the close economic, political and social ties between Canada and the U.S., which came to be epitomized by their previously mentioned "special relationship," Ottawa was well aware of the risks such close connection represented to it—well before the Nixon Shock took place. True, the special relationship, based on the diplomatic culture developed by the two countries and encapsulated in the term "partnership" in the overall bilateral relationship, constituted a genuine asset, especially for Ottawa. Particularly significant for Canada was that said partnership precluded issue linkage, which meant that it did not need to fear retribution from its more powerful neighbor on unrelated matters when it adopted policies that ran counter to Washington's preferences on a different issue area.[4] For Washington, this restraint was fundamental in building rapport with its northern neighbor. Thus, for instance, in the mid-1960s, president Johnson made it explicit to Congress that in the negotiation of the Canadian–American Automotive Products Agreement he valued maintaining Ottawa as a (junior) partner more than obtaining economic benefits for his country's automotive industry.[5]

Washington's munificence notwithstanding, Ottawa, as suggested, considered that it was in a vulnerable position. Indeed, over a decade before Nixon's unexpected economic measures, prime minister John Diefenbaker, anxious about his country's close economic relationship with its southern neighbor, had expressed its desire to redirect a substantial portion of its foreign trade from the United States to the United Kingdom.[6] Similarly, the year before the Nixon administration's announcement of its New Economic Program, the Trudeau government issued a foreign policy review noticing the dangers the close economic association with the United States entailed for Canada, and calling for the diversification of its economic and political relations; it was in this context that the Nixon Shock took place.

By this time, in any event, the Canada–U.S. special relationship was in its last days. In addition to the president's unaccustomed conduct, the transgovermental network that had been in charge of the bilateral affairs had been displaced by other actors, mainly south of the border.[7] Significantly, though, the relationship largely continued to be characterized by the U.S. abstaining from engaging in overt issue linkage.[8] Furthermore, throughout the whole period under review (1970–2016), beyond some momentary exceptions, Washington maintained a mostly liberal foreign economic policy, particularly regarding trade, as shown in the previous chapter. Ottawa, for its part, also kept its close economic ties to its southern neighbor during the five decades in question, despite repeated attempts to do otherwise.[9] As Paul Gecelovsky and Christopher J. Kukucha observe, from the late 1960s to the first decade of the 21st century, "Canadian trade policy is characterized by a high degree of continuity."[10]

This is not to suggest that Ottawa's trade policy did not change throughout the period covered here; it did evolve—as the Third Option in the 1970s and signing of the Canada–United States Free Trade Agreement in the late 1980s unmistakably attest. However, it is worth remembering that Canada's close engagement with the international economy has been a constant;[11] not in vain has it been called "a trading nation."[12] Now, as in any country in the world, foreign economic policy in general and commercial policy in particular have always been embedded in domestic politics. Multiple government agencies, individuals, interest groups and high public officials vie over the appropriate policy to be pursued. The Canadian case, moreover, has one more layer of complexity: its peculiar federal system, one in which the provinces possess ample political and economic resources—a feature which has meant that provincial governments have been important actors in the trade policy debate. Thus, the federal government has had to navigate—and use—the country's insertion in the international economy, and particularly its economic intercourse with the southern neighbor, to accommodate diverse economic and political demands emanating from the provinces; that is what has made trade policy a particularly complex political matter in Canada.[13]

But despite the contentious nature of its trade policy, Canadian policymakers have known that international commerce is fundamental to their country's welfare; hence, for instance, a Canadian, Dana Wilgress, was chairman (1946–1948) of the GATT negotiations.[14] The centrality of international free trade not only for Canada's economy, but for its foreign policy was commented on decades later by an Ottawan official in a tone reminiscent of Schelling's remark cited in Chapter 3 (about trade being "what most international relations are about") when he noted: "Canada's external policies and its foreign activities must relate directly to our national interest, and that interest is 90 per cent oriented toward trade and commerce."[15] The 1982 merging of the trade portfolio into the Department of External Affairs, resulting in the Department of Foreign Affairs and International Trade (DFAIT), only made this connection explicit.

Given the nature of the bilateral relationship and the overall continuities mentioned in both countries in the foreign economic policy realm during the 1970–2016 period, it is not that surprising that harmonious economic relations were indeed the norm. True, there have been some perennial thorny issues in the economic relationship, such as dairy products, fish and lumber, but they are by far the exception rather than the rule (and arguably those issues reflect different deep-rooted conceptions of the role of the state in the economy in each country).[16] Said patterns speak volumes about Washington's thick economic statecraft toward its northern neighbor.

There were times, however, when for whatever reason, things went out of the ordinary, and both countries had to adjust their economic intercourse. These times do not necessarily constitute periods of crisis; they might as well be windows of opportunity to reinforce the bilateral relationship. In what follows, I will look into several of these situations, focusing on US actions and/or responses, as this is a work devoted to Washington's power relations with its hemispheric neighbors as instantiated by its economic statecraft, not by the other countries' power relations. In the following three sections, I review both quiet, regular, tranquil economic relations, as well as more contentious, critical, or simply unusual moments in the political economy of Canada–United States economic relations. Among the instances reviewed are the US reaction to Canada's nationalist economic policies in the 1970s, the negotiation of the bilateral free trade agreement in the 1980s, the normalcy of economic relations in the 1990s, and the more confrontational cases of softwood lumber and the Keystone pipeline. The cases reviewed will illustrate not only the fluid nature of US power over its northern neighbor, but also how its relational nature and authoritative components operate.

1) 1971–1989

President Nixon's July 1971 suggestion that "economic power will be the key to other kinds of power … in the last third of this century," and the measures he subsequently announced revitalized Canadian economic nationalism.[17] While not a direct result of the US president's policies, it is telling that that same year Ottawa created the Canada Development Corporation, whose purpose was to purchase foreign assets in Canadian firms, particularly in mining and industry. Two years later, Pierre Elliott Trudeau's government established the Foreign Investment Review Agency (FIRA), whose task was to screen new foreign investment (with the stated aim of making sure that it would benefit the country). In 1975 Parliament founded another crown corporation, Petro-Canada, so that the government could get a foot not only in one of the country's key economic sectors, but particularly in one where US control exceeded 60%.[18] In 1980, the government announced its National Energy Program (NEP), which encompassed the Trudeau government's tripartite objective of increasing Canada's energy security, Canadianization, and a fairer distribution of resources in the country.[19] As a high Petro-Canada official would put it later,

> The Canadian government, reflecting a mood of the Canadian people which has been concerned about foreign ownership for a long time, has expressed this concern in measures such as the Foreign Investment Review Agency and through the creation of Petro-Canada.[20]

All the previous Canadian initiatives should be seen in the context of prime minister Trudeau's "Third Option," mentioned in Chapter 2. With the 1970 white paper *Foreign Policy for Canadians* as prelude, in the Fall of 1972, the Canadian government unveiled its "options for the future"—which encompassed the famous third one: "to develop and strengthen the Canadian economy and other aspects of its national life and in the process reduce the present Canadian vulnerability"; this was the alternative the document recommended should be pursued. Trudeau's government eagerly embraced the suggestion.[21]

The third option in general, as well as the initiatives mentioned above—Canada Development Corporation, FIRA and Petro-Canada, National Energy Program—were clearly at odds with Washington's traditionally preferred, leave-it-to-the-market, economic policies.[22] What follows illustrates the United States' reaction to its northern neighbor's heightened economic nationalism—a phenomenon to which Washington's own deeds had certainly contributed.

At a Senate Hearing on "U.S. economic relations with Canada" held in March 1982, US officials expressed their "concern[ed] about Canadian practices,"[23] as they go "against our basic philosophy," particularly "that foreign investment in general is good for both parties."[24] More specifically, according to a high official at the US Commerce Department, Canada's interventionist policies went against his government's "advocacy of free-market-oriented policy."[25] Furthermore, for the US government, "these new measures represent a marked change from the way our two countries have conducted business".[26] Ottawa's adoption of these policies was a letdown for the United States, but not exclusively in an economic sense; it appeared to be also for sentimental reasons, as its people felt "so close" to its northern neighbor—and not only geographically.[27] For Washington, "Canada is a country we that look to set a higher standard";[28] it was seen by its neighbor as "an economically developed country and a key player in the international economic system,"[29] as a true (junior) partner.

Washington also objected to Canada's interventionist policies because they were "no longer in keeping with Canada's international undertakings."[30] According to US officials, Canadian actions "undermine[d] the international norms"; this was a cause of concern as well because of the "impact" this could have "on other countries."[31] The demonstration effect was particularly worrisome to Washington. As Marc E. Leland, assistant Secretary for International Affairs at the Treasure Department put it,

While these measures are objectionable in principle, they are even more disconcerting in that they are indicative of a general trend by governments to intervene in trade and investment flows. The proliferation of these measures undercuts our efforts to achieve a liberalization of the world economy.[32]

As Robert D. Hormats, assistant secretary for Economic and Business Affairs at the State Department stated, "we look to Canada to set a good example."[33]

Washington's plan of action, though, was not simply to retaliate against Canada, but rather to engage with it and "press for changes."[34] Not that such a tactic (i.e., retaliation) was never considered, but in the end it was not used.[35] As Raymond J. Waldmann, assistant secretary for International Economic Policy at the Commerce Department explained,

> we have not been subjecting them to a reciprocity standard nor do we imply retaliation in a narrow kind ... rather, we are seeking to have Canada adhere to its existing international obligations and ... to a higher standard.[36]

Accordingly, US pressure was to be exercised mainly through multilateral channels "to enlist the support of others."[37]

Thus, at the above-mentioned Senate Hearing, a State Department official lamented that although the Canadian government was "keenly aware of our views" it had "shown little willingness to make any significant modifications to meet our specific concerns"; therefore, "we reluctantly concluded that we must take our case to the GATT."[38] Despite the displeasure expressed, and the actions that Washington had undertaken or planned to undertake to get Ottawa to change what it considered to be ill-advised economic policy, it was confident that reason would prevail, as this was "still a matter among friends."[39] Canada, for its part, had indeed let its neighbor know that they would accept the international commerce body's rulings.[40]

But regardless of the GATT's decision (a GATT panel found that the Canadian policy was inconsistent with Article III:4 of the Agreement);[41] Ottawa was also aware that escalating or maintaining its confrontation with Washington (as well as with the domestic actors opposed to its interventionist policies) was not in its best interest. Thus, finance minister Allan MacEachen announced in late 1981 that Canadianization measures would not be increased and that FIRA would not go further; indeed, investment regulations were interpreted in a laxer fashion.[42] By 1983, the Third Option was a thing of the past. Significantly, this was still during the Trudeau years—a signal of things to come.

Under the Progressive Conservative Brian Mulroney government, which came to power in September 1984, the undoing of Trudeau's signature policies gained momentum. Thus, FIRA's criteria were further diluted; in June 1985 new legislation, the InCan Act, effectively repealing FIRA came into force, and changed the agency's name to "Investment Canada." As the minister introducing the InCan Act in parliament pointedly noted, the government wanted to deliver "a message to the world that, once again, Canada welcomes investment."[43] Along the same lines, the Progressive Conservative government privatized Canada Development Corporation in 1986 and, four years later, it announced plans to privatize Petro-Canada—although it did so gradually. In 1991, the government sold 30% of the company's shares and some more the next year (sign of the [new] times, it was Jean Chrétien's Liberal government that got Petro-Canada listed it in the New York Stock Exchange in 1995—at which point it was government-owned only in 19%; two years later the government sold more of its shares. Paul Martin's Liberal government sold the remaining stock in government's hands).[44] By the late 1980s, the Progressive Conservative government had eliminated the National Energy Program.

But not only did the Mulroney government embark on the undoing of its predecessor's (well, strictly speaking, its predecessor was the John Turner legislature, but it lasted less than three months) trademark programs; he also initiated a crusade against government-owned enterprises—of which there were over 300, worth more than $57 billion, when it came to power.[45] It was clear that, in both the ideational and the political realm of Canada, market-friendly forces had the upper hand. This would have significant consequences for the country's relationship with its neighbor in the years to come.

The conservative, pro-market ideological affinity between prime minister Mulroney and president Reagan set the relationship between their two countries on a promising course. The prime minister had indeed campaigned on the need to "refurbish relationships with the United States."[46] And soon after his election Mulroney told the *Wall Street Journal*: "good relations, super relations with the United States will be the cornerstone of our foreign policy."[47] It would then seem not surprising that at their March 1985 summit in Quebec City the mood was optimistic—with both leaders paying musical homage to their common Irish background; president and prime minister committed themselves to explore the issue of freer trade between their countries. The pledge was consistent with candidate Reagan 1979's campaign proposal for the creation of a North American Accord between his country and its two neighbors (an idea at the subsequently dismissed by both president López Portillo and prime minister Trudeau).[48] The 1984 Canadian election marked an important turning point in Ottawa–Washington relations, but also for the political economy of North America and, of course, that of Canada.

However, Mulroney had previously explicitly excluded the possibility of entering into a free trade agreement with its neighbor; when campaigning for his party's leadership in 1983, he declared that Canada "could not survive" such an association with the United States, a position he reiterated during the 1984 election campaign.[49] Now, Mulroney's position on the matter was clearly not an ideological one, as suggested before, but rather political: Canadian history showed that advocating free trade with the economic powerhouse across the border was an electoral non-starter. Prime minister Laurier's 1911 losing bid for reelection over free trade with the United States was very likely in Mulroney's mind—as it had been in that of any other aspiring Canadian politician ever since. Thus, politics got in the way of openly launching the free trade idea early on in Mulroney's government.

But by the mid-1980s, the stage was set for what up to then had been unconceivable. In addition to the increasingly protectionist mood in Congress since early in the decade, which made Canadian exporters uneasy,[50] by that time it had become evident among the business and political class that Trudeau's economic policies had not delivered. Thus, in 1982, prime minister Trudeau appointed the Royal Commission on the Economic Union and Development Prospects for Canada, known as the Macdonald Commission (after its chair, Donald Macdonald). It produced its report in August 1985; among other things, it recommended negotiation of a free trade agreement with the United States.

In the previously noted context of rising US protectionism and 24 Sussex's ideological affinity with the White House, Mulroney announced his decision to follow the recommendation three weeks later—an announcement that came as no big surprise (already in January 1985 the Mulroney government had published *How to Secure and Enhance Access to Export Markets*, a discussion paper that established the necessity of improving trade relations with Washington;[51] as the Commission's chair wrote later, "a decision had been taken by Mr. Mulroney and his colleagues during the months before the final Report became public").[52] Subsequently, the prime minister called the US president to suggest their countries pursue free trade negotiations. Even if not unexpected, this was, as noted, a pronounced departure from the Canadian conventional wisdom regarding relations with its neighbor. But it was also quite a noticeable parting from its multilateral tradition, focused on GATT in trade-related matters; that is why Ottawa had avoided general bilateral trade agreements with Washington (it only had two, on automobiles and defense goods, with its neighbor).[53] But by the mid-1980s, several factors had coalesced to make this epochal change possible—to take, as the Macdonald report put it, a "leap of faith" and enter into a comprehensive free trade arrangement with the United States.[54]

Reagan responded favorably to the Canadian initiative. However, mindful of the prevalent mood in the Hill, the president sent the notification of his intention to move forward with his neighbor's initiative to Congress months after receiving the proposal (December). In April next year, president Reagan had to personally plead to the leaders of the Senate Finance Committee so that they would give a green light to the start of the negotiations;[55] the vote in the Committee couldn't have been narrower for a favorable outcome: 10–10 (i.e., the score meant that fast-track authority was granted). Negotiations started in May and concluded in October 1987.[56]

Ottawa's objectives in the negotiation were fairly straightforward: guaranteeing access to the huge US market. This simple goal, however, was complicated by the fact that its attainment implied changing US trade remedy rules;

thus, disputes regarding fair trade laws would no longer be adjudicated by US courts, such as the US Court of International Trade or the Court of Appeals, but by a binational panel. To many in Washington, this meant meddling with US sovereignty—something that made the Canadian endeavor a challenging task. Washington's objectives, however, also impinged on Canadian sovereignty; one of them—if not the most important one—was to address what it considered unfair trade practices on its northern neighbor's part: subsidies and industry support.[57] Other than this, Washington's main focus was on tariff reduction.[58]

But whereas the Canadians were well aware that the crux of the negotiating process was political (needless to say, the free trade debate within Canada was an intense political matter, revolving to a large extent on the threat it might represent to the country's identity),[59] and approached it as such, for the US negotiators it was mostly a technical, commercial matter—and a rather small one, at that.[60] This is not to suggest that the economics of the vast trade and investment agenda were a breeze—after all, it took over 20 rounds of negotiations to discuss matters such as investment, government procurement, rules of origin, and non-tariff barriers;[61] furthermore, many of the economic issues being negotiated impinged upon cultural, political and social matters.

However, the technical component of the talks was not where the real challenge was. The two negotiating teams did not seem to be on the same page in this regard. As Clayton K. Yeutter, the US trade representative, declared after the negotiations had concluded: "For the Canadian negotiators ... the strongest priorities were political; for us, the priorities were economic."[62] For the Canadians—not only government officials, but the public in general—the negotiations were a major item in the political agenda, in marked contrast with the scant attention the Americans paid to them.[63]

Nonetheless, high US officials were well aware that for their country the bilateral pact also had a large political component. Reaching a deal with Ottawa was intended to send a message to the world regarding Washington's leadership, particularly in the realm of free trade—something particularly important in the context of the incipient GATT's Uruguay Round. Furthermore, Canadian officials had made sure to convey to their US counterparts that their countries' close relationship on extra-economic matters, such as security or energy, could be endangered should their historical "leap of faith" fail.[64] Thus, in addition to ideological affinities, difficult economic circumstances and political obstacles, there was also a convergence of political interests that made the proposal viable.

After almost a year and a half of formal negotiations, talks concluded, as noted, in October 1987. More precisely, they ended late at night on 3 October—that is, only moments before the Congressional deadline for fast track authority. Fittingly, the negotiations were brought to a successful end only by the intervention of *political* principals. As anticipated, the main difficulties were not trade-related; as the *New York Times* noted when the negotiating process was coming to an end, "nearly 80 percent of all goods traded between the two countries are already tariff-free, and the rest are subject to modest levies averaging 5 to 10 percent on the Canadian side and half as much in the United States."[65] In a show of brinkmanship, the Canadians had walked out of the table just days before the deadline over US rejection to discuss the dispute settlement mechanism they sought. Their move worked. US treasury secretary James Baker intervened, making an enticing proposal; he told the Canadian negotiators after the final details had been worked out, around 10 in the evening: "All right, you can have your goddamn dispute settlement mechanism. Now we can send the report to Congress."[66] Disputes involving laws to enforce trade would now be adjudicated by a five-member panel.[67]

The Canadians were mostly pleased with the result (as in any negotiation, both sides had to make significant concessions). Prime Minister Mulroney confided to his cabinet the next day that he thought his team had "outsmarted the United States," but he urged them not to boast about it.[68] Canadian chief negotiator Simon Riesman, though, later declared that his country "'took the pants off' his team's counterparts."[69] Metaphors aside, many in Capitol Hill were indeed uncomfortable with the terms of the deal. Some members of the US Finance Committee were also unhappy about it being closed by politicians, rather than by professional trade negotiators because, in their view, it had debilitated their country's position; for them this had been the result of Ottawa's manipulative tactics.[70]

The Canadians had certainly played their cards well. In the final hours of the negotiating process, Mulroney had let Baker know that he would call president Reagan at Camp David to tell him about his disbelief that the U.S. could close arm deals with its "worst enemies, the USSR, but can't do a trade deal with their best friends, the Canadians."[71] Similarly, Canadian ambassador to Washington Allan Gotlieb made the case to Baker that the trade deal was in Washington's long-term interests, with which the secretary concurred.[72] Furthermore, the historic sense of partnership between the two countries, and not only on economic matters, also contributed to make top officials decide to go ahead with the agreement.[73] For the Reagan administration, the Canada–United States Free Trade Agreement (CUSFTA) was indeed a milestone.

Although in Canada there had been no clear popular majority for the trade agreement (polls generally showed citizens being evenly divided on the matter),[74] the November 1988 elections produced, at least in Parliament, a clear mandate for it. Mulroney's Progressive Conservative government obtained 169 of the 295 seats in the House of Commons (although the governing party won only 43% of the votes cast, against 53% for the Liberals and New Democrats).[75]

In a veritable leitmotif of Canadian foreign economic policy, in 1989, the same year CUSFTA went into effect, the Mulroney government unveiled "Going Global," its strategy for the decade to come; its objective of reducing Canada's dependence on the US market indeed sounded familiar.[76] But only four years later, when the Liberal Party, the same party that had so vehemently opposed CUSFTA, came to power it endorsed the pact's enlarged version: the

North American Free Trade Agreement (NAFTA)—a topic that I will review in the next chapter.

2) 1990–2000

The Liberal's about-face on NAFTA tells a lot about the order of things in the Canada–United States relationship during the "interregnum." The 1990s, most of which were under the leadership of the Liberals in Ottawa (Chrétien, since November 1993, as noted) and of the Democrats in the Washington (Clinton, since January 1993), were a calm, cooperative and pragmatic decade in the bilateral relations between the two countries—particularly in economic affairs.

As suggested, the Liberals had opposed CUFSTA in particular and, more generally, Mulroney's close relationship with Washington. The latter was a stand that had solid popular backing, as most Canadians perceived the Progressive Conservative Party was too close to the United States. Accordingly, Chrétien's promised "Canada will not be the 51st state of America," and that his government would be "less cozy" with Washington;[77] the Liberals' triumph at the polls in 1993 was to a large extent predicated on this issue. Although formally he delivered—it was not until February 1995 that Chrétien had his first separate meeting with Clinton— and created a sense of greater foreign policy detachment vis-à-vis its Southern neighbor,[78] the Liberal prime minister managed to maintain a mostly cooperative relationship with his American counterpart on the myriad issues of the bilateral agenda—as well as to meet frequently with the US president in less attention-grabbing multilateral fora.[79]

Both the finalization of the intense trade debates of the late 1980s—with CUSFTA—and early 1990s—with NAFTA—as well as the end of the Cold War certainly contributed, from Ottawa's perspective, to the generally more cordial and business-like relationship of the decade. But there was also the fact that, on many aspects, the two countries had become closer. By the mid-1990s, not only had Canadian anti-Americanism substantially declined,[80] but also, and more relevant to my argument, Canada's thick economic statecraft, and particularly its trade policy, had undergone profound changes. For starters, Ottawa fervently adhered to the Washington Consensus.[81] Furthermore, along with its neighbor, Canada became an active promoter of hemispheric economic integration, negotiating agreements with Chile and Costa Rica and promoting the Free Trade Area of the Americas (FTAA).[82] Tellingly, in 1998, Canada was relocated from the "European and Eurasian Affairs" section, to the "Western Hemisphere" one of the US State Department.[83]

The overall cordial state of Canada–United States relations during the 1990s did not, of course, preclude some disputes to persist and others to emerge during that decade. Regarding the former, trade issues were paramount. These, however, as a former US diplomat put it, referring to their occurrence in those years, "are akin to dermatological conditions: They don't kill you, but they are irritating and they never go away."[84] Regarding the latter, some of them had to do with the post-Cold War transitional phase of world politics, where the United States was the undisputed global leader. Ottawa was well aware of Washington's unilateralist tendencies, and it was willing to spend some of its middle power capital to counter them.[85] Thus, for instance, on the foreign policy front, Canada's leadership—orchestrated by its unswerving US critic, foreign affairs minister (since 1996 and until 2000) Lloyd Axworthy—on international issues such as anti-personal mines, the International Criminal Court, and human security, was more often than not a point of friction with the United States. Other diplomatic differences had to do with their respective engagement with third countries, such as Bosnia and Cuba.

The latter case was especially significant, as during this time emerged an issue that was related to US foreign economic policy affecting Canada: the Cuban Liberty and Democratic Solidarity Act of 1996, commonly known as the "Helms-Burton Act." Some analysts consider this rift as "the best evidence" of the extent to which the Canada–United States relationship was not all that positive during the decade.[86] The law's purpose was to intensify US economic sanctions against the island by punishing foreign companies conducting business with Cuba, particularly when involving property that was confiscated by the revolutionary regime from US citizens (as well as from formerly Cuban citizens that became US citizens). The legislation was clearly extraterritorial—a fact that was rejected by the international community and by the Canadians in particular. The act was also controversial within the United States, where it had failed to pass in Congress in previous incarnations, and where president Clinton had threatened to veto it. However, due to the downing of two Cuban exile planes by Cuban airliners in February 1996, the initiative gathered steam again, passed Congress, and president Clinton ended up signing it on 12 March that same year. After its passage, foreign minister Axworthy questioned "whether it is appropriate for any country unilaterally to take measures intended to force other countries to agree with its foreign policy."[87] Similarly, Canada's minister of foreign trade called the legislation "particularly offensive," and pointedly complained about US leadership: "as the leader of the movement to freer trade, the United States cannot say 'The world should follow this path, except when we tell them not to.'"[88] Late in 1996, Canada's Parliament passed amendments to previous anti-extra territoriality legislation ("An Act to amend the Foreign Extraterritorial Measures Act"), and the Canadian government joined the European Union in challenging the US measure at the World Trade Organization. It is worth noting, though, that the Helms-Burton Act was not fully carried out, thanks in part to president Clinton's intervention through waivers, and later through its amendment ("Trade Sanction Reform and Export Enhancement Act").[89]

Thus, the mere fact that the Helms-Burton Act is considered as the high point of Canada–United States conflict during the 1990s actually helps make the point that the relationship during those years was rather smooth. There were of course other problems in the bilateral economic relationship, the "irritants"

referred to above, in areas such as agriculture, cultural industries and the lumber industry; as suggested, they were of a relatively modest magnitude, dealt with at the bureaucratic transgovermental level, and therefore did not preclude the overall positive intercourse between Ottawa and Washington throughout the decade. Thus, for instance, a few months after the passage of Helms-Burton, the two countries signed the "United States–Canada Shared Border Accord," intended to make the border more efficient and, three years later, they redoubled on border cooperation through the establishment of the Canada–United States Partnership.

Thus, already in 1994, John Kirton wrote that during the post-Cold War period, the Canada–United States interaction had "become an even more intense, cooperative, and close partnership."[90] Also in 1994, David Layton-Brown and Joseph T. Jockel noted that the relations between the two countries could be "described as calm … comfortable and unruffled."[91] Particularly on economic matters, Sidney Weintraub observed at the time: "There is perhaps no bilateral relationship more mutually beneficial than that between Canada and the United States."[92] At the decade's end, Stéphane Roussel wrote that the bilateral relationship "remained for the most part serene."[93] In a similar tone, for David T. Jones, an Ottawa-based US diplomat, the relationship during those years was "essentially collegial."[94] In general, as a former US ambassador to Canada put it, relations between Ottawa and Washington conformed to what he called "the wheel that didn't squeak" theory, referring to the smooth market integration between the two countries.[95]

The overall positive state of the relationship, however, was obtained not only because of skilled diplomacy and shared values amongst the leadership in the two countries; it also had a lot to do with the economic boom the US economy underwent during the decade. The prosperity of the United States made the post-CUSFTA and post-NAFTA years more rewarding for the bilateral relationship. In this regard, it is important to recall that, as noted, despite having been opposed to both CUSFTA and NAFTA, the Liberals came to embrace free trade. The change of heart worked.[96] During the 1990s, bilateral exchange in goods and services, as well as US investment in Canada, increased drastically;[97] significantly, the dispute settlement mechanism pushed by Canada in CUSFTA and later incorporated into NAFTA proved an valuable instrument for Ottawa.[98] Even on the perennial conflict around softwood lumber, the two countries reached a (temporary) deal in 1996.[99] Furthermore, CUSFTA-modeled NAFTA became a showcase in the international trade scene—with Ottawa being one of its proud promoters.[100] On this, the Chrétien's legislatures were in sync with the two Clinton administrations. This in turn bolstered Ottawa's conviction (and incentives) that further regional integration was the way to go. The collegial character of the relationship during the 1990s obviously does not negate the fact that it was, at bottom, a power relationship—one in which Washington continued to play the central role.

3) 2001–2016

The power milieu in which the economic bilateral relationship is embedded became more prominent during the 2001–2016 period—if only because contention makes power more conspicuous. Not that conflict became the central feature in Ottawa–Washington relations, but during these years disputes in important areas came to the surface. The US-led invasion of Iraq was perhaps the most visible rift, but there were plenty of others in the economic, political and security realms as well (e.g., Canada initially rejected the United States' 2001 security perimeter idea, and, a few years later, it rebuked its neighbor on missile defense; the softwood lumber dispute reemerged, and the Mad Cow disease conflict arose).[101]

No doubt a contributing factor to the more distant relationship between Canada and the United States was the arrival to power of the Republican party under George W. Bush's leadership. The new administration's unilateralism (as evinced, for instance, by the country's withdrawal of the Kyoto Protocol and the Iraq war), as well as the major influence both the Christian right and the neo-conservatism movement exerted on it, didn't sit well with Chrétien's Liberal government. Furthermore, the "great recession" caused by the financial crisis that took place in the dawn of Bush Jr.'s administration, in addition to the damage inflicted (to different extents) to the economy of both countries, also brought difficulties to the bilateral relationship (more on this below).

But beyond the discrepancies brought about by the change of parties in power or international events, the foreign economic policy of Canada and the United States was broadly in sync. As noted, both countries had been part of the (by then vanishing) Washington Consensus, and were now pursuing "competitive liberalization," based to a large extent on CUSFTA–NAFTA successes. This meeting of minds increased with the arrival in Canada of the Conservative Party (formed by the merger of the Progressive Conservative Party and the Canadian Alliance), commanded by Stephen Harper, in February 2006. Thus, for instance, in the foreign economic realm, the Harper government released "Seizing global advantage," its trade strategy, in which it reiterated its commitment to "an ambitious bilateral agenda."[102] It is worth noting that, by that time (2006), Ottawa and Washington still maintained the largest bilateral trade relationship in the world, although in the following year China toppled Canada as the largest origin of US imports.[103]

This change of course had to do with China's emergence as an economic powerhouse, but it was also partially related to the "security tax" that the US fixation on security after 9/11 had come to represent for North American trade.[104] As Paul Cellucci, former US ambassador to Canada put it in 2003, "security trumps trade" in the bilateral relationship.[105] The commercial friction the US stand meant was to some extent taken care of with the establishment of the already mentioned (in Chapter 2) Security and Prosperity Partnership (SPP) in 2005. Although pushed by Washington mainly for its security agenda, the SPP also contained elements intended to facilitate economic exchange; in this regard, it was a mostly technical agreement, dealing with regulatory and procedural fixes, intended to build on NAFTA.[106]

It was in this context of limited upgrading in the bilateral (and trilateral, as México was also part of SPP) economic relationship that one of the perennial thorns in it was (temporarily) removed: softwood lumber trade (despite its recurrent nature, it is worth noting that the lumber dispute is not a representative case of the Canada–United States trade relationship; it is rather an extreme one, as shown by the fact that over 95% of bilateral trade is not contentious).[107] After a 1996 agreement on the matter (the third one since 1982) establishing quotas for Canadian exports expired in 2001, the issue of whether or not Canadian provinces were subsidizing their lumber industry resurfaced. That same year, at the request of the US lumber industry, the Department of Commerce launched an investigation which concluded, a year later, that Canadian firms were not only receiving subsidies, but were also involved in price fixing (i.e., dumping). The disputes went both to NAFTA panels and the WTO, with most of the rulings going on Canada's favor, although they were not final. It was at the North American Leaders Summit in Cancún, in March 2006, that president Bush and prime minister Harper agreed on the outlines of a deal; the agreement was subsequently worked out and presented in July. It established (among other things) that Canada would receive about 80% of the tariffs paid to the United States, and that no further tariffs would be imposed.

Even if the matter was a minor one for the overall bilateral relationship, and specifically for the economic component of it, it was a highly symbolic one for Canadian politics. The leadership of the Liberal party, and most of its members, were against it. As one of them warned, "If you give in to a bully on softwood lumber, which Canadian industry will be next?"[108] But the Liberal leadership was not successful on its attempts to thwart the lumber deal: on 12 September, the two countries' trade authorities signed the agreement in Ottawa, which subsequently passed in the House of Commons. Although it was widely acknowledged that it was the best deal Canada could get on the matter—and an improvement over the 1996 one[109]—there was also recognition that it was one skewed in Washington's favor.[110] The agreement was to last six years, with a possible two-year extension, if both parties agreed to it; the deal was indeed renewed and, thanks to a clause preventing US producers from filing anti-dumping or countervailing suits against Canadian firms for one year after the end of the agreement, legal battles on the lumber front were prevented until October 2016.[111]

Despite the fact that an agreement on this matter had been reached, the relationship was afflicted by other economic disputes. One of those cases was the controversial extension of the Keystone Pipeline, known as Keystone XL. The plan to build the addition, whose purpose was to send oil from Alberta to Texas, was announced on the eve of the 2008 financial crisis (on July of that year). The project faced multiple complaints from environmental groups, due the potential environmental damage an accident could bring to the areas it went through, but also because it ran counter to the Obama administration's energy and global warming policies. After a prolonged legal and political debate, in December 2011, Congress passed a bill stating president Obama had to make a decision within 60 days; on 18 January 2012, the president rejected Keystone XL. Four months later, TransCanada filed a new application for the northern portion of the project; in January 2015 the Senate passed a bill approving the construction of the pipeline extension, but Obama vetoed it the following month. The legal battle lingered on: after the Obama administration announced, in November 2015, its final decision to turn down TransCanada's new application, the Canadian company announced in January 2016 its decision to file a claim under NAFTA's Chapter 11 (on 24 January 2017, president Trump signed a memorandum instructing its administration to reconsider Keystone XL, and two months later issued the permit for it).[112]

There were many factors at play during the protracted battle over Keystone. One was of course the divergence on economic and energy policy between the governments in Ottawa and Washington; a second one was the cold relationship between Harper and Obama, and a third one was US domestic politics.[113] But Washington's understanding of its leadership on international affairs, particularly on climate change, weighed heavily in its decision to finally snub its traditional ally. For a snub it was. Harper had gone on record in 2011 to declare that the decision to approve Keystone XL was a "complete no-brainer," and two years later, in September 2013, the prime minister stated that he would not "take no for an answer" from the US government.[114] Obama's decision certainly hurt the bilateral "special relationship," something his administration took into account before announcing it.[115] But US world leadership on environmental matters was more important, especially when the decision was to be announced shortly before the 2015 Paris Conference on Climate Change. As the November 2015 State Department's "Record of Decision and National Interest Determination" noted, US "credibility" was "a major factor in determining U.S. foreign policy success"; that is, since other countries looked up to the U.S., how it was "viewed" on the matter by them could be expected to have an effect "across a range of foreign policy priorities."[116]

As suggested, in parallel to the evolution of the Keystone XL case, the "great recession" unfolded across the globe. In order to contain its effects, in early 2009 the Obama administration pushed through Congress the "American Recovery and Reinvestment Act." The $787 billion stimulus package contained a "Buy American" provision, which banned the use of Canadian products such as iron and steel on procurement for municipal and state projects worth about $280 billion. Canadians were not happy and, in addition to expressing their concern, started to retaliate.[117] Negotiations to obtain an exemption to Canadian firms started in August, and ended successfully in February 2010, with the U.S. excluding Canadian companies from most of the Buy American provision, and Canadian provinces agreeing to a 1996 WTO clause on free trade at the sub-federal level they had previously opposed.[118] A year after the agreement on Buy American had been reached, Ottawa and Washington announced, as if to emphasize that the time of acrimonious disputes was a thing of the past, the already mentioned (in Chapter 2) "Beyond the Border" initiative, whose purpose was to address security, trade and travel issues in a collaborative fashion; in addition, in February 2011 both countries also created the "Regulatory Cooperation Council," aimed at aligning their regulatory approaches while supporting market openness. A market openness that, as noted in the previous paragraph, was subordinated to wider foreign policy concerns. As US secretary of state John Kerry would later put it: "foreign policy today is economic policy"—a clear statement on the exercise of power through economic statecraft.[119]

4) Conclusions

As the previous narrative evinces, the alleged decline of US power as instantiated in the economic realm—at least as it regards its northern neighbor—has not been a straightforward phenomenon. Throughout the whole period (1971–2016) the two countries' relation of material capabilities, as measured by GDP, remained pretty much constant: the US economy was about 12 times bigger than the Canadian one.[120] Similarly, Canada's dependence on the US market for those years did not change much: the percentage of exports to the United States went from 66 to 74.[121] Brute facts, thus, do not seem to shed much light on the political economy of United States–Canada relations; that is, mere indicators by themselves do not tell much about the power Washington has been able to exercise over Ottawa in the last five decades.

Looking at the practice of Washington's economic statecraft in the three sub-periods illuminates the ebb and flow of the power relationship between the United States and Canada. Thus, it is clear that early in the first one (1971–1989), as the "special relationship" was coming to a close, and Ottawa became more sensitive to the risks involved its asymmetrical economic relationship with its southern neighbor, it set to do something about it, to wit, the Canadianization of its economy. As was to be expected, Washington did not take that well. Significantly, though, the question was not only—or arguably, mainly—about economic matters. For Washington considered Ottawa's behavior not only a departure from long-established practice on an area that affected its interests, and in that sense something akin to disloyalty, but also a bad example for other countries. Accordingly, the United States' attempted not only to reverse Canada's economic measures or at least to ameliorate its effect on the US economy, but also to send a message, both to Canada and the international community, that it was not going to simply sit while its major partner, and not only on economic affairs, went against what Washington believed were best practices in domestic and international economic affairs. The target of US economic statecraft on this matter was thus Canadian economic policy, particularly as it regarded foreign investment and energy. An important part of the costs Washington incurred by attempting to influence Ottawa's behavior was political: it could be perceived as a bully not just by its neighbor, but also by wider international community. Hence the non-coercive and multilateral means the United States resorted to.

As illustrated, Trudeau's efforts at distancing its country from the southern neighbor through nationalist economic policies had been pretty much abandoned by the mid-1980s—partially as a result of US influence attempts, but more fundamentally of the character of the structural economic relationship and the changing economic and political mood in Canada. Furthermore, in the last half of that decade an ambitious effort in the opposite direction (from those of the early 1970s) started: the establishment of a free trade agreement with the United States. As expected, Washington's reaction to this bold Ottawan initiative was of the contrary sign from that initiated about a decade earlier: it duly welcomed it. It could be said that Canada made hers this long-standing US influence attempt—for it was clear that free trade between the two countries had long been an item in the US agenda, as exemplified by Reagan's then still-recent call for a North American Accord. Now, the exercise of power not being necessarily a zero-sum game, the fact that Washington was able to get Ottawa to adopt policies it wanted did not mean that the latter "lost"; by the late 1980s, both countries' values and interests regarding free trade had converged.

This convergence only increased during the second sub-period, 1990–2000, as described above. Leaving aside Ottawa's discontent with Washington's unilateralist moves during the interregnum (the Helms-Burton Act), and economic disputes during this sub-period, it is clear that Canada was in synch with its southern neighbor regarding the Washington Consensus' ample spectrum of economic—and, to some, extent political—affairs. United States' hegemony vis-à-vis its northern neighbor on economic doctrine and practice did indeed seem to fit well with the image of the unipolar moment.

Finally, during the last sub-period (2001–2016) the contentious nature of the relationship the two countries had lived during the early 1970s made a comeback. This time, however, the issue was perhaps more political than economic, as US unilateralism during the Bush administrations had returned, with a vengeance. Beyond the usual economic disputes, mainly in the commercial relationship, the largest economic quarrel, to wit, the Keystone XL Pipeline, took place (mostly) under a Canadian conservative government. In the case in question, though, once again what mattered to Washington was not merely the economic aspect of the intended Canadian investment, but the underlying political one; the United States wanted to show world leadership on environmental affairs. Thus, at least until the end of the Obama administrations—the period that falls within the scope of this work—United States' economic statecraft toward Canada denoted both the deep intertwinement of the two countries' political economies, but also the ascendance Washington enjoyed over Ottawa in the overall bilateral relationship.

Notes

1   Molot 2003: 33; Hilliker and Donaghy 2005: 42–43.
2   Herdes 1971.
3   Gecelovsky and Kukucha 2011: 40.
4   Keohane and Nye 2012: 148; Bow 2009: 164, 168.
5   Holsti 1971: 383, note 9.
6   Kinsman 2001: 66; Hart 2002–2003: 35.
7   Bow 2009: 169.
8   Keohane and Nye 2012: 148; Bow 2009: 171.
9   Clark 2016: 238, 241; Finlayson and Bertasi 1992: 29, 32.
10   Gecelovsky and Kukucha 2011: 40.
11   Barbee 2015: 393.
12   Hart 2002–2003: 25.
13   Ibid.; Gecelovsky and Kukucha 2011: 40; Barbee 2015: 394; Lusztig 2006.
14   Hudec 1998: 104.
15   In Cooper, Higgott and Nossal 1994: 40.
16   Anderson 2003: 101; Austen 2018.
17   Herdes 1971; Thompson and Randall 2008: 238.
18   Ibid.: 240.
19   Laxer 1983: 74.
20   In James and Michelin 1989: 61.
21   Sharp 1972.
22   Kinsman 2001: 68.
23   U.S. Senate 1982: 4.
24   Ibid.: 17.
25   Ibid.: 22.
26   Ibid.: 15.
27   Ibid.: 35.
28   Ibid.: 4.
29   Ibid.: 26.
30   Ibid.: 15.
31   Ibid.: 4.
32   Ibid.: 19.
33   Ibid.: 36.
34   Ibid.: 5.
35   Thompson and Randall 2008: 255.
36   U.S. Senate 1982: 39.
37   Ibid.: 5.
38   Ibid.: 11.
39   Ibid.: 16.
40   Ibid.: 37, 40.
41   GATT 1984.
42   Thompson and Randall 2008: 256.
43   In Glover et al. 1985: 83–84.
44   Cohen et al. 1995; Yusufali and Pratt 2013; Boardman and Vining 2012: 4.
45   Whittington 1985.
46   Rowen 1984: 2/3.
47   In Barton 2012: 38–39.
48   Barry 1995: 5.
49   Burns 1988a: A7; Burns 1987: D1, D4.
50   Tomlin 1989: 263, 270; Doern and Tomlin 1991: 25.
51   Gecelovsky and Kukucha 2011: 43.

52   Macdonald 2005: 10.
53   Hart 1994: 49.
54   Gotlieb 2004: 19.
55   Doern and Tomlin 1991: 39.
56   Tomlin 1989: 272–273; Gherson 1988: 5.
57   Tomlin 1989: 274; Gherson 1988: 14.
58   Mulroney 2007: 570.
59   Wilkinson 1986/1987: 215.
60   Silk 1987: D2.
61   Hart 1994: 422.
62   Silk 1987: D2.
63   Rasky 1987a: D1.
64   Rasky 1987b: D5.
65   Burns 1987: .
66   Mulroney 2007: 572.
67   Famsworth 1987: 41, 53.
68   Mulroney 2007: 577.
69   Famsworth 1987: 41, 53.
70   Rasky 1987b: D5.
71   Mulroney 2007: 572.
72   Gotlieb 1998: 529.
73   Famsworth 1988: E4.
74   Martin 1988: 12; Burns 1987: D1, D4; Hart 1994: 88.
75   Burns 1988b: 10.
76   Gecelovsky and Kukucha 2011: 43.
77   In Jones 2001: npn; in James and Doran 2006: 397.
78   Doran 1997: 172-3.
79   Kirton 1994: 462; Roussel 2000: 144.
80   Granatstein 1996: 285.
81   Anderson 2003: 95.
82   Morici 1996: 496; Roussel 2000: 146; Lusztig 2006.
83   Thompson and Randall 2008: 339.
84   Jones 2001: npn.
85   Nossal 1997: 180.
86   Thompson 2003: 6.
87   In Nossal 1997: 189.
88   In ibid.: 190.
89   Roussel 2000.
90   Kirton 1994: 454.
91   Leyton-Brown and Jockel 1994: 449.
92   Weintraub 1994: 473.
93   Roussel 2000: 143.
94   Jones 2001: npn.
95   In Clarkson and Banda 2004: 320.
96   Roussel 2000: 145.
97   Clausing 2001: 678.
98   Haggart 2001; Molot 2003: 48.
99   Thompson and Randall 2008: 286.
100   Kukucha 2003: 60; Mulroney 2018: 2.
101   Moens 2010: 7, 25.
102   Government of Canada 2009: 5.
103   Fergusson 2011: npn.

104   Hufbauer and Schott 2004.
105   In Fergusson 2011: 22.
106   Moens and Cust 2008: 1, 5.
107   Duchesne 2007: 40.
108   Canadian Press 2006.
109   Duchesne 2007: 39.
110   Hoover and Ferguson 2017: 8; CTV Canada 2006.
111   Ibid.: 2.
112   Baker and Davenport 2017; Krauss 2017.
113   Garossino 2015; Bakx 2015.
114   McCarthy 2012; Wyld 2013.
115   Bloomsberg News 2015; Department of State 2015: 25.
116   Department of State 2015: 26–27.
117   Faiola and Montgomery 2009; Schott 2009: 151.
118   Moens 2010: 9; McKinney 2010: 241.
119   In Heyman 2013: 2.
120   BEA 2019; World Bank 2019.
121   OEC 2019.

References

Anderson, G. (2003). The compromise of embedded liberalism, American trade remedy law, and Canadian softwood lumber: Can't we all just get along? *Canadian Foreign Policy Journal*, *10*(2), 87–108.

Austen, I. (2018, June 11). Trudeau's challenge: Managing Trump and domestic politics. *New York Times*.

Baker, P., & Davenport, C. (2017, January 24). Trump revives keystone pipeline rejected by Obama. *New York Times*.

Bakx, K. (2015, November 13). Keystone XL denial all about politics, says former ambassador. *CBC News*.

Barbee, I. (2015). Canada's trade policy: In search of a roadmap. *American Review of Canadian Studies*, *45*(4), 392–412.

Barry, D. (1995). The road to NAFTA. In D. Barry, M. O. Dickerson & J. D. Gaisford (Eds.), *Toward a North American community? Canada, the United States, and Mexico* (pp. 3–15). Boulder, CO: Westview Press.

Barton, R. (2012). *Ties that blind in Canadian/American relations: Politics of news discourse*. New York: Routledge.

BEA (2019). Gross Domestic Product [GDPA]. FRED. Retrieved from https://fred.stlouisfed.org/series/GDPA

Bloomsberg News (2015, January 25). How keystone XL soured the 'special relationship' between Stephen Harper and Barrack Obama. *National Post*.

Boardman, A., & Vining, A. (2012). A review and assessment of privatization in Canada. *SPP Research Papers*, *5*(4), 1–31.

Bow, B. (2009). *The politics of linkage: Power, interdependence, and ideas in Canada-US relations*. Vancouver, BC: UBC Press.

Burns, J. F. (1987, September 14). U.S. and Canada split as end of talks nears. *New York Times*.

Burns, J. F. (1988a, October 3). Canada faces national vote On U.S. Trade. *New York Times*.

Burns, J. F. (1988b, December 18). Canada begins final battle over trade pact. *New York Times*, p. 10.

Canadian Press (2006, September 8). Liberals confirm they'll reject softwood deal. *CTV News*.

Clark, S. (2016). Steady march toward greatness? Tracing the evolution of Canada's international position. *Canadian Foreign Policy Journal, 22*(3), 228–248.

Clarkson, S., & Banda, M. (2004). Congruence, conflict, and continental governance: Canada's and Mexico's responses to paradigm shift in the United States. *American Review of Canadian Studies, 34*(2), 313–347.

Clausing, K. A. (2001). Trade creating and trade diversion in the Canada-United States free trade agreement. *Canadian Journal of Economics, 34*(3), 677–696.

Cohen, M. G., Morrison, J., & Smith, D. (1995). Dismantling social welfare: Chronology of federal govt. cutbacks, 1985–1995. *CCPA Monitor, 3*(4), 9–12.

Cooper, A., Higgott, R., & Nossal, K. (1994). *Relocating middle powers: Australia and Canada in a changing world order*. Vancouver, BC: UBC Press.

CTV Canada (2006, September 12). Emerson and U.S. counterpart ink softwood deal. *CTV News*.

Department of State (2015). *Trans Canada keystone pipeline, L-P-application for presidential permit: Record of decision and national interest determination*. Washington, DC: U.S. GOP.

Doern, G. B., & Tomlin, B. W. (1991). *Faith & fear: The free trade story*. Toronto, ON: Stoddart Publishing.

Doran, C. F. (1997). Style as a substitute for issue articulation in Canada-U.S. relations. *American Review of Canadian Studies, 27*(2), 167–178.

Doran, C. F. (2006). Canada-U.S. relations: Personality, pattern, and domestic politics. In P. James, N. Michaud & M. O'Reilly (Eds.), *Handbook of Canadian foreign policy* (pp. 389–410). Lanham, MD: Lexington Books.

Duchesne, É. (2007). Lumbering on: The state of the Canada-U.S. trade relationship. *American Review of Canadian Studies, 37*(1), 35–55.

Faiola, A., & Montgomery, L. (2009, May 15). Trade wars brewing in economic malaise. *Washington Post*.

Famsworth, C. H. (1987, December 12). U.S.-Canada trade pact's details listed. *New York Times*, pp. 41, 53.

Famsworth, C. H. (1988, June 5). How congress came to love the Canada free-trade bill. *New York Times*, p. E4.

Fergusson, I. F. (2011). *United States-Canada trade and economic relationship: Prospects and challenges* (Report No. RL33087). Washington, DC: Congressional Research Service.

Finlayson, J. A., & Bertasi, S. (1992). Evolution of Canadian postwar international trade policy. In A. C. Cutler, & M. W. Zacher. (Eds.), *Canadian foreign policy and international economic regimes* (pp. 19–46). Vancouver, BC: UBC Press.

Garossino, S. (2015, February 25). How Harper's disastrous diplomacy crushed Keystone XL. *National Observer*.

GATT (1984). *Canada – Administration of the foreign investment review act*. Report of the Panel, adopted on 7 February (L/5504-30S/140).

Gecelovsky P., & Kukucha C. J. (2011). Foreign policy reviews and Canada's trade policy: 1968–2009. *American Review of Canadian Studies, 41*(1), 37–52.

Gherson, G. (1988). Washington's agenda. In D. Cameron (Ed.), *The Free trade deal* (pp. 1–15). Toronto, ON: James Lorimer & Company.

Glover, G., New, D., & Lacourcière, M. (1985). The investment Canada Act: A new approach to the regulation of foreign investment in Canada. *The Business Lawyer, 41*(1), 83–98.

Gotlieb, A. (1998). Negotiating the Canada-U.S. free trade agreement. *International Journal*, 53(3), 522–538.

Gotlieb, A. (2004). *Romanticism and realism in Canada's foreign policy*. Paper presented at the Benefactors Lecture, Toronto, ON: C.D. Howe Institute.

Government of Canada (2009). *Seizing global advantage: A global commerce strategy for securing Canada's growth & prosperity*. Ottawa, ON: Minister of Public Works and Government Services Canada.

Granatstein, J. L. (1996). *Yankee go home?: Canadians and anti-Americanism*. Toronto, ON: HarperCollins Publishers.

Haggart, B. (2001). *Canada and the United States: Trade, investment, integration and the future* (No. PRB 01-3E). Ottawa, ON: Government of Canada Economics Division.

Hart, M. (1994). *Decision at midnight: Inside the Canada-US free-trade negotiations*. Vancouver, BC: UBC Press.

Hart, M. (2002–2003). Lessons from Canada's history as a trading nation. *International Journal*, 58(1), 25–42.

Herdes, J. (1971, July 7). Nixon sees strong rivalry from 4 other 'Economic Superpowers'. *New York Times*.

Heyman, B. (2013). *Testimony before the senate committee on foreign relations*. Washington, DC: U.S. GPO.

Hilliker, J., & Donaghy, G. (2005). Canadian relations with the United Kingdom at the end of empire, 1956–73. In P. Buckner (Ed.), *Canada and the end of the empire*. Vancouver, BC: UBC Press.

Holsti, K. J. (1971). Canada and the United States. In S. L. Spiegel & K. N. Waltz (Eds.), *Conflict in world politics* (pp. 375–396). Cambridge, MA: Winthrop Publishers.

Hoover, K., & Fergusson, I. F. (2017). *The 2006 U.S.-Canada Softwood Lumber Trade Agreement (SLA): In Brief* (Report No. R44851). Washington, DC: Congressional Research Service.

Hudec, R. (1998). The role of the GATT secretariat in the evolution of the WTO dispute settlement procedure. In A. Dunkel, J. Bhagwati, & M. Hirsch (Eds.), *Uruguay round and beyond: Essays in honour of Arthur Dunkel* (pp. 101–120). Ann Arbor, MI: Michigan University Press.

Hufbauer, G. C., & Schott, J. J. (2004). The prospects for deeper North American economic integration: A U.S. perspective. In *C.D. Howe Institute Commentary 195*. Toronto, ON: C.D. Howe Institute.

James, P., & Michelin, R. (1989). The Canadian national energy program and its aftermath: Perspectives on an era of confrontation. *American Review of Canadian Studies*, 19(1), 59–81.

Jones, D. T. (2001, November 01). Canada and the US in the Chrétien years: Edging towards confrontation. *Policy Options Politiques*.

Keohane, R. O., & Nye, J. S. (2012). *Power and Interdependence* (4th ed.). Boston, MA: Longman.

Kinsman, J. (2001). Who is my neighbour? Trudeau and foreign policy. *International Journal*, 57(1), 57–77.

Kirton, J. (1994). Promoting plurilateral partnership: Managing United States-Canada relations in the post-cold war period. *American Review of Canadian Studies*, 24(4), 453–472.

Krauss, C. (2017, March 24). U.S., in reversal, issues permit for keystone oil pipeline. *New York Times*.

Kukucha, C. (2003). Domestic politics and Canadian foreign trade policy: Intrusive interdependence, the WTO and the NAFTA. *Canadian Foreign Policy Journal*, 10(2), 59–85.

Laxer, J. (1983). *Oil and Gas: Ottawa, the provinces and the petroleum industry*. Toronto, ON: James Lorimer & Co.

Leyton-Brown, D., & Jockel, J. T. (1994). Introduction: Weathering the calm: The state of the Canada-U.S. relationship, 1995. *American Review of Canadian Studies, 24*(4), 449–451.

Lusztig, M. (2006). The evolution of liberalization in Canada's trade policy. In P. James, N. Michaud & M. J. O'Reilly (Eds.), *Handbook of Canadian foreign policy* (pp. 245–268). Oxford: Lexington Books.

Macdonald, D. (2005). The commission's work and report: A personal perspective. In D. Laidler & W. Robson (Eds.), *Prospects for Canada: Progress and challenges 20 years after the Macdonald commission* (pp. 5–12). Ottawa, ON: C.D. Howe Institute.

Martin, D. (1988, January 17). Free trade pact spurs debate in Canada. *New York Times*, p. 12

McCarthy, S. (2012, September 06). Keystone pipeline approval 'complete no-brainer,' Harper Says. *Globe and Mail*.

McKinney, J. (2010). US-Canadian economic relations, twenty years after the USA-Canada free trade agreement. *British Journal of Canadian Studies, 23*(2), 233–246.

Moens, A. (2010). Skating on thin ice: American-Canadian relations in 2010 and 2011. *Fraser Institute Digital Publications* (April).

Moens, A. with Cust, M. (2008). Saving the North American security and prosperity partnership: The case for a North American standards and regulatory area. *Fraser Institute Digital Publications* (March).

Molot, M. A. (2003). The trade-security nexus: The new reality in Canada-U.S. economic integration. *American Review of Canadian Studies, 33*(1), 27–62.

Morici, P. (1996). Editorial: Assessing the Canada-U.S. free trade agreement. *American Review of Canadian Studies, 26*(4), 491–497.

Mulroney, B. (2007). *Memoirs, 1939–1993*. Toronto, ON: Douglas Gibson Books.

Mulroney, B. (2018). *Notes for testimony before the United States senate committee on foreign relations hearing*. Washington, DC: U.S. GPO.

Nossal, K. R. (1997). "Without regard to the interests of others": Canada and American unilateralism in the post-cold war era. *American Review of Canadian Studies, 27*(2), 179–197.

OEC (2019). Visualizations: Export destinations. *The Observatory of Economic Complexity* (Accessed on May 13, 2019).

Rasky, S. F. (1987a, September 24). Canadians walk out at U.S. trade talks. *New York Times*, p. D1.

Rasky, S. F. (1987b, October 5). Broad terms of pact reflect American goal of free trade. *New York Times*, p. D5.

Roussel, S. (2000). Canadian-American relations: Time for Cassandra? *American Review of Canadian Studies, 30*(2), 135–157.

Rowen, H. (1984, December 9). Canada in transition. *Washington Post*.

Schott, J. (2009). Trade policy and the Obama administration. *Business Economics, 44*(3), 150–153.

Sharp, M. (1972). Canada-U.S. relations: Options for the future. *International Perspectives*, Special Issue, Autumn.

Silk, L. (1987, October 7). Economic scene: Trade benefits for both sides. *New York Times*.

Thompson, J. H. (2003). Playing by the new Washington rules: The U.S.-Canada relationship, 1994–2003. *The American Review of Canadian Studies, 33*(1), 5–26.

Thompson, J. H., & Randall, S. J. (2008). *Canada and the United States: Ambivalent allies*. Athens, GA: The University of Georgia Press.

Tomlin, B. (1989). The stages of prenegotiation: The decision to negotiate North American free trade. *International Journal, 44*(2), 254–279.

U.S. Senate (1982). *U.S. economic relations with Canada.* Hearing before the Subcommittee on International Economic Policy of the Committee on Foreign Relations, March 10. Washington, DC: U.S. Government Printing Office.

Weintraub, S. (1994). Current state of US-Canada economic relations. *American Review of Canadian Studies, 24*(4), 473–488.

Whittington, L. (1985, August 30). Despite Mulroney's Pledge, Canada's business ownership thrives. *Washington Post.*

Wilkinson, B. W. (1986/1987). Canada-United States free trade: The current debate. *International Journal, 42*(1), 199–218.

World Bank (2019). Gross domestic product for Canada [MKTGDPCAA646NWDB]. FRED. Retrieved from https://fred.stlouisfed.org/series/MKTGDPCAA646NWDB

Wyld, A. (2013, September 28). Stephen Haprer "won't take 'No' for an answer" on Keystone XL pipeline. *Common Sense Canadian.*

Yusufali, S., & Pratt, L. (2013). Petro-Canada. *The Canadian Encyclopedia.* Retrieved from http://www.thecanadianencyclopedia.ca/en/article/petro-canada/

Chapter 6

United States' Economic Statecraft toward México

México–United States economic relations have been perhaps no less intricate than those reviewed in the previous chapter, but in this case, the nature of the interaction has been quite different.[1] Part of the reason for this difference is that the wider context in which the economic relationship is embedded is of a different character; O'Gorman's above-cited "great American dichotomy" starts precisely at the United States' southern border. Furthermore, the historical legacy (e.g., México's loss of over half of its territory to its northern neighbor, US armed political intervention in México in the early 20th century) have made the economic intercourse with the Colossus of the North more sensitive to México than to Canada.

But as in the Ottawa–Washington case, the start of the period this work deals with also brought interesting events in the bilateral relationship—not least because of the shared Nixon Shock. Thus, just like Canada, México established foreign investment controls in the aftermath of the Nixon Shock (also in 1973). In the Mexican case, the abrupt change in US policy contradicted what secretary of state William Rogers had said about the bilateral relationship: that it was founded on "communication and exchange" and "the mutual respect for national identity and dignity".[2] But as in Canada's case, México's decision was not a direct response to the US president's unexpected action. Two years earlier, in September 1969, Nixon had abruptly ordered "Operation Intercept," a move intended to stop the traffic of drugs across the border by searching every vehicle trying to cross it northward. As a result, Mexican exports were greatly affected; the drastic measure lasted for about ten days, being abandoned after complaints from the Mexican president and an interview between México's ambassador to Washington and Nixon.[3] Thus, just like Ottawa, México City was well aware of the risks and potential surprises its relationship with its northern neighbor represented.

Also as in the previous case, the mode of the economic relationship between the two countries changed greatly during the period, even if the underlying inequality of the economic interaction did not. Like the previous chapter, this chapter is divided in three main sections, each corresponding to the sub-period established in the introduction (1971–1989, 1990–2000, 2001–2016) and a concluding section. The intervals also cover regular and critical economic interactions; thus, for instance, I review Washington's reaction to México's first attempt at GATT membership in the late 1970s, the negotiations leading to the North American Free Trade Agreement in the early 1990s, and the discussions regarding cross-border trucking access in the first decade and a half of this century. As in the previous chapter, the purpose of the cases reviewed is to illustrate both the fluid nature of US power, as well as its relational nature and authoritative components.

1) 1971–1989

In February 1973, México's Congress passed the Law to Promote Mexican Investment and to Regulate Foreign Investment. The new legislation specified the economic sectors reserved for the state, such as communications and energy, and promoted the Mexicanization of the economy by limiting foreign ownership in all industries (although the newly minted National Foreign Investment Commission could grant exceptions).[4] Washington knew in advance about the restrictive legislation. When its ambassador, Robert H. McBride inquired about it to a Mexican high official four months before the law was passed, the latter answered that, indeed, México was changing the rules, and went on to note: "Not only in Mexico but in the whole world, the topic of foreign investments should be raised";[5] furthermore, he added that just like labor regulation "is applicable as an indisputable principle of social justice in the internal politics of each country," so the principle of foreign investment regulation "is also applicable in international relations."[6] President Luis Echeverría had indeed already taken the matter to the international community in his proposed Chapters of Economic Rights and Duties of States at the April 1972 United Nations Conference on Trade and Development.[7] Washington of course did not like México's policy, nor its international activism on the matter.

Paradoxically, however, there was an implicit recognition, both in the law and in the president's discourse, that the relatively closed economic model embraced by México decades before was drawing to a close—and that in the upcoming change, a good economic relationship with the northern neighbor was bound to be fundamental.[8] As the Mexican president had privately warned his US counterpart in June 1972, American capital in his country and in the rest of Latin America would be needed to prevent "a great deal of social disorder."[9] Thus, despite the restrictive legislation, US investment kept flowing into México; with the advent of the new economic model some ten years later (more on this below), investment rules would be greatly relaxed in 1989—and four years later a new Foreign Investment Law would practically do away with all the restrictions established in 1973.[10]

On the commercial side, the bilateral relationship also had some contentious moments, but for most of the period it was tranquil. México's government was well aware that access to the US market was essential for its development purposes, and that the policy followed by its northern neighbor on this matter had been rather benign, an "act of grace" as president Gustavo Díaz Ordaz acknowledged to president Lyndon B. Johnson in the late 1960s.[11] During the period, México sent an average of 69% of its exports to the United States (66% in 1971, 74% in 1989)[12]. But just as in the investment front, there were also quarrelsome episodes; perhaps the most salient of them was the one involving the sale of Mexican gas to the United States. In August of 1977, the Mexican government signed an agreement to supply natural gas to six American companies; accordingly, México started the construction of a gas duct. The problem was that the deal went against US energy policy (according to which the price of Mexican oil should not exceed the existing price paid to Canada); accordingly, the Carter administration asked the Mexican government not to sign the agreement. Towards the end of that year, a conflict arose regarding the price, and the gas duct's construction was suspended. President López Portillo declared that the U.S. had "left us hanging."[13] Meanwhile, the head of the US Department of Energy, James Schlesinger, declared that México would eventually sell the gas to his country at the price they named. PeMéx Oil's director, Jorge Díaz Serrano, retorted that México could wait two or three years for that to happen. This dispute severely damaged the bilateral relationship.[14] Regardless, before the period proclaimed by PeMéx's director had passed, México began to sell natural gas to the United States—on the terms demanded by Washington.[15] More importantly, however, bilateral energy collaboration and trade continued after the ill-fated transaction.[16]

In addition to the conflicts over energy resources, throughout the Lopez Portillo administration there were persistent problems related to subsidies on export products, countervailing measures, the lack of the injury test benefit in US tariff laws, as well as the workings of the Generalized System of Preferences.[17] Washington considered these constant irritants to be largely México's fault. As a State Department memo noted in February 1977:

> The GOM's [Government of México's] active participation and leadership role in international efforts by the Third World to formulate group positions for negotiations with the developed countries on economic questions has limited the flexibility Mexico has in seeking solutions to bilateral trade issues.[18]

However, the United States was not worried that México's stand could affect the overall relationship. As a CIA document put it a few months later, "Since most Mexican administrations have believed that Mexico's economic health is dependent upon maintaining good relations with the US, foreign policy toward the US has been consciously pragmatic and non-ideological in content and non-contentious in style."[19]

But by that time, as noted, it had become evident that México's closed economy was not sustainable; thus, the country began taking the first steps toward liberalizing its trade, particularly with its northern neighbor, early in the López Portillo's administration. In 1977, México signed the first bilateral trade pact of any relevance in recent decades: the Agreement on Trade Matters.[20] That same year, import permits were replaced by tariffs in the majority of custom codes. Additionally, in 1978, México began to negotiate with the Secretariat of GATT a preliminary protocol for its entry.[21] México's intention to join the international trade regime was consistent with earlier statements made by president López Portillo; even before taking office, he referred to the United States as the best and most logical trade partner for México. At Lopez Portillo's first meeting with president Carter, the former highlighted the complementarity of the two nation's economies. Privately, López Portillo even suggested the possible convenience of México joining the GATT.[22] There was of course a convergence of positions on the matter, as the United States had been, since the mid 1970s, trying to convince its southern neighbor to join the international trade regime;[23] Washington was pleased with México's new stand.[24]

The official announcement was made in late 1978, and the negotiating process began the following year. The likelihood of success and a positive decision from México seemed to be great. In addition to the president's support for a change in trade policy, the new approach was favored by important business groups and several cabinet members—including his Treasury Minister and future successor, Miguel de la Madrid.[25] This support notwithstanding, on 18 March 1979—at the 41st anniversary celebration of the oil nationalization—president López Portillo announced that México would not be joining the GATT. Foreign Trade Deputy Minister, Héctor Hernández, confided his own confusion and desperation about his president's decision to US embassy officials.[26] Washington was taken by surprise about the unexpected change of heart, and it moved swiftly to defuse the widespread perception that it had inappropriately exerted too much pressure on its neighbor—pressure that, allegedly, had eventually backfired. Thus, US ambassador Julian Nava declared two months after López Portillo's about-face that "Mexico's decision not to join the GATT must be respected as hers and hers alone to make. No one—and I want to repeat that—no one is putting pressure on Mexico to reconsider her decision."[27]

While México's determination was a disappointment for Washington, it tried to accommodate its neighbors preference for bilateral dealings. Thus, for instance, in June 1980, Robert Krueger, US Coordinator for Mexican Affairs at the State Department noted: "While we would have preferred to deal with our important trade with Mexico in a multilateral and technical context through the GATT, we await Mexican proposals for bilateral trade negotiations with much interest."[28] México was indeed more interested in dealing with its northern neighbor on a reciprocal manner—but even here, México's preference was to negotiate sectoral agreements, not an overall one. Thus, as noted in the Canada chapter, when still as a presidential candidate Ronald Reagan launched the idea of a North American Accord, México dismissed it; for president López

Portillo, such an arrangement would limit his country's "sovereign ability to decide on the application of its economic policies."[29] Thus, Washington went along with México's more circumscribed preference for incremental steps toward economic integration.[30]

But beyond México's cautious approach toward its powerful neighbor, the economic context in which López Portillo decided to postpone joining GATT was important. By 1980 the oil boom was at full march, making of México's newly discovered oil reserves an important player in the world energy market. Thus, shortly after announcing the back out on GATT, the Lopez Portillo administration suggested it would utilize oil as its negotiating weapon in trade dealings. In late 1980, Washington proposed a new agreement for notifying and consulting, which required both nations to give the other warning before taking action that might negatively affect the commercial interests of the other. The agreement was not successful, but the following year, as a result of the presidential summit held at Camp David, the Joint Commission for Trade and Transactions (CCCT) and the Binational Commission were created.[31] While the CCCT was not very productive and turned out to be quite ephemeral (ceasing to exist two years after its establishment), the Binational Commission turned into an institutionalized forum which served as a mechanism for consulting at higher levels priority items on the bilateral agenda. Regardless of its efficacy, the creation of both commissions made it clear that México was exercising its newfound bargaining power at the negotiation table. Washington's accommodation of its southern neighbor was all the more remarkable given that, in the early 1980s, its trade policy was still quite unambiguous: the promotion of a global trading system.

Unfortunately for México, the oil boom, as well as its strengthened negotiating position, was short lived. In 1981, the international price of oil suffered a steep fall, thus provoking a serious crisis in the country's oil-dependent economy (hydrocarbons represented 67% of exports in 1980).[32] Due to this external shock, as well as to other structural economic problems, México had to devalue its currency in February 1982—and then again six months later. While the causes of the crisis were fundamentally domestic in origin, the Mexican government believed Washington shared responsibility for it, as despite evidence of upcoming problems in México's finances, US economic authorities had been slow to respond.[33] In February 1982, México's Treasury Minister, Jesús Silva Herzog, and México's Central Bank president, Miguel Mancera Aguayo, started making monthly visits to Washington. México was attempting to keep key actors like Donald Regan, head of the Treasury Department, Paul Volcker, Chairman of the Federal Reserve, Alden W. Clausen, president of the World Bank, and Jacques de Larosière, director of the International Monetary Fund (IMF), informed regarding financial developments in the country so that they could provide timely assistance.

According to Volcker, however, Washington determined at the outset that México had to begin talks with the IMF to get a loan, and that México had to undertake economic reforms. By Volcker's account, Silva Herzog promised that "as soon as the new president is in control of the situation, México would seek an arrangement with the IMF," since López Portillo was entirely opposed to any arrangement with the international organization (six years earlier, Washington had supported its southern neighbor when, due to current account problems, it had to devalue its currency [the peso went from its 22-year-long parity of 12.5 to the dollar, to 19]; the United States provided México with financial backing from the Treasury and the Federal Reserve, and also arranged for substantial [about 1.2 billion dollars] IMF assistance, which was contingent on a package of austerity measures to be taken by the Mexican government— hence López Portillo's opposition to resorting again to the intergovernmental financial institution.[34] For him, the IMF, and Washington through it, had been "meddling in our economic decisions").[35] The problem was that the next president would not take office until December.

Furthermore, the Reagan administration had expectations that the economic crisis hitting México would force it to adopt policies more aligned with its government. One document, apparently approved by deputy secretary of state, Thomas Enders, which alluded to such expectations, was filtered to the press; it stated that México finding itself without "wind in its sails" would be expected to adopt a "less adventuresome" foreign policy, and a "less critical" stance regarding US policies.[36]

On 6 August, the Mexican government established the dual control system for exchange rates, and considered declaring a moratorium. At the time, México had less than US$100 million in international reserves, and it had debt payments to make the next week amounting to US$700 million.[37] The Treasury Minister had to face his counterparts in Washington with an ultimatum: financial aid or moratorium. México was paradoxically in a relatively strong negotiating position, since its threat was believable, and the repercussions of suspending its debt service could unleash devastating results for the international financial system— and for the U.S. one in particular.

On Thursday 12 August, Silva Herzog spoke with his counterpart Donald Regan and with Volcker, to update them about the dramatic situation México's finances were in. The response was an invitation to visit Washington immediately.[38] Once in the US capital, upon receiving warnings from the US treasury secretary that México had a "serious" problem, Silva Herzog replied: "No, … we (the U.S. and México) have a serious problem." In fact, US banks were creditors for more than half of México's debt, and by that time the threat of moratorium was not simple rhetoric from Mexican financial authorities.[39] As the *New York Times* pointed out: the Mexican crisis "has global dimensions" with "particularly important implications for the United States."[40]

That weekend México received two billion dollars from the US Treasury. Two bilateral agreements were signed: one for the billion-dollar financing of grain imports (which made clear that the financial crisis had implications in other arenas), and another for an advance payment for the same amount on the sale of Mexican oil to the United States for its strategic reserves. It was the latter agreement that would stress the political economy of the bilateral relations the most. The problems that arose had little to do with the normal features of commercial transactions of this type (price or delivery time), and plenty to do with politics. The US negotiating team insisted on a lower than market price per barrel, to which the Mexican team was utterly opposed. Ultimately, instead of continuing to debate on barrel price, an agreement was reached wherein México would pay a surcharge on the interest rate on the advance payment. Although this symbolic switch helped break the impasse, the extremely high interest rate proposed by the US team almost broke negotiations. México ended up paying almost twice the current rate of interest: 38%.[41] As the head of the US Federal Reserve later admitted:

> [The] implied interest was egregiously high, reflecting the need to satisfy the Yankee trading instincts of Budget Bureau and Energy Department officials far removed from any sense of the larger issues at stake and more than slightly sensitive to the possibility of subsequent political criticism. The Mexican oil officials, who would have to pay, were understandably furious.[42]

However, the bailout would not be limited to the two billion dollars that were negotiated; the size of the Mexican crisis would require much more. Thus, the Federal Reserve would deliver a package of US$1.85 billion, taken from its reserves and from the Exchange Stabilization Fund, from other developed countries' central banks, and from the Bank for International Settlements of Basel, Switzerland.[43] As one banker noted, it was clear "how much clout México still has" in Washington;[44] México would receive a three-month moratorium on its debt.

Furthermore, in late 1982—with López Portillo still in office but with de la Madrid as president-elect—México reached an agreement with the IMF which allowed it a line of credit for US$3.7 billion. The agreement with the IMF, which did include an economic program for México approved by the financial institution, had been a condition imposed by Washington during the negotiation of its assistance.[45] Shortly after taking office—as had been anticipated by Silva Herzog—the de la Madrid administration reached a deal with Washington and the IMF by which several public bodies and private organizations of the crediting countries would advance funds to México so that debt service would be secure. Two debt restructuration packages, also with Washington's assistance, were reached just in the following two years.[46]

President de la Madrid appreciated the help provided by the Reagan administration on foreign debt, but he felt that Washington had not understood the magnitude of the problem his government was experiencing.[47] México would need further agreements to deal with its debt problem in the following years, such as the Brady Plan (named after US treasury secretary Nicholas Brady), an arrangement mostly intended for Latin America and in which México was among the first to take part.[48] US support in the multiple stages of the debt crisis was of course not gratuitous nor uninterested, and the dealings on this matter with its southern neighbor were always tense; however, in comparison with other aspects of the bilateral relationship, the overall economic interaction developed without major conflicts. Furthermore, compared to the treatment other countries of the hemisphere received from Washington on this and other matters, it seemed that México had in fact developed a sort of "special relationship" with its northern neighbor.[49]

The debt crisis had made clear that finding a way out of the economic situation México found itself in would involve a transition into a new model of growth. The success of the new economic paradigm entailed a more prominent insertion of México into the international economy, an arena where the United States was still the dominant player. An open economic model was needed to allow México to achieve a trade balance surplus, so that it could pay the service on its external debt and regain economic growth. The previously postponed change of course on economic matters, both internal and external, would take place simultaneously with the development of the debt crisis, mostly during the de la Madrid's administration, from 1982 to 1988. Illustrative of the radical change undertaken during those years in the economic model in the internal realm was the privatization of government assets, a measure that counted with Washington's blessing; thus, of 1,155 state enterprises that existed when de la Madrid's administration began, only 412 were left toward the end.[50] On the external front, and particularly on the new openness toward foreign investment, one case, also to Washington's liking, is instructive: the permission granted to US company I.B.M. to have total property rights—instead of the standard 49%—over a new plant in México.[51]

US foreign economic policy toward México evolved swiftly, as its southern neighbor reconsidered its place in the international economy. By the end of 1984, both governments announced the "Statement of Intent to Negotiate a Framework of Principles and Procedures for Consultation Regarding Trade and Investment Relations." The declaration projected future reductions in the barriers to trade (tariff and non-tariff) and a new handling of foreign investment.[52] In April 1985, by way of the "U.S.–Mexican Understanding on Subsidies and Countervailing Duties," México obtained the injury test benefit (that is, the burden was on US firms to show that Mexican practices caused or were likely to cause injury to their industry, before retaliation was taken), and in exchange it agreed to modify subsidies on exports.[53]

Thus, when the de la Madrid administration announced, in November 1985, that it would consider joining GATT, it did not come as a great surprise.[54] By then México had already unilaterally ended the import permits for the vast majority of the tariff codes.[55] As noted, since 1980, as Treasury Minister, de la Madrid had favored México's entry to the international organization. The entry agreement obtained was actually a continuation of the trade talks already held with Washington, since the GATT stipulated that protocols of accession should be negotiated by the applicant countries and their principal commercial partners.[56] México's trade liberalization was swift: in the 1985–1986 period, relative to the total, the value of imports requiring tariffs dropped from 83% to 28%.[57] Washington responded positively to México's new commercial practices.[58] One year after joining the GATT, México and the United States signed the "Understanding on Trade and Investment," which gave greater security to Mexican products entering the northern market. The agreement would serve as a sort of map for future negotiations, and included a consultation mechanism with a peremptory duration of 30 days, at the end of which the parties were allowed to take the matter to international forums. After the above-mentioned Framework Agreement, sectoral agreements were made, such as that for the textile industry in 1988. Moreover, the next year, already under the administrations of George H. W. Bush and Carlos Salinas, México and the United States entered into the Comprehensive Agreement to Facilitate Trade and Investment Talks.[59] The collapse of the Soviet Union would provide further incentives to México to attune not only its economic but also its overall relationship with the country that was now the undisputed victor of the Cold War.[60]

2) 1990–2000

The end of the Cold War indeed had a direct effect on México's relations with Washington: it prompted the former to enter into a free trade agreement with the latter. Although not incongruous with México's new economic path, the move was certainly groundbreaking for México's nationalist foreign policy. It was also unexpected. Carlos Salinas had rejected the possibility of starting such a partnership during his electoral campaign, and also during his first months in office. Then, during a trip to Europe to attend the 1990 edition of the World Economic Forum in Davos, he realized that the changes occurring in Central and Eastern Europe were grabbing the attention of foreign investors, plus the emergence of commercial blocks, threatened the flow of international capital to México—something on which the new development model depended.[61]

Ostensibly the goal of the envisioned treaty was to insure access for Mexican products to the US markets via pre-established rules. In this manner, according to México's leaders, México's exports would no longer be held hostage to the political comings and goings of its neighbor. Salinas' about-face caused some uproar in México, but mainly among the political class (popular support for the agreement was, surprisingly, 67%.[62] Ironically, the image México's nationalist administrations had promoted of Washington as the principal threat to sovereignty became, to some extent, an obstacle to the integrationist project.[63] A 1991 leaked confidential memo from US ambassador John Dimitri Negroponte, to undersecretary Bernard Aronson, was no help. In the memo Negroponte affirmed, "a FTA [Free Trade Agreement] would institutionalize acceptance of a North American orientation to Mexico's foreign relations."[64]

On the foreign front, president Salinas was sanguine. He knew his proposal, although unexpected, would be agreeable to his US counterpart. After all, at their first meeting—before taking office—with president Bush in Houston, the latter had already proposed the creation of a free trade area between the two countries. At the time, president-elect Salinas rejected the idea.

But by 1990 things had changed. The previous year México had restructured its debt under the above-mentioned Brady Plan, and by the start of the new decade the Washington Consensus, of which México was a poster child, had just been canonically articulated.[65] It was thus not surprising that Bush would accept Salinas' daring proposal. The start of the negotiations was announced on 10 June that year at a presidential meeting held in Washington. The scope and limitations of this treaty were clear already: two elements relevant in México–U.S. economic interdependence would be excluded, due to the sensitivities they raised in each country: migration (for the U.S.) and oil (for México). Three months later, Canada joined the talks.

Given the authoritarian nature of the Mexican political regime, the real battle over NAFTA was to take place in the United States. Canada's decision was of secondary importance to both the United States, which already had a FTA with it, and México, which had scant economic relations with Ottawa. Significantly, debate taking place in the north revolved, to a large extent, around sovereignty issues—principally due to threats posed by growing economic integration with México. For example, Republican Patrick Buchanan found NAFTA to represent "a loss of American sovereignty."[66] The former presidential candidate would later contend that "No matter the cash benefits, we don't want to merge our economy with Mexico, and we don't want to merge our country with Mexico."[67] This political stand was of course impregnated with xenophobic and racist overtones.[68] But there was also economic anxiety at play; in 1990–1991 the US economy was going through a recession, and therefore it was not surprising that labor unions were steadfast in their position against NAFTA. The 1992 presidential candidate Ross Perot would launch a campaign against the agreement, warning about the "the giant sucking sound" that the trade deal would produce when all jobs would be "sucked" away from the United States toward México. According to a survey taken at the time, 63% of the US public believed the Texan businessman.[69] The larger business associations, on the other hand, favored a formalization of the two countries' economic integration, and they lobbied Congress intensively in favor of the agreement.[70]

The negotiations finished on 12 August 1992, and the agreement was initialized by the three principal negotiators—with the presence of the three countries' leaders—in San Antonio, Texas, two months later. However, the proximity of the US presidential election complicated the deal's ratification. A month before the elections, Democratic Party candidate Bill Clinton made an important speech supporting the trade agreement—if it included treatment on three matters of concern among his supporters: the environment, labor standards, and compensation measures for workers displaced by sudden increases in Mexican imports.[71]

Following the Democrats' victory in November that year, the negotiation process was re-launched in January 1993. This part of the process was not for the treaty itself, but rather for the parallel agreements to be made for labor and environment, and for the inclusion of specific Mexican concessions (e.g., for sugar and citrus producers). With the signature of the parallel Agreements for Environmental and Labor Cooperation for North America, in September 1993, NAFTA was finally ready for the congressional vote in Washington and México City—although for México the decisive vote was held in Washington: its own process for approval, as suggested, was taken for granted (the one in Ottawa had taken place in June).[72] However, just weeks before Congress' decision, it seemed that NAFTA was going to be a failed venture: the administration lacked the votes to pass it.[73] But with intense pressure and coaxing from the White House, when the House voted on it—on 17 November—it survived: 234 legislators voted in favor and 200 against. Of the "yes" votes, 132 were republican and 102 were democrat's.[74] Three days later, the Senate gave the agreement a greater margin: 61 in favor and 38 opposed.[75] One week after the decisive vote in Washington, México's Federal Senate approved NAFTA with 56 in favor (from the governing PRI [Institutional Revolutionary Party] and the center-right opposition PAN [National Action Party]) and two against (from the left of center PRD [Party of the Democratic Revolution]).

As noted, CUSFTA served as the blueprint for the new agreement. With NAFTA, the three countries committed themselves to a general and immediate removal of all quantitative restrictions on trade, and to treat as national the goods and services originating in member countries. The treaty created a 10-year timeline according to which Canada would eliminate 99% of its tariffs, the U.S. 98.7%, and México 98.5%. In addition, the U.S. allowed México to maintain the benefits of the Generalized System of Preferences, and the cuts in Mexican tariffs would be gradual. Thus, the tariffs on approximately 80% of Mexican exports to the U.S. were immediately reduced and México only had to do the same on 41.1% of goods imported from the United States.[76] For Mexican agricultural products that were especially sensitive domestically (beans, corn and milk) a 15-year protection period was granted. A very significant component of the treaty is Chapter 11, regarding investment. This section not only includes an innovative investment regime among the three partners, but also creates a dispute resolution mechanism with a tribunal made up of three arbitrators selected by the disputing parties. Moreover, considering the guidelines created for issues such as national treatment, expropriation, and transfers, Chapter 11 represents a significant switch in the traditional Mexican posture on foreign investment (by virtue of the North American Agreement on Environmental Cooperation the Commission for Environmental Cooperation was created. The binational institution, for México and the U.S., the North American Development Bank, was also established. Likewise, by mandate of the North American Agreement on Labor Cooperation the Commission on Labor Cooperation was created). Canada's cherished Chapter 19, on dispute settlement mechanisms, became NAFTA's ... Chapter 19. The agreement went into effect on 1 January 1994. NAFTA became the template for US trade agreements to come.[77]

In general terms, as much as CUSFTA worked for Canada, NAFTA worked for México (as much as a trade—and investment—agreement could work, that is, not to solve the country's myriad development problems, but to increase its exports and attract foreign capital). Thus, trade did grow notably after the deal went into effect: from US$102.8 billion in 1994 to US$256.2 billion in 2000. In the same period, Mexican imports rose in value from US$50.8 billion to US$108.8 billion, and Mexican exports from US$51.943 billion to US$147.4 billion.[78] Similarly, US investment in México grew substantially after NAFTA went into effect; for instance, US$3,503 million in 1993 vs. US$7,348 million in 1999.[79]

Also as in CUSFTA, while NAFTA made bilateral trade growth possible, it did not end disputes in every area. Problems involving sugar, tomatoes and cross-border cargo trucking, to name a few, persisted. But despite of these frictions, NAFTA has permitted the debate for their resolution to take place within previously convened upon rules. As Antonio Ortiz-Mena has observed, with NAFTA México received the assurance that there are "significant limits on US unilateral conduct."[80] For Gustavo Vega Cánovas, on balance, the agreement has been positive: it "has served the purposes for which it was negotiated."[81] It was thus not surprising that, in the final days of his administration, on 21 November 2000, with NAFTA already in its seventh year, president Zedillo granted the *Águila Azteca* award (insignia class) to five US NAFTA promoters.[82]

Not a year had passed since NAFTA had gone into effect, when the political economy of México and the United States would become again deeply intertwined—this time in a much more challenging situation, as noted. The process of economic reform initiated in 1982 had been carried in the context of a profound crisis, not only regarding foreign debt, but also inflation rates and the value of the peso. Although some of these problems had subsided during the Salinas administration, the current account turned into a red light; foreign factors, such as the increase of US interest rates, were no doubt an element, but an overvalued peso was a crucial cause of it. Furthermore, major domestic political problems during 1994, such as the 1 January uprising of the Zapatista movement in the southern state of Chiapas, the assassination of Luis Donaldo Colosio, the frontrunner in the presidential electoral process that was to take place in August, and that of the Secretary General of his party a few months later, further complicated the country's troubles with its current account: foreign investors' confidence in the country started to evaporate.

Thus, following Colosio's murder, Washington made available a credit line (swap) for six billion dollars. The following month, the brand new NAFTA partners signed the North American Framework Agreement (NAFA), which made the swap permanent (Canada would also put down around US$750 million as part of the agreement). The day after the first political magnicide, Deputy Secretary of the Treasury Larry Summers sent a memo to treasury secretary Lloyd Bentsen informing him that México "expects some words from the Treasury Secretary that might calm the press." The Secretary did put out a communiqué stating: "We have every confidence that México is on the right economic path."[83] Even one month later, on 26 April, Summers declared that México's currency was safe; but in an internal memo he informed Bentsen that "Mexico's dependency on the financing of its large account deficit [sic— should read 'current account'] from largely volatile investment remains a serious problem."[84]

Similarly, a couple of weeks later, a Treasury department official visited México to meet Pedro Aspe, México's Treasury Secretary at the time, and Miguel Mancera, still-president of *Banco de México*; following these meetings, he reported that the volatility in portfolio investments had become a serious problem for Mexico.[85] Even the Chairman of the Federal Reserve, Alan Greenspan, informed Mexican officials of the "necessity" that their country adjust its exchange rate policy if pressures on the peso continued. According to another Federal Reserve officer, who held talks with a Central Bank officer in México, he was informed by the Mexican official that the country's central bank would be making adjustments if the pressures on the peso persisted following the August elections, probably in late September of the same year.[86] In August, following an agreement reached in this direction (i.e., México would modify their exchange policy if pressures on the peso persisted following presidential elections), the US government and the Bank for International Settlements made another swap arrangement with México. While pressure did decline, however, foreign capital did not flow at the same rate it had before.[87]

Concerns remained in Washington regarding the sustainability of México's exchange rate policy. In late September, an internal memo by Summers questioned the decision against a policy change. The next month, a document prepared for Greenspan, in preparation for meetings he would hold with Mexican officials, suggested he warn them that they "should not count on the U.S. for financial support via the Federal Reserve and Treasury lines to sustain an inappropriate exchange rate."[88] By this time, both the Federal Reserve and the Treasury Department were quite worried by the Mexican authorities' insistence on defending the exchange rate policy.[89] Even as late as 18 November, another Treasury Department report challenged the use of declining international reserves, and warned treasury secretary Bentsen about the peso's weakness.[90]

Precisely the weekend of 19–20 November, a meeting was held between the outgoing and incoming administration in México regarding the convenience of adjusting exchange rate policy. During that time, high US Treasury

Department officials were consulted, and they indicated that neither they nor the Federal Reserve President saw any alternative to a change in said policy—although treasury secretary Lloyd Bentsen made it clear to his counterpart that the final decision was México's.[91] The decision taken at the meeting was that the peso would not be devalued. But a month later the situation had turned unsustainable. México's international reserves held only US$6,500 million, in contrast to the $26,000 million held nine months earlier.[92] With only 19 days in power, the Zedillo administration, through its treasury secretary Jaime Serra Puche, announced a 15 percent expansion of the floatation band. The administration's attempt to administer the peso's depreciation without the support of other complementary measures lacked credibility in the markets, and within two days the dollar not only reached its maximum permitted value, but the reserves in dollars were depleted by five billion dollars. The same day the measure was announced, 19 December, a Treasury Department memo noted as a troublesome sign that México should decide to change their exchange rate policy before Christmas without consulting them.[93] Three days later, a floating exchange rate policy was adopted.

Serra Puche met with investors in New York the same day the floating exchange rate was announced. The Treasury Secretary tried to explain the new measures, avoiding at all costs the term "devaluation." The investors felt they had been fooled and the meeting ended in failure.[94] On this same day, the Mexican government also drew on its NAFA swap credit lines mentioned above. With its currency still falling, the Zedillo administration cancelled the sale of "tesobonos" (México's treasury bonds) on 27 December 1994. México was unable to finance new domestic deficit.[95] Two days later, Serra Puche was replaced by Guillermo Ortiz. The new head of the Treasury announced a greater openness to foreign bank involvement—a measure resisted by México during the NAFTA negotiations, but which was now inevitable.[96] México needed to bring in capital and convince foreign investors to keep their money in the country. As deputy secretary Summers would later observe: "By early January, México was on the brink of default."[97]

On 2 January 1995, the US government announced an $18 billion bailout, of which US$9 billion would come from the US contribution to NAFA (including an additional US$3 billion); $1.1 billion Canadian dollars would come from Ottawa, also within the NAFA framework; US$5 billion from the Bank for International Settlements and US$3 billion more from international banks. These funds covered the value of the *tesobonos*, but did not cover the value of the certificates of deposit (CDs) held by local banks. Even considering the international reserves, México could only cover around half of the obligations it held that would come up for payment in 1995. This is why México decided to seek other sources of funding in Washington, and turn to the IMF again.

Given the bleak situation unleashed by the Mexican financial crisis, president Clinton met with his new treasury secretary, Robert Rubin, deputy secretary

Summers and some advisors in the Oval office on 11 January 1995. Although not all would back his decision, Clinton followed the advice of the two principal officials of the Treasury department and chose to prepare a bailout program.[98] He announced that the "United States is committed to doing what we can to help Mexico through what I believe should be a short-term crisis".[99] On 12 January, the US president met with leaders of both houses of Congress—both Republican—as well as leaders of the democratic factions, with the goal of reaching agreement on the bailout for México, for a maximum of US$40 billion. This figure wasn't arbitrary: it was calculated to be twice what México could possibly require; the message intended was that México had full US support.[100] Mexican markets responded favorably to the announcement. However, in spite of the support Clinton obtained from the Republican and Democratic leadership, a revolt by lawmakers from both parties soon revealed the uphill road that the president's proposal faced ahead—and Mexican markets fell again.

On 19 January, Clinton referred to the Mexican crisis as "plainly also a danger to the economic future of the United States."[101] Similarly, treasury secretary Rubin (who had succeeded Bensten on 23 December) would suggest a few days later the possible scenario of a 30% increase in Mexican immigrants to the U.S. if the package was not passed.[102] México's crisis had crossed the Rio Grande again—just as Silva Herzog had made clear to his American counterpart Donald Regan, 13 years before.

On 26 January, it was announced that México had requested an 18-month stand-by credit from the IMF for $7.8 billion (amounting to 300% of México's quota). In spite of this, by the end of the month neither Clinton's promise nor the agreement with the IMF could calm the markets; international investors were still unconvinced by the policies proposed by the Mexican government to accompany the funding support. On 31 January, when it was clear that Clinton's bailout package would not be approved by Congress in time, Clinton announced that he would draw on the Exchange Stabilization Fund to offer up to $20 billion in credit. That same day he communicated with Mexican president Zedillo to inform him about the plan he had put into action.[103] The Mexican president made a national announcement where he promised that with Washington's aid, "the problems of capital liquidity in our economy will be fully overcome," and he praised his US counterpart "for his solidarity and the absolute respect he has shown the Mexican people and their government."[104]

After intense lobbying by deputy secretary Summers, the Managing Director of the IMF, Michel Camdessus, announced that the fund would increase the stand-by credit lines for México to US$17.8 billion, an unprecedented amount in the history of the institution.[105] In addition, México would receive US$10 billion from the Bank for International Settlements, one billion from Canada, and credit lines from the World Bank and the Inter-American Development Bank, which together added three billion dollars. European leaders were not entirely in agreement to committing resources to a country that, in their consideration, was a problem for the U.S. to handle. Thus, six European members of the IMF's Board of Governors abstained from voting on the rescue package.

México signed four financial agreements to obtain the aid from the United States: the framework agreement, the oil agreement, the mid-term stabilization agreement, and the guarantee agreement.[106] The framework agreement established that México would commit itself to presenting a financial plan to the US Treasury Department (as well as annual updates) as soon as the Stabilization Fund resources were available. Additionally, this agreement stated that the US Treasury Department could retain the funds' provision if México did not uphold its part of the bargain, either by not ful-filling the pact made with the IMF for the credit line the institution would provide, or by not fulfilling the economic measures announced by the Mexican government when the agreements were made.[107] The agreement also stated that the Mexican finance officials would not use international reserves to stabilize the exchange market, and that the government would make financial information more transparent.[108] Particularly delicate was the loan obtained through the Exchange Stabilization Fund, since it required guaranteed payment; it was agreed that México would deposit resources obtained from oil sales by PeMéx and its two exportation subsidiaries at the Federal Reserve Bank of New York. This meant that Washington would have automatic access to these resources if México did not complete the agreed upon payments.[109]

As treasury secretary Rubin would say, México had to "meet strict targets […] and provide timely transparency."[110] Secretary of State Christopher went further and described the package as one which contained "strong and hard terms which will protect the integrity of the loan," although he recognized that he and the Treasury Secretary had both stated "frequently that this transaction need not be loaded down with conditions which are not economic."[111] But non–economic factors were of course at play. Former Federal Reserve head, Paul Volcker, noted that

> one of the reasons why it is important to try to ease this adjustment and provide some support, is that the political system has become more open, more reliable, and less corrupt, and it is very much in our interest to foster that development.[112]

For his successor, Alan Greenspan, the bailout was the "least-worst" option his country had in order to face the bleak international economic horizon created by the Mexican crisis.[113] In his words, "if this were strictly about México, I would say there is absolutely no reason to make a rescue package."[114] But the Chairman of the Federal Reserve did accept that it was "important to the United States, politically" to help its southern neighbor, since the political and economic "model" of transitioning from a rigid system of state intervention towards one of free markets, was México.[115]

As a General Accounting Office's report would later note, by virtue of the agreements the United States and the IMF possessed "a degree of influence over Mexican economic policy that did not exist before the onset of the financial crisis."[116] Even if in the context of the Washington Consensus there was a broad, tacit agreement between Mexican and US negotiators regarding the type of economic policy that México would follow, the United States' proposals were certainly more radical; ultimately, the Mexican negotiators did yield.[117] But as with the 1982 debt crisis, the negotiations were successful in immediate terms: México obtained the financial resources it required. Thus, towards the end of his administration, on 10 July 2000, president Zedillo awarded the *Águila Azteca* (sash class, higher than the insignia awarded to NAFTA promoters) to the then-former IMF Director, Michel Camdessus, "for the help he provided México in financial matters."[118]

3) 2001–2016

In contrast to the Ottawa–Washington case, in which the relationship became more distant with the arrival of George W. Bush to the White House, in the México City–Washington relationship, the immediate effect of this factor was the opposite. Furthermore, the arrival to power in México of an administration that for the first time in over 70 years did not come from the party that emerged victorious from the 1910 Mexican Revolution, one that, moreover, was headed by the conservative PAN, gave México a "democratic bonus" abroad, one that the new administration was willing to cash in its relationship with its northern neighbor. Thus, for instance, before taking office Vicente Fox was received in the White House by president Clinton (in August 2000), and the first international trip made by his successor, president Bush, was to México (in February 2001). Furthermore, president Fox was the first State leader received by Bush in a state visit (in September 2001); the US president would declare at the time that the most important relationship for his country was that with México.[119] It was in this cordial bilateral context that their two countries started negotiating what came to be known as the "enchilada completa" (the whole enchilada), an ambitious plan to deal with the persistent migration problem, one that, as noted, had been left out of the NAFTA negotiations.

But the 9/11 terrorist attacks would transform the bilateral agenda's priorities—at least from Washington's perspective—and the relationship cooled substantially. Like Ottawa, México City did not support their common neighbor in the invasion of Iraq, but president Fox went further and rubbed its government estrangement from the United States on the matter on national television as the hostilities started. On the international economic scene, China's displacement of México as the second exporter to the United States in 2004[120] fueled anxieties in México City; however, as noted, with Washington's focus on the security agenda, the progress achieved in what in México's perspective should have been a NAFTA Plus but ended up being the 2005 Security and

Prosperity Partnership (SPP) was quite modest, as suggested in the previous chapter. The 2008 financial crisis not only greatly impacted the commercial relationship, with trade falling in 2009 from 367 billion to 305 billion, that is, 17%, but also México's economy which, in contrast to Canada's, fared worse than the U.S.'s, falling by 6.5 percent.[121] To complicate this further, it was in this context that Democratic presidential candidate Barack Obama promised to re-negotiate NAFTA—a promise that, fortunately for México, he quickly forgot about once he took office (although the Bush-era-associated SPP did fall through the cracks after 2009).[122] The permanence of the trade agreement notwithstanding, localized problems in the trade relationship persisted throughout the period (more on this below).

But beyond the lack of progress in further economic integration and the persistence of trade irritants, bilateral economic links continued to grow; between 2000 and 2010 Mexican exports to the United States had grown by 69 percent, while Mexican imports from the northern neighbor had increased by 47 percent.[123] Furthermore, a true believer in the by-then agonizing Washington Consensus, México was one of the most active promoters of free trade agreements around the world: by 2016, it had signed 12 free trade agreements, covering 46 countries—second only to ... Chile. More relevant for this work, México was an enthusiastic promoter of the already mentioned Free Trade Area of the Americas (FTAA) from its formal start at the 1998 Summit of the Americas in Santiago, Chile, to its veritable demise in 2005 in Mar de Plata, Argentina; throughout this period, México consistently sided with Washington. Later, México (in 2012) joined the United States in the (failed) Trans-Pacific Partnership, in the hope of modernizing NAFTA through the backdoor, also as noted in the previous chapter.

President Enrique Peña Nieto's efforts (2012–2018) tried to "de-securitize" the bilateral agenda (during Felipe Calderón's administration [2006–2012] the bilateral relationship had been dominated by anti-drug trafficking collaboration, as epitomized by the Mérida Initiative, launched by presidents Calderón and Bush in October 2007), by pushing for closer cooperation on economic matters. Thus, in May 2013, presidents Peña Nieto and Barack Obama announced the establishment of the High Level Economic Dialogue (HLED), intended to deal with strategic economic and trade priorities. It was to meet once annually at the cabinet level, headed by the Treasury secretary on the Mexican side and vice president Joseph Biden on the US side[124]). The HLED held three meetings (plus one video conference) from 2013 to 2016, and focused on issues such as border development, communication, energy, transport and the strengthening of the North American Development Bank. Among the most remarkable results are trade facilitation mechanisms, the construction of border facilities, and a notable increase in student exchange programs. Overall, however, the HLED's achievements were rather modest.

As in the Canadian case, the institutionalization of the economic relationship did not prevent disputes from emerging. Among the ones that persisted during the 2001–2016 period are those related with cross-border trucking and tomato. I now briefly review each of them for illustrative purposes.

One of the most persistent NAFTA irritants, cross-border trucking problems, actually started a long time before the trade agreement was born. In 1982, Washington issued a moratorium on the granting of licenses to both Canada and México, citing safety concerns as well as lack of equal treatment; whereas the issue with Canada was promptly solved, the one with México lingered on through the NAFTA negotiations. The agreement provided for Mexican motor carrier companies to receive licenses to operate in the four border states as of 18 December 1995 (three years after NAFTA's signing) and in the rest as of 1 June 2000.[125]

But three days before the first part of the agreement was to come into effect, president Clinton, under pressure from the Teamsters union, postponed its commencement; although the president cited security reasons for its decision, it was clear that he had taken it for political reasons. Luis de la Calle, a former NAFTA negotiator and high-level public official in the Zedillo administration (1994–2000), recalls that the same day the moratorium on Mexican trucks was to end, "we got a call from (U.S. Trade Representative) Mickey Kantor saying the U.S. was backing down under pressure from the Teamsters."[126] Thus, from 1995 to 2001 Mexican trucks were able to go up to 25 miles from the border (from that point on, the goods had to be transferred to a Teamsters Union-operated truck; in the meantime, México closed its market to US land carriers and initiated an arbitration procedure.[127]

The February 2001 arbitration panel's report found that the United States was in breach of the agreement, although it noted that Washington could impose different operating requirements to Mexican trucks from those that it applied to its own and to Canadian units.[128] Although the Bush administration signaled its intention "to live up to our NAFTA obligations"[129] and comply with the panel's ruling, between that year and 2006, Congress approved various measures that prevented it from fully honoring its obligations.[130] In November 2002, the Bush administrations started granting access to Mexican trucks, but it was taken to court by environmental and labor organizations; although the opposition's legal recourse was first sustained, the Supreme Court reversed that decision in June 2004.[131]

It was not until 2007, though, that real progress was made. On that year, the Bush administration initiated the Cross Border Demonstration Program. According to this pilot program (it was set up for one year, but it lasted 18 months), up to 100 permits for trucking companies from both countries were to be issued, allowing them to go beyond the previous 25-mile limit; 27 Mexican firms, and 10 US ones, took part in it. The pilot program was a compromise, as it did not allow Mexican trucks operate within the United States (that is, they could not pick up cargo in it).[132] In February 2009, the Federal Motor Carrier Safety Administration (FMCSA) issued a report evaluating the demonstration program; although it was favorable, noting, for instance, that Mexican drivers in the program had equal or better scores that their US counterparts, president Obama signed the FY 2009 Omnibus Spending Bill, effectively terminating the demonstration program.[133] The administration argued that its intention was to create a new arrangement that would take into consideration Congress's "legitimate concerns," as well as its NAFTA obligations, but the Mexican government didn't buy it.[134] México's ambassador to Washington saw protectionist intentions in the move, which came to be known as "Obama's first trade war."[135]

Indeed. México immediately announced that, using the rights the arbitration panel had granted it to take retaliatory measures, it was imposing tariffs (ranging from 10% to 45%) on 90 agricultural and industrial products worth $2.4 billion in exports. In 2010, México added 26 products to the list, causing extensive damage to some US producers; a bipartisan 56-member group of representatives contacted the Obama administration, asking it to bring closure to the dispute. Along the same lines, 150 firms—including major ones such as General Electric and Walmart—sent a letter to president Obama noting that México's "retaliation is already impacting the ability of a broad range of U.S. goods to compete in the Mexican market".[136] México's punitive tactic worked. In March 2011, president Calderón and president Obama announced a new agreement on the matter. Six months later, Mexican trucks were again crossing the border, and México ended retaliatory tariffs on US products.[137] The program expired in October 2014, but the next FMCSA further expanded the rights Mexican trucking companies have in the United States—a measure challenged again by the Teamsters; by the end of 2016, they had not been successful.[138]

Disputes regarding tomato go back even further than those related to trucking. Already in 1968, a conflict had arisen when Florida authorities tried to set the size specifications of the fruit; a decade later, another battle regarding Mexican exports surfaced, this time with Florida producers charging their Mexican counterparts were engaging in dumping during the winter season.[139] The issue kept coming back during the 1980s and early 1990s, but it took a turn for the worse as NAFTA liberalized Mexican tomato imports. Thus, for instance, by the end of the decade, imports were almost 50% greater than at the start of it.[140] A deal was reached in 1996. The US Commerce Department suspended an inquiry into Mexican dumping in exchange for México setting a reference price floor for its winter tomatoes.[141] The suspension was re-evaluated in 2002, when floor prices were established as well for summer tomatoes; México renewed this export restraint six years later.

As this last agreement was set to expire on 31 December 2012—an election year—the Obama administration, under pressure from Florida growers, accepted to review it in June (2012). As the *Wall Street Journal* put it, "President Obama proved he'll use trade law as a campaign weapon."[142] Since Florida was a swing state, it made electoral sense for the administration to pander to its tomato growers, but, as Gary Clyde Hufbauer, former Deputy Assistant Secretary for International Trade and Investment Policy at the Treasury Department suggested at the time, it did not make that much sense in light of the broader bilateral relationship with the southern neighbor; as he put it, "we also have a lot of fish to fry with México."[143] Mexican ambassador Sarukhan, also warned that a trade war would damage the bilateral relationship.[144] Furthermore, pointing to the recent cross-border trucking case just reviewed, the diplomat threatened: "When México aims, México hits the target."[145]

In September, Washington decided to preliminarily finish the agreement, staring a 270-day period for a final decision to be reached. But México did not stand still. It threatened to reciprocate US protectionist measures; furthermore, it recruited powerful allies in the United States, such as Walmart and over 300 agribusinesses who were afraid of being collateral damage if a trade war with México ensued.[146] Four months after the mid-term elections, in February 2013, México and the United States reached an agreement. In exchange for higher reference price in the established tomato categories, and the addition of new ones, also with reference prices, the Mexican producers would be able to sell tomatoes again in the United States.[147]

4) Conclusions

The account above suggests that, as in the case covered in the previous chapter, the supposed economic decline of the United States since the early 1970s has not manifested itself, an least not in a linear fashion, in the relationship with its southern neighbor. Although during the 1971–2016 period the ratio of material capabilities between the two countries did change some, with México's economy going from 3.4 as a percentage of the US economy in 1971 to 5.8 in 2016, its trade dependency (measured in terms of the percentage of it exports going to the United States) in the US market increased, passing from 66% in the former year to 81% in the latter.[148] Brute facts alone, as in the bilateral relationship reviewed before, fail to enlighten the dynamics of the United States–México political economy. For that we need to look at the practice of US thick economic statecraft during the last five decades.

US foreign economic policy toward México during the first sub-period (1971–1989) reflected both that, unlike Ottawa, México City was not considered a (junior) partner and that, at the end of the day, it was in Washington's interest to support its southern neighbor's economy—even if heavy-handedly. Thus, while making its views known, the United States reacted with restraint toward its southern neighbor's nationalist policies of the early 1970s, such as the law on foreign investment. Similarly, US economic statecraft on the matter of México's aborted entrance into GATT went in the same direction. But on other matters of more immediate concern to Washington, such as the failed gas deal of the late 1970s, the United States played hard ball. Washington was well aware that its influence attempts would not necessarily work in the short term, and it was willing to pay the cost of engaging in coercive foreign economic policy—as it did in the gas case—but it was confident, given the lopsided character of the relationship, that it would most likely emerge victorious. The 1982 debt crisis episode illustrates well both the United States' heavy-handedness and its interest on an economically and politically stable México. The succeeding treatment provided to México City on the matter, especially through the Brady Plan, showed that perhaps, as noted, México had a sort of tropicalized "special relationship" with Washington.

That the United States was playing the long-term game regarding the fundamental matter of the nature of the bilateral relationship, as it referred to its economic component, was made clear in the 1990s, the Washington Consensus' decade. Both in the NAFTA negotiations and in the 1995 bailout, the United States again showed that it wanted to bring México into its economic fold. In the first case, for all the domestically complicated trade deals can be, it was clear that Washington stood to win both economically and politically from signing an agreement with its southern neighbor; the second case was even harder to sell domestically, but it allowed the United States to not only save its interests and the stability of the international financial system of which it was custodian, but also to present itself as a responsible and reliable economic partner. US influence attempts on both instances, though, had the goal of preserving a functioning market economy, one that would more closely resemble its own, south of the border.

The last sub-period (2001–2016), with the broad guidelines of what domestic and foreign economic policy should be, and without any major (homemade) crisis in México (the 2008 one was a different story), the United States and México enjoyed a more stable economic relationship. With domestic politics intruding more prominently in the bilateral relationship, Washington foreign economic policy toward its southern neighbor was rather passive, eschewing its southern neighbor's interest in deepening the economic partnership. But with México being as economically dependent on its northern neighbor as it was at the beginning of the period (circa 1971) and with a much more market-oriented political economy, it was clear that its ascendancy over México City had hardly diminished during the period.

Notes

1   In this chapter I draw on Santa-Cruz 2012.
2   In *Comercio Exterior* 1970: 387.
3   Doyle 2003a: 47.
4   Whiting 1992: 98–99.
5   Ibid.: 97.
6   Ibid.: 98.
7   UN 2012.
8   Whiting 1992: 93; Urquidi 1987: 190.
9   Doyle 2003b.
10   Aguila et al 2012: 94; Lustig 2002: 173;Vega Cánovas 2003: 199.
11   Department of State 2004: 745.
12   OEC 2019.

13   In Castañeda and Pastor 1989: 470 and 471
14   Purcell 1981: 382; Story 1982: 775.
15   Aguayo 1998: 180; Cowan 1979.
16   Grayson 1979: 452.
17   Rico 2000: 165; Bennett 1989: 136.
18   Department of State 1977.
19   Central Intelligence Agency 1977b.
20   Vega Cánovas 2009: 53.
21   Tello 2007: 684; Bennett 1989: 126.
22   Central Intelligence Agency 1976a; Central Intelligence Agency 1976b; Central
      Intelligence Agency 1977a.
23   Purcell 1981: 382; Greene 1994: 125.
24   Story 1982: 775.
25   Ibid.: 775 and 780; Castañeda and Pastor 1989: 291.
26   Brzezinski 1980.
27   Story 1982: 776.
28   Krueger 1980: 75.
29   Barry 1995: 6.
30   Brzezinski 1979.
31   Bennett 1989: 135–137.
32   Lustig 2002: 64 and 65; Nafinsa 1990.
33   Lustig, 1997: 34.
34   Fagen 1977: 695.
35   In Marín 1982: 6.
36   Riding 1982a; Buendía 1982.
37   Gurría 1993: 29; Taylor 1985: 162.
38   Smith 2000: 62.
39   Riding 1982b; Astié-Burgos 2007: 262 and 263.
40   New York Times 1982.
41   Gurría 1993: 31.
42   Volcker in Lustig 1997: 41.
43   Bennet 1982.
44   Riding 1982b.
45   Bennet 1982
46   Gurría 1993: 53–56.
47   Bush 1987.
48   Marichal 2003: 475.
49   Santa-Cruz 2010
50   Tello 2007: 678 and 679; Werner et al. 2006: 87.
51   Meislin 1985.
52   Erb and Greenwald 1989: 176 and 177.
53   Greene 1994: 128; Rico 2000: 165; Lustig 2002: 179.
54   Reuters 1985.
55   Zabludovsky 2005: 60.
56   Romero 2003: 195; Bennett 1989: 139.
57   Werner et al. 2006: 90.
58   Rico 2000: 164.
59   Lustig 2002: 179.
60   Purcell 1997: 140.
61   Salinas de Gortari 2000: 9.
62   Heredia 1994: 20; Nevitte and Basáñez 1998: 158; González 2010: 241. Cf. Salinas de
      Gortari 2000: 65; Astié-Burgos 2007: 326.

63 Aguayo and Reyes Heroles 1991: 21.
64 *Proceso* 1991: 7.
65 Williamson 1990.
66 In Weintraub 1996: 135.
67 Buchanan 1993: C1.
68 Wiarda 1994: 117.
69 Destler 2005: 200.
70 Mills 1993: 1; Montaño 2004: 54.
71 Destler 2005: 198.
72 The Canadian Senate put NAFTA to vote on 23 June; 47 legislators approved and 30 rejected the treaty; Fagan 1993.
73 Blumenthal 1993.
74 Rosenbaum 1993a: A–1.
75 Rosenbaum 1993b: 22.
76 Puyana and Romero 2004: 403; Von Bertrab 1996: 113; Astié-Burgos 2007: 339.
77 Cox 2008: 1530.
78 DOTS: International Monetary Fund. Direction of Trade Statistics Online Database.
79 Secretaría de Economía 2019.
80 Ortiz Mena 2008: 158.
81 Vega Cánovas 2009: 84.
82 Los Pinos 2000.
83 Bentsen in D'Amato 1995: S9349.
84 Summers in D'Amato 1995: S9349.
85 GAO 1996: 84.
86 Ibid.: 87.
87 Ibid.: 13.
88 In Lustig 1997: 50.
89 GAO 1996: 90.
90 In D'Amato 1995: S9349; Weintraub 2000: 117.
91 GAO 1996: 95.
92 Gamez 1994.
93 Weintraub 2000: 104 and 105; GAO 1996: 71, 72 and 98.
94 De Palma 1994.
95 Ibid.; GAO 1996, 73.
96 Weintraub 2000: 107 and 110.
97 U.S. Senate 1995: 363.
98 Clinton 2004: 641 and 642.
99 Chandler and Robberson 1995.
100 Weintraub 2000: 117.
101 Sanger 1995.
102 Weintraub 2000: 139.
103 Beltrán del Río 1995a: 12.
104 In Ortega Pizarro 1995b: 9.
105 GAO 1996: 127 and 128; Beltrán del Río 1995a: 8; De Palma 1995.
106 Woods 1998: 153 and 154.
107 GAO 1996: 122.
108 *La Jornada* 1 February 1995.
109 *El Universal* 22 February 1995.
110 In U.S. Senate 1995: 358.
111 In Beltrán del Río 1995a: 14 and 15; *La Jornada* 1995.
112 In U.S. Senate 1995: 345.
113 Ibid.: 354.

114   Beltrán del Río 1995b: 8.
115   In U.S. Senate: 76 and 77.
116   GAO 1996: 126.
117   Lustig1997: 62.
118   Los Pinos, press release number 2295, 10 July 2000.
119   White House 2001.
120   Chávez and Marín 2007: 931.
121   https://www.census.gov/foreign-trade/balance/c2010.html
122   Ward 2008.
123   https://www.census.gov/foreign-trade/balance/c2010.html
124   Shear and Archibold 2013.
125   Medina 2012: 9; Edson 2010: 324.
126   Dibble 2014.
127   Alexander and Soukup 2010: 318; Carbaugh 2011: 3.
128   Frittelly 2010: 1.
129   In Alexander and Soukup 2010: 320.
130   Carbaugh 2011: 5.
131   Villarreal 2018: 25.
132   Medina 2012: 9; Frittelli 2010: 3; Villarreal 2018: 25; Carbaugh 2011: 5.
133   Carbaugh 2011: 6.
134   In Alexander and Soukup 2010: 324.
135   Ibid. 2010: 326.
136   In Ibid. 325.
137   Villarreal 2018: 26.
138   Ibid.; Cassidy 2017.
139   Johnecheck, Wilde and Caswell 2010: 504.
140   Ibid.: 505.
141   Rosenzweig 2012.
142   Wall Street Journal 2012.
143   In Strom and Malkinp 2012.
144   In Villarreal 2018: 28.
145   In Hotakainen 2012.
146   Strom 2013.
147   *Reforma* 2013; Villarreal 2018: 28.
148   Sources for GDP: World Bank 2019; BEA 2019. Source for trade: OEC 2019.

References

Aguayo, S., & Reyes Heroles, F. (1991). TLC Responde Serra. *Este País* (2), 15–30.

Aguayo Quezada, S. (1998). *Myths and [Mis]Perceptions: Changing U.S. elite visions of México*. San Diego, CA: University of California/COLMEX.

Aguila, E. (2012). *United States and México: Ties that bind, issues that divide*. Santa Monica, CA: RAND.

Alexander, K., & Soukup, B., (2010). Obama's first trade war: The US-Mexico cross-border trucking dispute and the implications of strategic cross-sector retaliation on U.S. compliance under NAFTA. *Berkeley Journal of International Law, 28*(2), 313–342.

Astié-Burgos, W. (2007). *Encuentros y desencuentros entre México y Estados Unidos en el siglo XX. Del porfiriato a la posguerra fría*. México: Miguel Ángel Porrúa

Barry, D. (1995). The road to NAFTA. In D. Barry, M. O. Dickerson & J. D. Gaisford (Eds.), *Toward a North American Community? Canada, the United States, and Mexico* (pp. 3–15). Boulder, CO: Westview Press.

BEA (2019). Gross Domestic Product [GDPA].

Beltrán del Río, P. (1995a). Washington impone su precio: Rígido control de la economía, y revisión, asuntos no financieros. *Proceso* (953), 7–15

Beltrán del Río, P. (1995b). A debate, en Washington, lo quedebe hacer el gobierno mexicano en materia de petróleo, política exterior, impuestas, migración y justicia. *Proceso* (952), 6–11.

Bennet, R. (1982, August 21). Bankers pressured to assist Mexico. *New York Times*.

Bennett, B. T. (1989). Las relaciones comerciales recientes de México y Estados Unidos: Resultados positivos y mayor cooperación. In R. Roett (Ed.), *México y Estados Unidos. El manejo de la relación* (pp. 125–150). México: Siglo XXI.

Blumenthal, S. (1993, November 29). The making of a machine. *New Yorker*, pp. 80–93.

Brzezinski, Z. (1979, January 18). *Memorandum from the White House (Brzezinski) for the special trade representative*. Washington, DC, (Carter Center Archives).

Brzezinski, Z. (1980). Memorandum for the president, from Zbigniew Brzezinski. Subject: Daily Report, 22 March (Carter Center Archives).

Buchanan, P. J. (1993, November 7). America first, NAFTA never. It's not about free trade, It's about our way of life. *Washington Post*, p. C1.

Buendía, M. (1982, August 11). Red Privada. *Excélcior*

Bush, G. H. W. (1987). Memorandum for the president from the vice president. "My Conversation with President De la Madrid of Mexico." Loreto, México, 27 December 1986, dated 15 June 1987, 3 (State Department Archives).

Carbaugh, R. (2011). NAFTA and the U.S.-Mexican trucking dispute. *Journal of International and Global Economic Studies*, 4(1), 1–10.

Cassidy, W. (2017, February 13). Mexican trucking past US border in crosshairs. *JOC*.

Castañeda G. J., & Pastor, R. (1989). *Límites en la amistad México y Estados Unidos*. México: Joaquín Mortiz/Planeta.

Central Intelligence Agency (1976a). Policy guidelines for the incoming administration of president-Elect Jose Lopez-Portillo. CIA-FOIA, 7 October (State Department Archives).

Central Intelligence Agency (1976b). Mexico under Jose Lopez-Portillo: Problems and prospects for US-Mexican relations. CIA, 16 December (State Department Archives).

Central Intelligence Agency (1977a). Summary of conversations between Carter and López Portillo. 14 February, 1 and 2 (Carter Center Archives).

Central Intelligence Agency (1977b). The forces for change in Mexican foreign policy. 2 June (State Department Archives).

Chandler, C., & Robberson, T. (1995, January 12). Clinton Pledges more financial help for México; Markets recover after offer to raise country's $9 billion credit line with treasury. *Washington Post*, p. A-19.

Chávez, F. J., & Marín, L. L. (2007). México y China: Competencia en el mercado de Estados Unidos. *Comercio Exterior*, 57(11), 931–944.

Clinton, B. (2004). *My Life*. New York: Alfred A. Knopf.

Comercio Exterior (1970). Desarrollo y resultados de la X junta Interparlamentaria México-Estados Unidos. *Comercio Exterior*, 20(5), 387–388.

Cowan, E. (1979, December 30). Importation of Mexican natural gas is given final approval by U.S. *New York Times*.

Cox, R. (2008). Transnational capital, the US State and Latin American trade agreements. *Third World Quarterly*, 29(8), 1527–1544.

D'Amato, A. (1995). *Mexico crisis report and chronology* (pp. S9349). Washington, DC: U.S. Senate.

De Palma, A. (1994, December 23). Crisis in Mexico: The overview; with Peso Freed, Mexican currency drops 20% more. *New York Times.*

De Palma, A. (1995, February 3). Mexican report details brush with insolvency. *New York Times.*

Department of State (1977). Department of State Briefing Paper. "U.S.-Mexico trade problems," 3 February (Carter Center Archives).

Department of State. (2004). *Relations of the United States, 1964–1968: South and Central America; Mexico* (Vol. XXXI). Washington, DC: U.S. Government Printing Office.

Destler, I. M. (2005). *American trade politics.* Washington, DC: Institute for International Economics.

Dibble, S. (2014, May 10). Nafta trucking vision unfulfilled. *San Diego Union Tribune.*

Doyle, K. (2003a). La operación intercepción: Los peligros del unilateralismo. *Proceso* (1380), 44–48.

Doyle, K. (2003b). *The Nixon tapes: Secret recordings from the Nixon White House on Luis Echeverría and much much more.* Transcript 27 (No. 735-1). National Security Archive: George Washington University.

Edson, A. (2010). Road block: The U.S.-Mexican trucking dispute. *Law and Business Review of the Americas, 16*(2), 323–332.

El Universal (1995, February 22). Al margen de condiciones políticas, los US20,000 millones. Dispondrá EU de los ingresos petroleros si México no cumple. *El Universal.*

Erb, G., & Greenwood, J. (1989). Aspectos del comercio bilateral entre México y Estados Unidos. In W. E. Glade & C. Luiselli (Eds.), *La economía de la interdependencia: México y Estados Unidos* (pp. 157–202). México: FCE.

Fagan, D. (1993, June 24). Report on Business Index, Summary Trade. *Globe and Mail*, p. B-1.

Fagen, R. (1977). The realities of U.S.-Mexican relations. *Foreign Affairs, 55*(4), 685–700.

Frittelli, J. (2010). *North American Free Trade Agreement (NAFTA) implementation: The future of commercial trucking across the Mexican Border* (Report No. RL31738). Washington, DC: Congressional Research Service.

Gamez, C. (1994, December 23). Caen las reservas al nivel de 1988. *Reforma.*

GAO. (1996). *Mexico's financial crisis: Origins, awareness, assistance, and initial efforts to recover.* Washington, DC: United States General Accounting Office.

González, G. (2010). Un siglo de política exterior Mexicana (1910–2010). Del nacionalismo revolucionario a la intemperie global. In M. A. Casar & G. González (Eds.), *México 2010, el juicio del siglo* (pp. 231–274). México: Taurus.

Grayson, G. (1979). Oil and U.S.-Mexican Relations. *Journal of Interamerican Studies and World Affairs, 21*(4), 427–456.

Greene, M. (1994). *The political economy of trade liberalization in Mexico: The de la Madrid Administration, 1982–1988.* (PhD thesis), London School of Economics and Political Science, London, United Kingdom.

Gurría, J. Á. (1993). *La política de la deuda externa.* México: FCE.

Heredia, C. (1994). NAFTA and democratization in Mexico. *Journal of International Affairs, 48*(1), 13–38.

Hotakainen, R. (2012, September 27). Risking trade war, administration sides with Florida tomato growers in dispute with Mexico. *McClatchy Newspapers.*

Johnecheck, W. A,. Wilde, P. E., & Caswell, J. A. (2010) Market and welfare impacts of COOL on the U.S.-Mexican tomato trade. *Journal of Agricultural and Resource Economics, 35*(3), 503–521.

Krueger, R. (1980). U.S.-Mexican relations. *Department of State Bulletin, 80*(2042), 74–77.

La Jornada (1995, February 1) Impondrá Washington medidas fuertes para garantizar el préstamo, advierte Christopher. *La Jornada.*

Los Pinos (2000, November 21). Press Release 2540.

Lustig, N. (1997). Mexico in crisis, the U.S. to the rescue: The financial assistance packages of 1982 and 1995. *UCLA Journal of International Law and Foreign Affairs*, Spring/Summer, 25–67.

Lustig, N. (2002). *México: Hacia la reconstrucción de una economía.* México: COLMEX/FCE.

Marichal, C. (2003). La deuda externa. In I. Bizberg & L. Meyer (Eds.), *Una historia contemporánea de México. Tomo I: Transformaciones y permanencias* (pp. 451–491). México: Océano.

Marín, C. (1982, August 23). Los convenios con el FMI son hipotecas de la soberanía contra los que JLP previno con frecuencia. *Proceso*, pp. 6–7.

Medina Ramírez, S. (2012). Apertura fronteriza al transporte de carga Mexicano: ¿fin del problema?. *Comercio Exterior, 62*(1), 9–11.

Meislin, R. (1985, July 24). Mexico, in reversal, to let I.B.M. build and own a computer plant. *New York Times.*

Mills, J. (1993, November 12). Business lobbying for trade pact appears to sway few in congress. *New York Times.*

Montaño, J. (2004). *Misión en Washington: 1993–1995: De la Aprobación del TLCAN al Préstamo de Rescate.* México: Editorial Planeta.

Nafinsa (1990). *La Economía Mexicana en Cifras* (Vol. 11). México: Nacional Financiera.

Nevitte, N., & Basáñez, M. (1998). Trinational perceptions. In R. Pastor & R. Fernández de Castro (Eds.), *The controversial pivot: The U.S. congress and North America* (pp. 147–179). Washington, DC: Brookings Institution Press.

New York Times (1982, August 25). In the shadow of the dollar; Bridging gaps in Mexico. *New York Times.*

OEC (2019). Visualizations: Export destinations. *The Observatory of Economic Complexity* (Accessed on May 13, 2019).

Ortega Pizarro, F. (1995, February 6). Agradecimientos a Clinton, encabezados por Zedillo y Televisa. *Proceso*, p. 9.

Ortiz Mena, A. (2008). El Tratado de Libre Comercio de América del Norte y la Política Exterior de México: Lo esperado y lo acontecido. In A. Covarrubias (Ed.), *Temas de Política Exterior* (pp. 125–159). México: COLMEX.

Proceso (1991, May 13). Memorándum del embajador Negroponte al Secretario de Estado. *Proceso*, (758), p. 7.

Purcell, S. (1997). The changing nature of US-Mexican relations. *Journal of Interamerican Studies and World Affairs, 39*(1), 137–152.

Purcell, S. K. (1981). Mexico-U.S. relations: Big initiatives can cause big problems. *Foreign Affairs, 60*(2), 379–392.

Puyana, A., & Romero, J. (2004). La estrategia comercial Mexicana ¿superando la fuerza centripeta estadounidense? *Foro Internacional, 44*(3), 392–429.

Reforma (2013, February 4). Reabre puertas EU a tomate nacional. *Reforma.*

Reuters (1985, November 26). Mexico and GATT. *New York Times.*

Rico, C. (2000). *México y el mundo: Historia de sus relaciones exteriores. Tomo 8: Hacia la globalización.* México: Senado de la República.

Riding, A. (1982a, August 14). U.S. and Mexico: Major rift emerges. *New York Times.*

Riding, A. (1982b, August 19). Mexico sets talks on its debt. *New York Times.*

Romero, J. (2003). Crecimiento y comercio. In I. Bizberg & L. Meyer (Eds.), *Una historia contemporánea de México. Tomo I: Transformaciones y permanencias* (pp. 155–221). México: Océano.

Rosenbaum, D. E. (1993a, November 18). House backs free trade pact in major victory for Clinton after a long hunt for votes. *New York Times*, p. A-1.

Rosenbaum, D. E. (1993b, November 21), Without earlier drama, trade accord is passed. *New York Times*, p. 22.

Rosenzweig, F. (2012, September 17). Versión estenográfica de la Conferencia de Prensa ofrecida a fin de detallar la situación de las exportaciones de tomate. Discurso: Sala de Prensa Secretaría de Economía.

Salinas de Gortari, C. (2000). *México. Un paso difícil a la modernidad*. México: Plaza and Janés.

Sanger, D. (1995, January 19). With opposition rising, Clinton pleads for Mexico rescue package. *New York Times*.

Santa-Cruz, A. (2010). *It depends upon what the meaning of the word 'Is' is: México-United States relations as a special relationship*. Paper prepared for the 2010 ISA conference, February 17–20, New Orleans.

Santa-Cruz, A. (2012). *Mexico-United States relations: The semantics of sovereignty*. New York: Routledge.

Secretaría de Economía (2019). Inversión Extranjera Directa en Mexico y en el Mundo: Carpeta de Información Estadística. DGIE, 29 de Mayo.

Shear, M. D., & Archibold, R. C. (2013, May 2). Obama arrives in Mexican capital to meet with new leader. *New York Times*.

Smith, C. E. (2000). *Inevitable partnership: Understanding Mexico-U.S. relations*. Boulder, CO: Lynne Rienner.

Story, D. (1982). Trade politics in the third world: A case study of the Mexican GATT decision. *International Organization, 36*(4), 767–794.

Strom, S. (2013, February 3). United States and Mexico reach tomato deal, averting a trade war. *New York Times*.

Strom, S., & Malkinp, E. (2012, September 27). Ammunition for a trade war between U.S. and Mexico. *The New York Times*.

Taylor, L. (1985). The crisis and thereafter: Macroeconomic policy problems in Mexico. In P. B. Musgrave (Ed.), *Mexico and the United States: Studies in economic interaction* (pp. 147–170). Boulder, CO: Westview Press.

Tello, C. (2007). *Estado y desarrollo económico: México 1920–2006*. México: UNAM

UN (2012). *Charter of economic rights and duties of states*. General Assembly Resolution 3281 (XXIX). United Nations Audiovisual Library of International Law.

Urquidi, V. L. (1987). ¿Sería viable un área de libre comercio en América del Norte? Notas acerca de la perspectiva Mexicana. In G. M. Bueno (Ed.), *México-Estados Unidos, 1986* (pp. 189–193). México: COLMEX.

U.S. Senate (1995). *The Mexican peso crisis*. Hearings before the Committee on Banking, Housing, and Urban Affairs, First Session on the Mexican Peso Crisis and the Administration's Proposed Loan Guarantee Package to Mexico, January 31, March 9, March 10, May 24, and July 14. Washington, DC: U.S. Government Printing Office.

Vega Cánovas, G. (2003). ¿Inversión contra soberanía? México y Canadá y el capítulo 11 del TLCAN. In B. Mabire (Ed.), *México-Estados Unidos-Canadá, 1999–2000* (pp. 197–242). México: COLMEX.

Vega Cánovas, G. (2009). De la protección a la apertura comercial. In I. Bizberg & L. Meyer (Eds.), *Una historia contemporánea de México. Tomo 4: Las políticas* (pp. 51–96). México: Océano COLMEX.

Villarreal, M. A. (2018). *U.S.-Mexico economic relations: Trends, issues, and implications* (Report No. RL 32934). Washington, DC: Congressional Research Service.

Von Bertrab, H. (1996). *El redescubrimiento de América. Historia del TLC.* México: FCE.

Wall Street Journal (2012, October 1). Rotten tomato fight: Obama again uses trade protection to help his re-election campaign. *Wall Street Journal*, p. A14.

Ward, A. (2008, March 3). Obama under fire over Nafta memo. *Financial Times.*

Weintraub, S. (1996). NAFTA and U.S. economic sovereignty. In J. Hoebing, S. Weintraub & M. D. Baer (Eds.), *NAFTA and sovereignty. Trade offs for Canada, Mexico, and the United States* (pp. 135–153). Washington, DC: The Center for Strategic & International Studies.

Weintraub, S. (2000). *Financial decision-making in Mexico. To bet a Nation.* London: Macmillan Press.

Werner, A., Barros, R., & Ursúa, J. (2006). Economía Mexicana: La transformación y desafíos. In L. Randall (Ed.), *Reinventar México: Estructuras en proceso de cambio* (pp. 81–104). México: Siglo XXI.

White House (2001). Remarks by president George Bush and president Vicente Fox of Mexico at Arrival ceremony. Retrieved from https://georgewbush-whitehouse.archives. gov/news/releases/2001/09/print/20010905-2.html

Whiting, V. R. (1992). *The political economy of foreign investment in Mexico: Nationalism, liberalism, and constraints on choice.* Baltimore, MD: The Johns Hopkins University Press.

Wiarda, H. J. (1994). The U.S. domestic politics of the U.S.-Mexico free trade agreement. In M. D. Baer & S. Weintraub (Eds.), *The NAFTA debate: Grappling with unconventional trade issues* (pp. 117–143). Boulder, CO: Lynne Rienner.

Williamson, J. (1990). What Washington means by policy reform. In J. Williamson (Ed.), *Latin American adjustment: How much has happened?* Washington, DC: Peterson Institute for International Economics.

Woods, N. (1998). International financial institutions and the Mexican crisis. In C. Wise (Ed.), *The Post-NAFTA political economy* (pp. 148–167). University Park, PA: Pennsylvania State University Press.

World Bank (2019). Gross domestic product [NY.GDP.MKTP.CD].

Zabludovsky, J. (2005). El TLCAN y la política de comercio exterior en México: Una agenda inconclusa. *ICE* (821), 59–70.

Chapter 7

United States' Economic Statecraft toward Central America

The countries of Central America have historically, that is, since the Latin American independence movements of the early 19th century, been considered as composing a larger unit. Indeed, between 1823 and 1839, Costa Rica, Guatemala, El Salvador, Honduras and Nicaragua constituted themselves as a state, the United Provinces of Central America (later called the Federal Republic in Central America). Notwithstanding the advent of the five distinct countries traditionally considered Central American (the above-mentioned, to the exclusion of two other countries which are also part of the isthmus: Belize, which gained independence from the United Kingdom only in 1981, and Panamá, which seceded from Colombia in 1903), and despite the obvious cultural, economic, political and social differences among them, they still regard themselves and are commonly treated as a region.[1] Thus, for instance, in 1908 these five republics established the Central American Court of Justice (which operated for ten years), in 1951 created the Organization of Central American States and, in the economic realm, instituted the Central American Common Market to pursue further integration in the early 1960s (Guatemala, El Salvador, Honduras, Nicaragua in 1960, and Costa Rica in 1962; Panamá joined in 2012).

Accordingly, the United States has viewed the Central American countries as an entity, as a system of client states that is in constant need of its patron's guidance.[2] For Washington, the isthmus has been part of its "third border"; as such, the region as a whole has been valuable for the United States mainly for strategic reasons.[3] The construction and control of the Panamá Canal in the early 20th century evinced the fusion of Washington's economic and geopolitical interests in the area (the 1977 signing of the treaties promising the return of the Canal to Panamá took place when its value, in both economic and military terms, had diminished considerably to the United States, and under an administration that had made a deliberate attempt to improve relations with Latin American countries).[4] By that time, the US companies had initiated their emblematic banana business in the region, but there was no question that purely economic interests were then, and have continued to be, of secondary importance to United States involvement in the area.

Central America's geopolitical value to the United States increased sharply with the advent of the Cold War. Thus, for instance, the overthrow of Jacobo Arbenz's nationalist government in Guatemala in 1954 had more to do with Washington's ideological war against the USSR in the context of the emerging domino theory, than with the Central American government's agrarian reform program that threatened the (US-based) United Fruit Company.[5] Once friendly governments in the region were in place, of which the Nicaraguan's one controlled by the Somoza dynasty became emblematic, the isthmus remained marginal to the global US foreign policy interests during the Cold War. In terms of foreign aid and investment, the area barely figured in the US radar.[6] Central America was indeed labeled a "low priority" area by the States Department in the late 1960s and early 1970s.[7]

Fearful that the region's backwardness could become a cauldron for political radicalism, the Nixon administration attempted to improve the lot of Central Americans by means of foreign assistance, but, in the president's words, with a "bankers' approach."[8] Nevertheless, the new methods hardly had an effect on the region's development. Fortunately, however, the 1971 Nixon Shock—particularly the 10% import surcharge—also had a scant impact on the region; its main exports, such as beef, coffee, fruit and sugar, were exempted from the punitive measure. On average, only 8.3% of the traditional 5 Central American countries' exports were affected by the surcharge, according to contemporary State Department estimates (in contrast, 50.2% of Mexican exports were affected).[9] Furthermore, the limited consequences of Nixon's protectionist measure was short-lived, as a later boom in commodity prices more than counteracted its effects.[10] Relative economic prosperity notwithstanding, some countries in the region did begin to undergo political upheaval in the late 1970s.

It was at this point that the isthmus occupied a central place in the US radar.[11] External shocks, such as the 1979 hike in the price of oil, the fall of other commodity prices, and increased interest rates, worsened—if to different extents—the fragile economic situation of the countries in the region, materializing the Nixon administration's fears at the beginning of the decade: political turmoil. The most important site of concern for Washington was of course Nicaragua, where, in July 1979, the Sandinistas put an end to the Somoza dynasty—but Central America being a system of "communicating vessels," as former Nicaraguan vice president Sergio Ramírez has described the region, political upheaval was bound to spread in the isthmus.[12] The Carter administration, true to its policies of (relative) non-intervention and promotion of human rights, tried to temporize with the Sandinista government, but the attempt did not work.[13] What followed was not only a sustained exercise of economic and political assault of the part of the Reagan administration on the Nicaraguan government, but also an increased level of intervention in the region as a whole. Thus, as the US ambassador to the United Nations, Jeane Kirkpatrick, noted in 1981, "Central America is the most important place in the world for the United States today."[14] Accordingly, politically oriented aid to the region increased dramatically during the 1980s—fourth-fold in real terms, compared to the previous decade.[15] Thus, for instance, US economic assistance to Costa Rica went from representing 0.3% of its GDP in 1980 to 2.0% in 1988; in El Salvador, the corresponding figures are 1.6% and 7.5%, whereas for Nicaragua they are 1.8% and 0.0% (zero point zero).[16] The increase and directionality of the economic support—from which Nicaragua was excluded—made sense, for as secretary of state Alexander Haig had pointed out, "in the formation of economic policy, in the allocation of our resources, in the discussions about international economic issues, a determinant factor will be the need to protect and promote our security."[17]

Regarding Nicaragua, upon taking office president Reagan made clear that he would resort to economic coercion to bring down the Sandinista regime. Thus, two days after his inauguration he reaffirmed the suspension of economic aid to the country, which had just been suspended by president Carter, when it had become clear that the Sandinistas were still sending arms to the Salvadorian rebels; later, despite evidence that the transfers had stopped, the Reagan administration permanently discontinued economic aid to Nicaragua. On the commercial front, also soon after his inauguration, Reagan made it harder for the Sandinista government to purchase US commodities, demanding cash instead of providing loans through the EXIM Bank, as had been customary. Furthermore, in 1983 the Republican administration reduced Nicaragua's portion of the US sugar quota by 90%—even though the sanction went against US GATT obligations. Nicaragua appealed, and a GATT panel ruled in its favor, but the Reagan administration ignored the multilateral trade body's decision.[18]

Escalating the extent of its economic duress against the Central American country, the Reagan administration embarked on a trade embargo. Despite its Justice Department's qualms—on the grounds that the sanctions went against the OAS and UN Charters—the government went ahead and, invoking the International Emergency Economic Powers Act, on 1 May 1985 Reagan declared a national emergency and prohibited all trade with Nicaragua. According to the US president, as stated in the Executive Order, "the policies and actions of the Government of Nicaragua constitute an unusual and extraordinary threat to the national security and foreign policy of the United States"; furthermore, as he noted in his message to Congress on the same matter, "The activities of Nicaragua, supported by the Soviet Union and its allies, are incompatible with normal commercial relations."[19] International condemnation of the US measure was widespread. European allies censured it, and México referred to it as "economic coercion."[20] Whereas at the Western Hemisphere, the OAS and the Caribbean Community (CARICOM) urged Washington to lift the embargo, at the global level the UN Security Council passed a resolution (11–1; 3 abstentions) denouncing it, as did the General Assembly (84–4; 37 abstentions). The embargo took a high toll on the Nicaraguan economy.[21]

Washington's policy of economic coercion was in addition to its more aggressive, if not blatant, attack on the Sandinista regime: economic warfare—something that, as discussed in Chapter 4, is usually considered to be beyond the economic statecraft pale. Thus, Washington supported (financially, and with training) a counter-revolutionary army, known as "Contras," which engaged in low-intensity warfare, primarily against farms and small villages. In addition, the Central Intelligence Agency turned to foreign agents to mine Nicaraguan ports.[22]

Meanwhile, as noted, the Reagan administration had also been using foreign economic policy, of the opposite sign from that directed at Nicaragua, in the rest of the region in general, but in one country in particular: El Salvador. From Washington's perspective, supporting one Salvadorian regime was critical to avoid a second leftist government in the isthmus, as the region's smallest country seemed to be the most likely country to follow the revolutionary path (the leftist Farabundo Martí National Liberation Front was established in 1980; in January 1981 it launched its first armed attack). Thus, the United States resorted not only to economic tools, but also to military assistance to support the right-wing government in San Salvador. Despite being the largest recipient of US funds in the region during the decade, US intervention did not solve the economic problems, and only worsened the political situation in El Salvador; per capita income in the country fell by about 15% in the 1980s, and 2% of its population died in the civil war that took place in those years.[23]

But Central America being a system of communicating vessels, the Reagan administration was aware from early on that its backward conditions had to be dealt with regionally. Therefore, it developed what, at least initially, appeared to be an ambitious attempt to alleviate the endemic development problems of the isthmus and its vicinity: the Caribbean Basin Initiative (CBI); this exercise in economic statecraft will be reviewed in the next section.

For several reasons, among which political strife, declining terms of trade, the breakdown of the Central American Common Market, and the debt crisis figure prominently, the 1980s were a disastrous decade for Central America: a "lost decade"—the region being, after all, part and parcel of Latin America, which endured the same fate.[24] A country of the isthmus, Costa Rica, was actually the first in the hemisphere to go into moratorium—in 1981, a year before México—and also one of the first ones to enter into the US treasury secretary Nicholas debt-reduction program (the Brady Plan, mentioned in Chapter 6).[25] It was precisely the hardships lived during these years that drove the Central American countries—with Washington's decisive instigation—to abandon the economic policies they had been following for decades and embrace, in the 1990s, the Washington Consensus.[26] With the Cold War behind and the defeat of the Sandinistas in the February 1990 elections by the US-backed Violeta Chamorro, the George H. W. Bush's administration could focus now on more conventional foreign economic policy matters on the region.[27] Thus, Washington deployed several market-based instruments and provided policy advise to encourage the transition to a more liberalized economic environment in the region. The opening of the Central American economies consolidated their dependence on the US market, which at the start of the decade (1990s) was already around 50%.[28] As the economic liberalization process was taking hold in the region, though, Washington decided to drastically reduce its aid to it; Central America was no longer a foreign policy priority, neither for the Bush or the Clinton administrations.[29] The Washington Consensus' years were ones of benign neglect of the region on the Northern Colossus' part; as the second section below will show, US economic statecraft toward the region was not very active during the 1990s.

At the dawn of the 21st century, Central America as a whole was in sync with Washington—and not only regarding economic doctrine. When the George W. Bush administration decided to invade Iraq in 2003, the isthmus contributed five of the seven Latin American states (33 in total) that supported it.[30] It would seem that by this time, the countries of the region were granting the United States the "gratitude" a State Department official argued in 1926 his country deserved from playing the role of "teacher," "doctor" and "policeman" in the area.[31] Central American backing in Bush Jr.'s military adventure, though, might not have been mere principled. Around that time the region was negotiating the Central America Free Trade Agreement (CAFTA) with the United States, a matter I will review in the third section of this chapter.

1) 1971–1989

Around the time of the Nixon Shock, US foreign economic policy tailored toward Latin America in general, and toward Central America in particular, was becoming a thing of the past. Washington's signature post-war program, the *Alliance for Progress*, irrespective of its virtues and defects, was no longer effective. It wasn't only the relatively large aid component—regardless of whether it was altruistic or interested—of the regional plan that was being phased out, the same went for any consideration of a distinctive economic statecraft toward the region.[32] By the second half of the 1970s, hemispheric economic policy, *tout court*, was out. As Assistant Secretary for International Affairs at the Department of the Treasury C. Fred Bergsten put it in 1978, "the U.S. does not have anything that you can call specifically a Latin American economic policy";[33] similarly, four years later, secretary of state George Shultz noted at the Organization of American States: "We are all members of the world economy and not dependent on the inter American system for the management of our economies in the same way we are for the preservation of peace."[34] Latin America, for its part, was also increasingly interested in dealing with economic matters on a global scale, as the 1970s proposals for the New International Economic Order and the 1981 International Meeting on Cooperation Development (North-South Summit) evinced.

It was in this context that a rather unexpected turn of events took place. In an about-face, the Reagan administration decided to launch a major initiative granting preferential trade treatment to Central American countries.

In light of the political instability striking the region—in addition to its backing of the Contra war against Nicaragua, Guatemala and, as noted, El Salvador were engaged in their own civil wars—and due to the increasing isolation Washington was being subjected to by other countries due to its support to right-wing dictatorships, in May 1981, the State Department reached out to Canada, México and Venezuela to try to partner with them in the establishment of a major aid plan for the isthmus. Ottawa, México City and Caracas, however, did not agree with Washington's take on the origins and solutions to the region's problems, and declined to participate.[35]

Thus, on 24 February 1982, in a speech at the Organization of American States, president Reagan announced his administration's Caribbean Basin Initiative (CBI). In his address, the president recognized that "at times we have behaved arrogantly and impatiently toward our neighbors," and that on occasions, "No matter how good our intentions were, our very size may have made it seem that we were exercising a kind of paternalism."[36] Echoing Nixon's thoughts on the relationship between material welfare and political stability, Reagan remarked that the "economic disaster [in the region] has provided a fresh opening to the enemies of freedom, national independence, and peaceful development;"[37] hence the importance of the US pledge to the countries of the Caribbean and Central America to help them "make use of the magic of the marketplace, the market of the Americas, to earn their own way toward self-sustaining growth."[38] More specifically, the "centerpiece" of the new program was one-way free trade for the selected countries.[39] In promoting the "magic of the marketplace" president Reagan was making clear that, for him, there was no distinction between domestic and foreign economic tenets; as he would tell his Council of Economic Advisors,

> the Administration's approach to international economic issues is based on the same principles which underlie its domestic programs: a belief in the superiority of market solutions to economic problems and an emphasis on private economic activity as the engine of non-inflationary growth.[40]

But just as his Secretary of State's intimation that there was no such thing as an inter-American economic system had made clear, president Reagan was well aware that the political stability of the isthmus was of paramount importance for his country; as he put it: "Make no mistake: The well being and security of our neighbors in this region are in our own vital interest."[41]

Washington's conception of the region, however, was a peculiar one. For "Caribbean Basin" was not an established cultural, economic or geographic concept. It was rather reminiscent of the State Department's suggestion, during the Roosevelt administration, to treat Iceland as part of the Western Hemisphere; the New Deal's president disapproved of the idea on the grounds that "the strain on the public idea of geography would be too severe."[42] Even if geography, as Tom Farer has noted, "is a perception, not a fact,"[43] there are limits to what is socially acceptable. Back to the 1980s, the newly defined term, Caribbean Basin, barely made it into "the public idea of geography" for, although in topographic terms the countries included bordered the Caribbean sea, it excluded Colombia and Venezuela, it comprised El Salvador—with coasts only on the Atlantic—and, for political reasons, it excluded Nicaragua.[44]

The CBI was also uncharacteristic in that, as noted in the intro, it broke with a long tradition in Washington's economic statecraft: the inclination for global trade policies. As Robert Pastor noted, the measure represented

> a sharp break in U.S. foreign economic policy—comparable in principle, if not in impact, to the shift in 1934 in the Reciprocal Trade Agreements Act, which tied the United States to the principle of reciprocity, most favored nation (MFN) treatment and declining tariffs, and to the movement in 1947 to multilateralism and the General Agreement on Tariffs and Trade (GATT).[45]

However tortuous the contours of the geographic area covered by the initiative might have been, it indeed was, as deputy secretary of state Kenneth Dam put it: "the first time that the United States has granted preferential economic treatment to an entire geographic region."[46] Certainly there must have been something the Reagan administration considered important enough to warrant creating a mostly idiosyncratic region while breaking with the country's well-established precedent in the management of the post-war international economic order.

That something was geopolitics. Not that geopolitics had been alien in previous US economic statecraft—as we have seen, it hadn't. But the open politicization of trade policy in particular, as opposed to foreign economic policy in general, or some other aspects of it, such as aid, was a bold and risky venture.[47] Reagan himself noted in his OAS speech that "Never before has the United States offered a preferential trading arrangement to any region."[48] In any case, the geopolitical threat the Reagan administration located in the initiative's target area was the incursion of what he would later refer to as the "evil empire": the Soviet Union. By the early 1980s, the USSR was indeed supporting the Sandinista regime, which in turn was supporting the FMLN guerrilla in El Salvador, but the claim that such backing represented a security threat to Washington required some ideological and missionary zeal. Republican Senator Robert Dole compared the initiative to the 1823 Monroe Doctrine, in that both shared the idea that "the new lands of this hemisphere must remain free from outside intervention in order to pursue their own destinies in peace," although he pointed out that "the nature of the threats, enemies, and solutions have changed markedly in 160 years;"[49] according to the lawmaker, the CBI, was about showing "purely and simply, that we are concerned about the countries to our south."[50]

As mentioned, in his speech announcing the program before the hemispheric organization, president Reagan stated that unilateral free trade was the "centerpiece" of CBI. More specifically, the idea was to grant duty-free entrance to the United States to the products of the (new) region, except textile and apparel, for a 12-year period. But there were five other components to the initiative. The second one was the provision of tax incentives for investment in the beneficiary countries; the third element was $350 million in economic assistance, the fourth was technical assistance and training to the private sector in matters such as export promotion, and the fifth was partnering with other countries, such as Canada and Venezuela—although, as noted, they had already declined the offer—to coordinate their efforts, and the sixth one some sort of special assistance to Puerto Rico and the Virgin Islands.

The initiative was welcomed by the impoverished countries who stood to benefit from the it, particularly by the Central American ones.[51] Interestingly, though, the reason for optimism seemed to lay more on the aid promised—a traditional element of US foreign economic policy—than in the one-way free trade, as 87% of the region's products exported to the United States already entered duty free under the System of Generalized Preferences—a fact recognized by president Reagan himself in his OAS address. But compared to the previous major US initiative in the Western Hemisphere, the *Alliance for Progress*, the CBI did not fare well—it was found lacking both in transformative vision and financial resources.[52] The new initiative's philosophy—and eventual instantiation—seemed to have more to do with a coaching course than with a development strategy; in the words of Peter McPherson, USAID Administrator, "What we have tried to create is a program that is based more on the development of an indigenous private sector ... so they can develop the institutional means for preserving political pluralism."[53] For Senator Dole, CBI had "little to do with creating new industries in the Caribbean or withholding or anything else";[54] it was about, as noted, showing that the U.S. cared about its neighbors.

The bill passed by Congress in August 1983, the Caribbean Basin Economic Recovery Act, which officially gave birth to the Caribbean Basin Initiative, was indeed disappointing. For starters, the so-called "centerpiece" of the initiative—one-way free trade—was limited, in the sense that the tariffs and non-tariff barriers that were susceptible to be removed (again, 87% of the region's exports already entered the United States duty free), were not. Furthermore, Washington ended up establishing import quotas on sugar.[55] The fiscal incentive to invest in the Caribbean basin failed to pass Congress, and instead a bizarre inducement was created: deductions for holding business conventions in the area.[56] CBI's aid component fared better, with Congress appropriating $350 million for emergency assistance in September 1982, and additional aid resources in the next months.[57] Not surprisingly, El Salvador was the main beneficiary of what, by historical standards, was a generous aid program to the countries of the Caribbean and Central America; the president's request to

Congress for the non-Caribbean country was $128 million—out of the $350 million noted—but the legislators reduced it to $75 million—keeping San Salvador still the largest recipient.[58]

Just weeks before the legislation enabling the CBI was passed, probably aware that it would turn out to be insufficient to achieve its stated objectives, and also trying to put some distance with the Central American imbroglio given the following year's electoral process, president Reagan created a National Bipartisan Commission on Central America, tasking former Secretary of State and National Security Advisor Henry Kissinger to chair it.[59] The Kissinger Commission, as the group came to be known, delivered its report in January 1984. It suggested a substantial increase in aid to the region—both economic and military—as well as expanding trading advantages. While it acknowledged that "just as Nicaragua was ripe for revolution, so the conditions that invite revolution are present elsewhere in the region as well," it also noted that "indigenous revolution" is not necessarily a security threat to the United States. Significantly, the Commission recommended that Washington engage on "a comprehensive regional settlement," building on the proposals already advanced by the Contadora group (formed in 1983 by Colombia, México, Panamá and Venezuela to counteract Washington's interventionist policies and bring peace to Central America), as well as continuous consultation with it.[60] As time went by and Reagan was re-elected in November 1984, the Kissinger's Commission's recommendations fell on deaf ears.[61]

Not surprisingly, CBI's results, like the bill passed by Congress, were rather disappointing. Its "centerpiece," one-way free trade, was in practice pushed to the margins, as the expected increase in exports from the region failed to materialize; instead, the more traditional and conspicuously politically biased aid element came to occupy the initiative's center stage.[62] After a widespread critical evaluation and complaints at home and abroad, CBI was amended in 1986, with the introduction of the Caribbean Basin Special Access Program for Apparel, which granted more favorable treatment to such category of products as well as to textiles.[63] CBI began a process of further expansion three years later. Congress again severely curtailed the benefits for the target countries requested by the administration—this time the recently inaugurated one of George H. W. Bush—thus, for instance, the 50% tariff reduction for products such as leather footwear and canned tuna fish, as well as the tariff elimination for some textile products, were rejected. On the other hand, lawmakers agreed to make the benefits granted to the Caribbean and Central American countries permanent. CBI II, as the slightly improved program came to be known, was finally passed in August 1990.[64] By this time, the situation in the region, or at least in the region that was the catalyst for CBI's emergence, Central America, was a very different one from that of 1982. Thus, for instance, Nicaragua, with the Sandinista regime gone, was now a beneficiary—although civil war continued in Guatemala and El Salvador (peace accords were signed in December 1996 for the first case, and in January 1992 for the second).

In what certainly was a self-serving overstatement arguing for the administration's proposal, Republican Senator Graham referred to the countries in the region as a "bloom in democracy," which needed US "economic assistance" and "encouragement." With the worst of the crisis over, economic assistance and encouragement, as we will see in the next section, would be in short supply during the 1990s.[65]

2) 1990–2000

As the 1990s began, with the Cold War practically over, and with definitively no "Soviet threat" in Central America, the United States soon lost interest in the region. If during the 1980s Washington disbursed about $9 billion to "contain communism"—a lot of it in non-productive activities, admittedly—spending levels in the following decade fell sharply.[66] Thus, for instance, economic assistance to Costa Rica went from $95.5 million in 1990, to $2.1 million in 2000, to El Salvador from $246.9 million to $44.4 million in the same years (as noted, civil war was still raging in the country), and to Nicaragua from $224.4 million to $33.9 million, also in 1990 and 2000 (all figures in current dollars).[67] The "unipolar moment" made Washington unmindful of his "third border."

The Central American countries, for their part, perceived the starting of negotiations between México and its two northern neighbors in 1990 as a threat, since their preferential access to the US market would vanish; accordingly, they lobbied Washington to also start trade talks with them.[68] In what appeared to be a sincere effort to accommodate the Central American leaders' requests, at the 1994 Miami Summit, president Clinton pledged to grant their countries the same commercial privileges as those México enjoyed with the trade pact, but his administration did not follow through.[69] According to a top Costa Rican trade negotiator, "for more than seven years the region put forward their intentions to negotiate an agreement, but an agreement was not a priority for Bill Clinton's administration."[70]

Despite Washington's indifference, Central America was able to recover some of the lost ground of the "lost decade," growing at an average annual rate of 4.3% during the 1990s.[71] The improved performance had to do, most of all, with the pacification of the region; but it was also related to the economic reforms that had been undertaken during the previous decade, as well as to the increase in exports to the United States.[72] The Washington Consensus had also permeated the isthmus, and not only at the level of the technocratic elites or politicians; market-friendly policies were popular among voters of the region during the 1990s.[73]

But it would not be until late in the decade, toward the end of the second Clinton administration, that Washington took some effective action regarding its economic statecraft toward Central America. In May 2000, the Caribbean Basin Trade Partnership Act (CBTPA), which extended trade benefits to textiles and matched some of the benefits México had obtained through NAFTA, was approved by Congress; such benefits were to last until 2008, until the (eventually failed) Free Trade Area of the Americas (FTAA) became effective, or until a free trade agreement was enacted between the beneficiaries and the United States.[74] This modest, incremental program (CBTPA), was the most remarkable economic initiative toward the region pursued by the United States during the decade.

3) 2001–2016

Just as the debate of the decline of US hegemonic power at the global level resurfaced again, the Clinton administrations' benign neglect of Central America was to some extent mended by its successor. Not that Washington had suddenly recovered interest in the region. The reason was rather that under George W. Bush's economic statecraft, the already-mentioned (in Chapter 4) policy of "competitive liberalization" gained prominence—and a free trade agreement with the isthmus fitted nicely with this strategy. Thus, although the Central American leaders had proposed to president Clinton negotiating a trade agreement since May 1997,[75] it was not until the idea was floated again in April 2001 that Washington obliged.[76]

As suggested, the change in Washington's foreign economic policy toward the region was not only a matter of goodwill. China was about to join the World Trade Organization (WTO; it did in December 2001), and US trade deficit in goods with the emerging Asian power was already on the rise.[77] Free Trade with the isthmus was functional in US Trade Representative Robert Zoellick's pragmatic approach of competitive, or gradual, liberalization—particularly at a time when the 11-year-old idea of a Free Trade Area of the Americas (it was included in president Bush's 1990 Enterprise of the Americas, and re-launched at Clinton's 1994 Summit of the Americas) was not gaining traction in the hemisphere. Accordingly, a USTR's office report noted that "Agreement between the U.S. and Central America on free trade would promote a greater convergence of positions at the FTAA negotiating table."[78] Geopolitics was also a factor in the proposed agreement. The already-noted (in Chapter 1) rise of the left in Latin America meant that the isthmus might become again an arena of ideological confrontation. Representative Dan Burton, Chairman of the Subcommittee on the Western Hemisphere, stated his pro-trade position toward the region by warning against Hugo Chavez' Venezuela making inroads in the area: "We are concerned about tyrants taking power ... This is our back-yard ... Central America is our backyard."[79]

But not all was Machiavellian calculation. Washington was also convinced that the liberalizing, pro-market foreign economic policy it had been promoting since the CBI was delivering positive results in Central America.[80] In a sardonic twist, US Trade Representative Robert Zoellick went on to accuse US critics of the agreement of ... imperialism! As he put it: "You'll pardon me if I have a little bit of an ironic smile when primarily people from the United

States decide to tell democracies in Central America what's good for them. We used to call that imperialism."[81]

Central American leaders, for their part, also had important inducements for attempting to secure a trade deal with its main export market—one which, moreover, the region was increasingly dependent on. Among the incentives the leaders faced were the emergence of China as an export powerhouse (particularly in the textile sector, and especially to the US market), the 2005 end of the Agreement on Textiles and Clothing, and the 2008 finalization of some trade concessions gained under the CBTPA. The region's leaders thus not only wanted a trade agreement—they also wanted it fast. But the popularity of free trade was not limited to the states' top echelons—it largely permeated the region's population (although, of course, there were also important sectors who opposed it).[82] Take the case of Nicaragua, where, for whatever reason (US economic coercion, the Sandinistas' blunders in the management of the economy, or both), pro-market governments where consistently elected for over three lustrums, starting in 1990; a similar case could be made for El Salvador.[83] This favorable attitude toward what came to be known as neoliberalism seemed to be associated with a positive vision of the United States among the isthmus' population. At the dawn of the 21st century, Central America was indeed the region in the hemisphere with the most favorable view of the Colossus of the North: above 70%, according to the most respected polling firm in Latin America, *Latinobarómetro*.[84]

The opening of negotiations leading to the Central America Free Trade Agreement (CAFTA, which would become CAFTA-DR, after the Dominican Republic joined) was officially announced in 2002, soon after Trade Promotion Authority—mentioned in Chapter 4—was granted to the Bush administration by Congress. The political standing of the proposed deal in the United States was quite different from the one it had in the isthmus. While most US citizens did not care about it, it faced strong opposition in a few very localized areas; among the economic sectors that resisted the trade pact were sugar, as well as textile and apparel.[85] The nature of the industries opposed to the new agreement (rudimentary, labor-intensive) pointed to the trivial impact it would have on the overall economy of the United States, dominated by technologically sophisticated and knowledge-intensive industries. But there was also a non (economic) interest-based opposition to CAFTA in the United States, which came mainly from human rights, labor and environmental groups—although, of necessity, they were not completely alien to the unions that opposed the agreement for pecuniary reasons. The Bush administration and the Republican-dominated Congress had to deal with this wider group of forces by making the case for both free trade and solidarity with Central America, while granting it some concessions.[86]

The compromises the Bush administration had to make to appease its domestic opposition came, more often than not, at the expense of the Central American parties (as well as of the Dominican Republic). But this does not mean that otherwise Washington took a soft position at the (international) negotiating table. As suggested, CAFTA-DR was intended to be a stepping stone in the process of competitive liberalization; but the idea was that it should also be a model for upcoming agreements, so there was need to set a high bar for future trading partners. This dual logic was dutifully applied by US negotiators in CAFTA. Thus, for instance, instead of using CBTPA as a baseline, as the Central Americans had assumed (apparently wrongly for, as noted before, when CBTPA was passed it was established that its terms would last until 2008, until the FTAA was enacted— hypothetically in 2005—or, as was expected to be the case, until a free trade agreement the beneficiaries and the United States came into effect), they disregarded it and started from a conventional tariff scenario; Reaganite, one-way free trade seemed to be a thing of the past.

Furthermore, the US team suggested building on the recently concluded (December 2002) U.S.–Chile Free Trade Agreement, which in turn was based on NAFTA. The agenda thus included extra-commercial items, such as intellectual property rights, investment protection, domestic business regulation and services.[87] As suggested, at the request of domestic opponents, negotiators also brought environmental and labor issues to the table. US trade negotiators also used CAFTA-DR to surpass the global trade regime's regulations—what came to be known as WTO-Plus.[88] Thus, for instance, under CAFTA-DR intellectual property in general, and the pharmaceutical industry in particular, received protection that went beyond what was established by the WTO.[89] As noted, the extra demands imposed on Central America and Dominican Republic were part and parcel of the "competitive liberalization" strategy; it remained to be seen if other countries and other fora would adapt to the US preferences the way these small countries did—in the meantime, though, Washington had used them as guinea pigs.

Not that Central America (and the Dominican Republic) did not resist, or that it did not get some concessions from their counterpart; they were also not forced by Washington into the agreement—after all, it was the region that requested the deal. During the negotiating process they were thus far from being passive agents. But the fact remains that the United States resorted to myriad kinds of pressure to get what it wanted from its potential partners—and not only on economic matters. Hence, for instance, the Bush administration twisted arms in Central America to join or at least sanction its "coalition of the willing" in the war against Iraq; all the isthmus countries but Guatemala, as well as the Dominican Republic, supported, in one way or another, the US-led coalition (Costa Rica requested Washington to remove it from a list of supporters it had produced after its Constitutional Court found that its inclusion went against the country's pacifist precepts).[90]

The United Sates, for its part, also made some concessions to its would-be partners. Thus, for example, Washington granted longer phase-out periods (of up to 20 years) to these countries than it had done to México or Chile (15- and 12-year periods, respectively); it also gave them special treatment on apparel (although the concessions were not the same for all countries). Additionally, Washington agreed to reinstate CBTPA-level access for the region's products.[91] Telling of the disparity between the parties involved, Washington provided financing and, indirectly, training to the Central American negotiating teams.[92] The agreement was negotiated speedily, in nine rounds that took place during 2003 [Costa Rica withdrew from the negotiations toward their end, but came back and finalized the agreement a few months later], and signed the following year.

In keeping with the "competitive liberalization" approach, CAFTA-DR became important for the Bush administration as it wanted to show the world, in the words of the US Trade Representative Zoellick, "our position as the global leader on trade."[93] But the debate over the deal became a major political issue when it came up for a vote in Congress; like NAFTA in the days preceding its November 1993 vote, it seemed CAFTA-DR was doomed to fail. Finally, thanks to a last-minute shift from a North Carolina Republican representative whose district had lost jobs in the textile industry, the deal was approved in July 2005 in the House; the final tally was 217 to 215 [it had already passed the Senate in late June by a wider margin: 54–45].[94] The agreement was enacted between 2006 and 2009 in its seven contracting parties [Costa Rica was the last one to ratify it, by means of a national referendum, in October 2007].[95] The region's exports to the United States grew considerably as a result of CAFTA-DR; they went from $19,452 in 2006 to $24,465 in 2016 [in millions of current dollars], an increase of 26% (the country that benefited the most during this period was Nicaragua, whose exports to the United States more than doubled).[96]

Also in 2007 the United States and Panamá signed their own free trade agreement, which had been in the making during the previous two and a half years; the canal country had preferred to negotiate separately from the countries involved in the CAFTA-DR process in order to underscore its special relationship with Washington.[97] Like CAFTA-DR, the United States-Panamá Free Trade Agreement is also "WTO-Plus."[98] Panamanian exports to the United States went from 718,958 in 2006, to 2,307,907 in 2016 [in thousands of current dollars], an increase of 321%.[99] It seemed that Washington was able to lock in free trade in the region. Interestingly, though, concurrently some countries of the region were hedging their bets, as they also got closer to an alternative scheme of economic (and political) integration: the Bolivarian Alliance for the Peoples of Our America (ALBA). As noted in Chapter 2, Fidel Castro and Hugo Chávez had signed the ALBA's constitutive agreement in December 2004—a month after negotiations leading to the Free Trade Area of the Americas had collapsed in Mar del Plata. Already in 2001, in the framework of the third Summit of Heads of State of the Caribbean Community, Chávez had made clear his intention to launch an alternative to both the Washington Consensus and the hemispheric trade agreement.[100] Nicaragua joined in the competing organization in 2007, and Honduras in 2008 (the following year Venezuela suspended oil shipments to Honduras, in response the coup d'etat against president José Manuel Zelaya; this effectively initiated the process to expel Tegucigalpa from ALBA; the Honduran parliament denounced the agreement in January 2010). In any case, Central American economic integration within ALBA did not flourish: by 2016, only Nicaragua belonged to the mechanism.

But the region's increasing commercial relationship with the United States did not translate into substantially better economic conditions for most people (only Costa Rica and Panamá were able to move to the "medium" category of the Human Development Index in the late 1990s).[101] To make matters worse, violence deteriorated in the isthmus; thus, the Bush administration included the region in its 2007 Mérida Initiative (mentioned in the previous chapter); the Obama Administration renamed that share of the program as Central America Regional Security Initiative. With yet another aid-focalized program sub-performing, in 2014 Washington launched a more comprehensive approach: the US Strategy for Engagement in Central America, focused on El Salvador, Guatemala and Honduras; the guiding principle of such a program was that economic, political and security matters are "mutually reinforcing and of equal importance."[102] As with previous aid programs, conditionality was part of the Strategy.[103] Thus, well into the second decade of the 21st century, the United States kept playing the role of patron for most of the countries of the region.

Conclusions

The previous pages show that, unlike the cases of Washington's economic statecraft toward Canada and México (where the former was seen as a junior partner and the latter as a subordinate whose strategic position warranted some sort of special consideration), in the one concerning the countries of the Central American region, the United States perceived them as children in need of guidance. During the whole period under study (1971–2016), both the material capabilities of the Central American countries, as measured by their joint GDP vs. the Colossus of the North (0.50% in the former year; 0.99% in the latter), as well as the region's trade dependency on the US market (for their export products) grew considerably (32% in 1971; 45% in 2016).[104] However, it is not this change that drove the dynamics of US statecraft toward the region (they are both minuscule from Washington's perspective, and in any case they moved in opposite directions, from the Isthmus' perspective, i.e., a stronger economy (potentially less dependent on the United States), but at the same time an export sector more reliant on the US market. Thus, one more time, brute facts are not a useful indicator of Washington's economic statecraft toward the region. The changes on the matter that actually took place had more to do with US' wider economic, political and security concerns.

Thus, during the first sub-period (1971–1989) Washington's change in the way it provided foreign aid to the region (Nixon's "banker's approach") did not work as expected and, by the early 1980s, the United States came up with an unprecedented trade policy measure intended to make the "magic of the market" work in the isthmus (and the Caribbean): one-way free trade. Now, Washington's motivation for the trade initiative was not only, or perhaps even mainly, economic: at stake was also the political stability of the region. Showing resolve in matters pertaining to its "second frontier" was clearly also a factor in Washington's decision to put together the special trade program, the Caribbean Basin Initiative (CBI). Thus, the US influence attempt was a composite one, including demonstrating that the Monroe Doctrine was still in effect, strengthening friendly regimes (e.g., El Salvador), and castigating hostile ones, particularly Nicaragua. The target was not the newly minted Caribbean Basin that gave name to the program, but rather the few states in which the initiative's benefit focused. Given the huge disparity between the economies of the beneficiary countries as a whole compared to that of the United States, the economic cost in which the latter incurred were minimal.

Similarly, the foreign economic policy of the opposite sign displayed by Washington toward Nicaragua required a modicum economic cost—although Washington had to pay dearly in reputational terms in the hemisphere and beyond (Caracas', Ottawa's, and México City's refusal to participate in the U.S.' CBI attest to these political costs). With its extremely coercive economic statecraft toward Managua, an approach that at times included economic warfare, the United States was attempting to remove the Sandinista regime. Although Washington's economic bullying did not work at first, it could be argued that it eventually did, when the candidate it supported in the 1990 electoral process emerged victorious.

Despite Central American's adhesion to the Washington Consensus, as noted, during the second sub-period (1990–2000) the region was mostly relegated by the United States. There was not more urgent political motivation to support the region—no need to show resolve or guard against security threats there during the unipolar moment. Thus, it was not until late in the period that Washington bothered to bring the Central American countries into the free trade fold through an agreement—even though, as seen before, they had been requesting it. Thus, both US influence attempts as well as the capital it was willing to spend on them during the 1990s were minimal.

The situation changed slightly during the last sub-period (2001–2016). Looking at the isthmus through the prisms of its wider trade policy of "competitive liberalization," Washington decided to oblige the countries of the region by following up on the free trade deal promise, while using the negotiating process as a stepping stone in its broader take on furthering free trade (regardless of whether or not the strategy pursued was the correct one or not). Thus, by negotiating CAFTA-DR the United States was not only trying to influence the political economy (both domestic and foreign) of the countries of the region, but also that of other countries, particularly the hemispheric ones, as they were part of the FTAA going during the first phase the CAFTA-DR negotiations. But as the political and security situation of the isthmus continued deteriorating, and the pink wave reached the area, Washington had to come again to the rescue of selected Central American countries, recognizing, as noted above, that economic, political and security affairs go hand in hand. The United States continued perceiving the region as one in need of guidance.

Notes

1 Granados 1986: 75, 80; Spalding 2014: 246.
2 Coatsworth 1994: 4–8; Cottam 1994: 23; Van Tassell 1997: 240–241.
3 Zorn and Mayerson 1983: 544.
4 Ford 1976: 387; LaFeber 1989: 219–220; Lowenthal 1983: 312.
5 Bulmer-Thomas 1988: 210.
6 Cruz 1995; Granados 1986: 93.
7 In Morley 1994: 65.
8 Brands 2008: 247.
9 CEPAL 1971: 8
10 Brands 2008: 253; Bulmer-Thomas 2003: 335.
11 Hakim 2011: 67.
12 Ramírez 1999: 274.
13 Coatsworth 1994: 157; Leogrande 1996: 330; Lafeber 1984: 7.
14 In Levin 1981: 34.
15 Hakim 1991: 4.
16 Spalding 2014: 36.
17 U.S. House of Representatives 1981.
18 Leogrande 1996.
19 Reagan 1985: 809–810.
20 In Leogrande 1996: 339.
21 Ibid.; GATT 1986.
22 Ramnarine 1993: 15; Leogrande 1996: 340.
23 Hakim 1991: 4; Spalding 2014: 43.
24 Cardemill et al. 2000: 34; Spalding 2014: 34–35; Hakim 1991: 4.
25 Sullivan 1993: XVIII.
26 Williamson 1988; Cardemill et al. 2000: 34; Cruz 2015: 45.
27 Spalding 2014: 56.
28 Lederman et al. 2002: 3; Weintraub 1991: 11.
29 Cruz 1995; Hakim 1991:6; Leogrande 1990: 621.
30 Lowenthal and Mostajo 2010: 573.
31 In Lafeber 1984: 25.
32 Weintraub 1997: 66.
33 U.S. Senate 1978: 121.
34 Shultz 1982: 30140.
35 Riding 1982: 641–643; Pastor 1982: 1043–1044.
36 Reagan 1982: npn.
37 Ibid.: npn.
38 Ibid.: npn.
39 Ibid.: npn.
40 In Bitar 1984: 28.
41 Reagan 1982: npn.
42 In Whitaker 1954: 160.
43 Farer 1993: 339.
44 Van Tassell 1997: 256.

45   Pastor 1982: 1044–1045.
46   In Polanyi-Levitt 1985: 236.
47   Feinberg and Newfarmer 1982: 133–134.
48   Reagan 1982: npn.
49   In Ramnerine 1993: 28.
50   In Potoker and Borgman 2007: 86.
51   Whittingham 1989: 88; Polanyi-Levitt 1985: 233–234.
52   Weintraub 1982: 128.
53   In Sanford 1983: 2.
54   Potoker and Borgman 2007: 86.
55   Whittingham 1989: 88–89; Lafeber 1984: 9.
56   Potoker and Borgman 2007: 86.
57   Hellinger and Hellinger 1983: 1.
58   Ramnerine 1993: 36; Polanyi-Levitt 1985: 232–233.
59   Lowenthal and Mostajo 2010: 584.
60   Kissinger Commision 1984.
61   Lowenthal and Mostajo 2010: 585.
62   Newfarmer 1985: 67; Whittingham 1989: 87.
63   Bakan et al. 1993:6.
64   Ibid.: 7–8; Whittingham 1989:91.
65   U.S. Senate 1990.
66   Sweeney 1998: npn.
67   Spalding 2014: 36).
68   Pregelj 2003: 1; González 2006: 4.
69   Sweeney 1998: npn.
70   In Condo et al. 2005: 8.
71   World Bank 2019a.
72   Lederman et al. 2002: 3, 9.
73   Spalding 2014: 53.
74   González 2006: 4; Potoker and Borgman 2007: 81.
75   Molina 2017: 218.
76   González 2006: 4.
77   Morrison 2018: 9–10.
78   USTR 2003: 2.
79   In Finley-Brook 2012: 633.
80   Andrews 2005; Potoker and Borgman 2007: 110–1; Spalding 2014: 157.
81   In Blustein 2004.
82   Spalding 2014.
83   Ibid.: 53.
84   Latinobarómetro 2017: 90.
85   Condo et al. 2005: 10.
86   Andrews 2005.
87   Cox 2008: 1530; Spalding 2014: 82, 84; Ricker and Stansbury 2006; Phillips 2005:18.
88   Cox 2008: 1536.
89   Ibid.: 1538; El País 2011; Spalding 2014: 82–83.
90   Valenzuela 2005: 60; Associated Press 2004.
91   Taconne and Nogueira 2004: ii, 31; Spalding 2014: 84.
92   Spalding 2014: 71.
93   In Finley-Brook 2012: 640.
94   Andrews 2005.
95   Spalding 2014: 61, 65–66, 128.
96   World Bank 2018.

97 Hornbeck 2012: 13.
98 Ibid.: npn.
99 World Bank 2018
100 Lamrani 2012: 347.
101 UNDP 2018.
102 In CRS 2019: 4.
103 Ibid.: 1.
104 The countries included are: Costa Rica, El Salvador, Guatemala, Honduras and
    Nicaragua; the most recent available data was used: 2015 for the cases of Guatemala
    and Nicaragua; 2014 for Honduras. Source for GDP: World Bank (2019b). Source for
    trade: OEC (2019).

References

Andrews, E. (2005, July 29). How Cafta passed house by 2 votes. *New York Times*.

Associated Press (2004, September 10). Costa Rica asks to be taken off U.S. list of Iraq
coalition partners. *Los Angeles Times*.

Bakan, A., Cox, D., & Leys, C. (1993). *Imperial power and regional trade: The Caribbean basin
initiative*. Waterloo, ON: Wilfrid Laurier University Press.

Bitar, S. (1984). United States-Latin American relations: Shift in economic power and
implications for the future. *Journal for Interamerican Studies and World Affairs*, *26*(1), 3–31.

Blustein, P. (2004, May 28). Trade vote won't be held before election: Central American
agreement could have been big campaign issue. *Washington Post*, p. E04.

Brands, H. (2008). Economic development and the contours of U.S. foreign policy: The
Nixon administration's approach to Latin America, 1969–1974. *Peace & Change*, *33*(2),
243–273.

Bulmer-Thomas, V. (1988). *Studies in the economies of Central America*. London: Macmillan
Press.

Bulmer-Thomas, V. (2003). *The economic history of Latin America since independence* (2nd ed.).
Cambridge: Cambridge University Press.

Cardemill, L., Di Tata, J., & Frantischek, F. (2000). Central America: Adjustment and
reforms in the 1990s. *Finance and Development*, *37*(1), 34–37.

CEPAL (1971). *Las Probables Repercusiones Sobre América Latina de la Nueva Política Económica
de los Estados Unidos. XII Reunión de CECLA*. Lima: CEPAL.

Coatsworth, J. (1994). *Central America and the United States: The clients and the colossus*. New
York: Twayne Publishers.

Condo, A., Colburn, F., & River, L. (2005). *The United States Central America Free Trade
Agreement (CAFTA): Negotiations and expected outcomes*. Costa Rica: INCAE Business
School.

Cottam, M. L. (1994). Images and intervention: Policies in Latin America. Pittsburgh, PA:
University of Pittsburgh Press.

Cox, R. (2008). Transaction capital, the US state and Latin American trade agreement. *Third
World Quarterly*, *29*(8), 1527–1544.

CRS (2019). *U.S. strategy for engagement in Central America: Policy issues for congress* (Report
No. R44812). Washington, DC: Congressional Research Service.

Cruz, A. (1995). Estados Unidos y Centroamérica: La Era del Comercio. *INCAE Business
Review*, *8*(2), 9–22.

Cruz, J. (2015). The root causes of the Central American crisis. *Current History*, *114*(769),
43–48.

El País (2011, February 5). Cable en el que se recoge las presiones de EEUU para que Guatemala vete una ley que planea impulsar los medicamentos genericos. *El País*.

Farer, T. (1993). A paradign of legitimate intervention. In L. F. Damrosch (Ed.), *Enforcing restraint: Collective intervention in internal conflicts* (pp. 316–348). New York: Council on Foreign Relations Press.

Feinberg, R., & Newfarmer, R. (1982). A bilateralist gamble. *Foreign Policy*, (47), 133–138.

Finley-Brook, M. (2012). Geoeconomic assumptions, insecurity, and 'Free' trade in Central America. *Geopolitics, 17*, 629–657.

Ford, G. R. (1976). *Public papers of the presidents of the United States: Gerald R. Ford, 1976–1977*. Washington, DC: U.S. Government Printing Office.

GATT (1986). United States-trade measures affecting Nicaragua GATT Panel Report L/6053.

González, A. (2006). Estados Unidos: La experiencia del tratado de libre comercio entre Centroamérica, Estados Unidos y República Dominicana. *INTAL-ITD: Documento de Divulgación, 42*.

Granados, C. (1986). Geopolítica En Centroamérica. *Cuadernos Políticos*, (46), 74–89.

Hakim, P. (1991). From cold war to cold shoulder? The US in Central America. *Harvard International Review, 13*(3), 4–6.

Hakim, P. (2011). The United States and Latin America: The neighbourhood has changed. *The International Spectator: Italian Journal of International Affairs, 46*(4), 63–78.

Hellinger, D., & Hellinger, S. (1983). *Supporting Central American and Caribbean development: A critique of the Caribbean basin initiative and an alternative regional assistance plan*. Washington, DC: The Development Group for Alternative Policies.

Hornbeck, J. F. (2012). *The U.S.-Panama free trade agreement* (Report No. RL32540). Washington, DC: Congressional Research Service.

Kissinger Commission (1984). *Report of the National Bipartisan Commission on Central America*. Washington, DC: U.S. Government Printing Office.

Lafeber, W. (1984). The Reagan administration and revolutions in Central America. *Political Science Quarterly, 99*(1), 1–25.

LaFeber, W. (1989). *The Panama Canal: The crisis in historical perspective*. New York: Oxford University Press.

Lamrani, S. (2012). The Bolivarian alliance for the peoples of our America: The challenges of social integration. *International Journal of Cuban Studies, 4*(3/4), 347–365.

Latinobarómetro (2017). *La era de Trump Imagen de Estados Unidos en América Latina*. Santiago: Corporación Latinobarómetro.

Lederman, D., Perry, G., & Suescún, R. (2002). *Trade structure, trade policy and economic policy options in Central America*. The World Bank, Latin America and the Caribbean Region.

Leogrande, W. (1990). From Reagan to Bush: The transition in US policy towards Central America. *Journal of Latin American Studies, 22*(3), 595–621.

Leogrande, W. (1996). Making the economy scream: US economic sanctions against Sandinista Nicaragua. *Third World Quarterly, 17*(2), 329–348.

Levin, B. (1981, March 16). Storm Over El Salvador. *Newsweek*, p. 34.

Lowenthal, A. (1983). Ronald Reagan and Latin America: Coping with hegemony in decline. In K. Oye, R. Lieber & D. Rothchild (Eds.), *Eagle defiant: United States foreign policy in the 1980s*. Boston, MA: Little Brown and Company.

Lowenthal, A., & Mostajo, F. (2010). Estados Unidos y América Latina, 1960–2010: De la pretensión hegemónica a las relaciones diversas y complejas. *Foro Internacional, 50*(3/4), 552–626.

Molina, E. (2017). Costa Rica y el Proceso de Producción del TLC: Estrategias de Socialización Profesional y Nuevas Élites Estatales. *Anuario de Estudos Centroamericanos, 43*, 189–223.

Morley, M. (1994). *Washington, Somoza, and the Sandinistas: State and regime in U.S. policy towards Nicaragua, 1969–1981.* Washington, DC: Cambridge University Press.

Morrison, W. (2018). *China-U.S. trade issues* (Report No. RL 33536). Washington, DC: Congressional Research Service.

Newfarmer, R. (1985). Economic policy toward the Caribbean Basin: The balance sheet. *Journal of Interamerican Studies and World Affairs, 27*(1), 63–89.

OEC (2019). Visualizations: Export destinations. *The Observatory of Economic Complexity* (Accessed on May 13, 2019).

Pastor, R. (1982). Sinking in the Caribbean Basin. *Foreign Affairs, 60*(5), 1038–1058.

Phillips, N. (2005). U.S. power and the politics of economic governance in the Americas. *Latin American Politics & Society, 47*(4), 1–25.

Polanyi-Levitt, K. (1985). The origins and implications of the Caribbean Basin initiative: Mortgaging sovereignty? *International Journal, 40*(2), 229–281.

Potoker, E., & Borgman, R. (2007). The economic impact of the Caribbean Basin Initiative: Has it delivered its promise? *Canadian Journal of Latin American and Caribbean Studies, 32*(64), 79–119.

Pregelj, V. (2003). *Caribbean Basin Interim Trade Program: CBI/NAFTA Parity* (Report No. IB95050). Washington, DC: Congressional Research Service.

Ramírez, S. (1999). *Adiós Muchachos: Una memoria de la revolución sandinista.* México D.F.: Aguilar.

Ramnarine, D. (1993). The political logic of the CBI. In A. Bakan, D. Cox, C. Leys (Eds.), *Imperial power and regional trade: The Caribbean Basin initiative* (pp. 11–44). Waterloo, ON: Wilfrid Laurier University Press

Reagan, R. (1982). Remarks to the permanent council of the organization of American states on the Caribbean Basin initiative. Ronald Reagan Presidential Library and Museum. Retrieved from https://www.reaganlibrary.gov/research/speeches/22482a

Reagan (1985). United States: Economic sanctions against Nicaragua. *International Legal Materials, 24*(3), 809–822.

Ricker, T., & Stansbury, B. (2006). The CAFTA chronicles: Strong-arming Central America, mocking democracy. *Multinational Monitor, 27*(1), 21–25.

Riding, A. (1982). The Central American quagmire. *Foreign Affairs, 61*(3), 641–659.

Sanford, J. (1983). *Caribbean Basin initiative* (Report No. IB82074). Washington, DC: Congressional Research Service.

Shultz, G. (1982). *Secretary of State Shultz OAS address. In congressional record – Senate,* December 13, 1982. Washington, DC: U.S. Government Printing Office.

Spalding, R. (2014). *Contesting trade in Central America: Market, reform and resistance.* Austin, TX: Texas University Press.

Sullivan, M. (1993). *The Caribbean Basin: Economic and security issues.* Study Papers submitted to the Joint Economic Committee Congress of the United States. Washington, DC: U.S. Government Printing Office.

Sweeney, J. (1998). Clinton's Latin America policy: A legacy of missed opportunities. *The Heritage Foundation.*

Taccone, J. J., & Nogueira, U. (2004). *Central American report* (Report No. 2). Buenos Aires: Institute for Integration of Latin America and the Caribbean.

UNDP (2018). Human Development Data (1990–2017). *Human development reports.* Retrieved from http://hdr.undp.org/en/data#

U.S. House of Representatives (1981). *Foreign assistance legislation for fiscal year 1982.* Hearing before the Committee on Foreign Affairs, March 13, 18, 19 and 23. Washington, DC: U.S. Government Printing Office.

U.S. Senate (1978). *Latin America.* Hearing before the Subcommittee on Western Hemisphere Affairs of the Committee on Foreign Relations, October 4, 5 and 6. Washington, DC: U.S. Government Printing Office.

U.S. Senate (1990). *Caribbean Basin initiative.* Hearing before the Subcommittee on International Trade of the Committee of Finance, February 9. Washington, DC: U.S. Government Printing Office.

USTR (2003). Trade with Central America: Strengthening democracy, promoting prosperity. Fact Sheets: January 08.

Valenzuela, A. (2005). Beyond benign neglect: Washington and Latin America. *Current History, 104,* 58–63.

Van Tassell, D. H. (1997). Operational code evolution: How Central America came to be "Our Backyard" in U.S. culture. In V. M. Hudson (Ed.), *Culture & Foreign Policy* (pp. 231–261). Boulder, CO: Lynne Riener.

Weintraub, S. (1982). A flawed model. *Foreign Policy,* (47), 128–133.

Weintraub, S. (1991). The new US economic initiative toward Latin America. *Journal for Interamerican Studies and World Affairs, 33*(1), 1–18.

Weintraub, S. (1997). US-Latin American economic relations. *Journal for Interamerican Studies and World Affairs, 39*(1), 59–69.

Whitaker, A. P. (1954). *The Western Hemisphere idea: Its rise and decline.* Ithaca, NY: Cornell University Press.

Whittingham, W. (1989). The United States government's Caribbean Basin initiative. *CEPAL Review,* (39), 73–92.

Williamson, R. (1988). Policies for the Americas in the 1990s. Bureau of Public Affairs. *Current Policy,* (1071).

World Bank (2018). Trade stats [export $US thousand]. World Integrated Trade Solutions. Retrieved from https://wits.worldbank.org/

World Bank (2019a). GDP [NY.GDP.MKTP.KD.ZG]. Retrieved from https://data.worldbank.org/indicator/ny.gdp.mktp.kd.zg

World Bank (2019b). Gross domestic product [NY.GDP.MKTP.CD]. Retrieved from https://data.worldbank.org/indicator/NY.GDP.MKTP.CD

Zorn, J., & Mayerson, H. (1983). The Caribbean Basin initiative: A windfall for the private sector. *University of Miami Inter-American Law Review, 14*(3), 523–556.

Chapter 8

United States' Economic Statecraft toward South America

Unlike the United States' North American neighbors or Central America, South America has not been at the center of Washington's radar. Both in political and economic matters, the region has historically occupied a distant third place in Washington's hemispheric concerns. Thus, for instance, 1823 Monroe Doctrine's co-author (if not intellectual creator) secretary of state John Quincy Adams, was chiefly concerned about the septentrional part of the hemisphere; as he put it, "It was one thing to tell Europe to keep its hands off the Western Hemisphere ... but it was another to join hands with those weak Latin governments in the spirit of equality and fraternal affection."[1] For him, "the world shall be familiarized with the idea of considering our proper dominion to be the continent of North America."[2]

Unlike Latin Americans, who consider the Western Hemisphere a continent, Adams—like his compatriots—viewed it as being constituted by more than one landmass. In a letter preceding the enunciation of the Monroe Doctrine, Adams thus wrote that "the American continents are no longer open for the settlement of New European colonies."[3] Significantly, Adams did not seemed to include México in North America; as he wrote,

> The whole continent of North America appears to be *destined by Divine Providence* to be peopled by one *nation*, speaking one language, professing one general system of religious and political principles, and accustomed to one general tenor of social usages and customs.[4]

Thus, during the 19th and 20th centuries, Washington's intervention in South America was lower than that in Central America and México.[5] Similarly, Christian Deblock and Sylvain F. Turcotte note that, in the early 21st century, South America can be thought of as the "third circle" of US interests in the hemisphere (with North America being the first, and Central America and the Caribbean the second).[6] As the disappointed Chairman of the House of Foreign Affairs Committee, Tom Lantos, put it in 2007: "The administration has put South America somewhere slightly ahead of Antarctica on its priority list."[7]

South America cannot of course be considered a single bloc, in the way we saw in the previous chapter Central America can. There are, in fact, two widely recognized political regions within South America: the Andean one—usually conceived of as comprising Bolivia, Colombia, Ecuador, Perú and Venezuela—and the Southern Cone, constituted by Argentina, Brazil, Chile, Paraguay and Uruguay. Furthermore, Brazil—the largest country in the area, both economically and geographically, one that is not a former Spanish colony but was the seat of an empire (Portugal's) for a few years—plays in some way an analogous role in the region to the one the United States plays in the hemisphere. Brazil and the other countries in the region, however, share some interests and values.[8] Hence, South American economic and political integration, even the development of a common identity, has been a recurrent theme in the region's history and political economy.[9]

The fact that South America has not historically been a priority for Washington does not mean, of course, that it has been exempted from what Abraham Lowenthal has called the United States' "hegemonic presumption: the belief in this country that the entire hemisphere was a rightful sphere of U.S. influence."[10] Washington's hemispheric-wide premise and policy in turn served to reinforce a sense of solidarity vis-à-vis the Colossus of the North among its southern neighbors. Thus, for instance, a couple of years prior to the 1971 Nixon Shock, Latin American countries issued the Viña del Mar (Chile) Consensus, a statement containing a "common position to jointly elaborate with the United States new bases for Inter-American economic and social cooperation."[11] When the US president's unexpected announcement came two years later, Latin America as a whole made a joint statement against said measure.[12]

But regardless of Latin American political camaraderie, the United States hegemonic presumption prevailed—at least during the first period (1970–1989) of this work. The first case to be reviewed here, Washington's foreign economic policy toward Chile during the government of leftist president Salvador Allende (1970–1973), makes clear that the dominance supposition was fully at work. As secretary of state Henry Kissinger would candidly put it, "I don't see why we need to stand by and watch a country go Communist due to the irresponsibility of its own people."[13] Washington's economic statecraft toward Chile would do an about-face with the arrival—via coup d'état—of military dictator Augusto Pinochet in 1973.

United States' lack of hemispheric solidarity, and more precisely its dismissal of the 1947 Inter-American Treaty of Reciprocal Assistance and support of the United Kingdom during the 1982 Falkland/Malvinas War, further increased its unpopularity in the region (Chile and Colombia did not support Argentina either).[14] Later in that decade, United States' attention to the region would be drawn in a more sustained fashion. The reason: the debt crisis. During this period, Washington's focus was, to a large extent, on the challenge presented by the government of Peruvian president Alan García; I review this juncture below.

Hemispheric relations improved substantially during the 1990s, the second period of analysis in this work. With the Cold War over at the global level, and the political milieu of the Washington Consensus at the hemispheric one, the United States embarked on a more amicable relationship with the countries of South America. Thus, for instance, the Andean Trade Promotion Act (ATPA), proposed around the time of the fall of the Berlin Wall, went into effect in late 1991. The new legislation eliminated tariffs on many products from Bolivia, Colombia, Ecuador and Perú. Like the CBI, the measure enacted by former Reagan's vice-president, George H. W. Bush, was also a one-way free trade program. But ATPA's objective was not only economic—its stated purpose was to reduce the production of coca (most of which ended up in the United States).

A few months after ATPA was implemented, and with NAFTA negotiations still under way, the latter's demonstration effect began. The North American agreement would become the new model of economic integration with the United States, and several countries showed interest in negotiating its own trade deal with Washington, or simply joining NAFTA. As the poster child of the political economy advocated by the Washington Consensus, Chile was quick to request the opening of trade talks with the United States; the latter, needless to say, was happy to oblige. Thus, during Chilean president Patricio Aylwin's visit to Washington in May 1992, president Bush declared that Washington would soon start free trade discussions with Santiago.[15] Already in November 1991, during a trip to South America, president Bush had intimated that Chile would be a good candidate for a free trade agreement with his country.[16] The agreement, however, would not materialize until a decade later; I review the initial moments below.

Economic reform, and particularly trade liberalization, would become the leitmotif of Washington's economic statecraft toward Latin America in general, and South America in particular. On this matter, there seemed to be no difference between the Bush (Sr.) and Clinton administrations. The 1994 Summit of the Americas, with the launching of the idea for the Free Trade Area of the Americas (FTAA) would become an appropriate emblem of the prevailing hemispheric mood. As Jeffrey Davidow, Assistant Secretary of State in charge for Western Hemisphere policy-making, noted when making the case for fast-track authority the Clinton administration lacked in 1997: since the FTAA had become "the cornerstone" of hemispheric relations,

For the United States to maintain our traditional leadership role in global economic policy, it will clearly require expeditious congressional approval of fast track procedures ... If we lose our ability to lead in the trade arena, we will increasingly lose our influence strategically, politically, and in other spheres of international relations.[17]

One of the other spheres in the hemisphere that was attracting increased attention from Washington during the 1990s was the security one, particularly as it related to drug smuggling. Going back to the concerns which crystallized in the 1991 ATPA, but now with a much clearer emphasis on military assistance, the Clinton administration secured congressional approval for Plan Colombia, which initially involved US$1.7 billion.

The arrival of George W. Bush to the presidency, which coincides with the start of the third period (2001–2016) in which this work is divided, brought renewed hope of Inter-American cooperation, particularly in the Southern Cone. There, the Argentinian government of Fernando de la Rúa was starting its second year with increasing economic difficulties. During his campaign, Bush had repeatedly chastised the Clinton administration for not delivering on his promises of a closer economic relationship with Latin America (Clinton failed to obtain fast-track authority for trade negotiations) and had promised to make the region a priority. As the economic situation in Argentina worsened during the first months of the Bush (Jr.) presidency, particularly regarding the twin deficits (i.e., in government spending and current account), de la Rúa's hope for US support, as well as that of his successor, Eduardo Duhalde, vanished.[18] Although it was clear that the new administration was willing to engage Congress more forcefully in order to make good on the president's father's promise (in the 1991 Initiative for the Americas) of a creating a free trade area "from Alaska to Tierra del Fuego," it was also clear that in the financial realm the thinking had changed. Thus, for instance, whereas the Clinton administration came to México's rescue in 1995 (as discussed in Chapter 6), six years later, Bush Jr. would refuse to do so in Argentina; I review this case below.

In consonance with its free trade "credo" (USTR Zoellick *ipse dixit*)[19] and its "competitive liberalization" approach, George W. Bush's administration would obtain Trade Promotion Authority (as fast-track authority was now called) in 2002, and deliver on signing the belated trade agreement with Chile in 2003. But Washington went further in promoting free trade in the region. The same year president Bush came to office, his administration set to renew and expand ATPA. The unilateral trade facilitation initiative was certainly wider, but not only on commercial matters—it now came to more explicitly include the fight on narcotics production, as its new name made clear: Andean Trade Promotion and Drug Eradication Act (ATPDEA). Congress approved the president's proposal, extending the unilateral trade benefits until 2005—date by which the FTAA was supposed to come into effect.

But the assumption that the FTAA would supersede ATPDEA turned out to be overly optimistic. Washington and Brasília, as co-chairs of what was supposed to be the last stretch of the negotiations leading to the hemispheric pact, could not reach an agreement, and the deal collapsed in 2005 in Mar del Plata (Argentina). Although there were 34 countries involved, significantly, as suggested, it was only two of them, the United States and Brazil, that led the process; this is the last case I review in this chapter. It is important to note, however, that the demise of the FTAA was not only due to Brasília's opposition to it—at least in the terms Washington wanted to negotiate it. The failure to reach an agreement was also related to the rise of left-leaning governments in South America; Hugo Chávez had taken office in 1998 in Venezuela, Nestor Kichner in Argentina in 2003 (Brazil's Luiz Inácio Lula da Silva also took office in 2003), and Tabaré Vázquez the same year the hemispheric trade negotiations came to a halt (Bolivia and Ecuador would also turn left within two years of the FTAA's passing away). By the time of the Mar del Plata summit, as William Leogrande has put it, "The convivial consensus Bill Clinton lauded at the first Summit had been replaced by starkly divergent visions of the hemisphere's future."[20] It was at this time that both talk of a "post-Washington Consensus" or "post-hegemonic" order in the region emerged,[21] but also that a sense of panic transpired in some quarters in Washington. As House Foreign Affairs Committee Chairman Lantos put it, "Now under our very noses our neighbors are staging a mini-revolt … We have ignored South America as a partner for far too long. We have allowed Chavez to define us to our neighbors."[22] Venezuela, under Hugo Chavez's "socialism of the 21st century" and its bankrolling of the nascent Bolivarian Alliance for the Peoples of Our America (ALBA, established in 2004, as noted in Chapter 2), had indeed become a major problem for Washington.

However, Washington's competitive liberalization strategy continued its course. After the accomplishment of the FTAs with Chile and Central America, the United States signed more trade agreements in the following years. After all, 29 out of the 34 countries represented at Mar del Plata were in favor of the FTAA—and several of them were in South America.[23] Thus, Colombia and Perú signed trade promotion agreements in 2006 (the former did not go into effect until 2012; the latter became effective in 2009). Furthermore, these were second generation, WTO-Plus, agreements; they included novel trade matters, such as e-commerce, and extra-commercial areas, such as intellectual property, government regulation and environmental and labor protections. The inclusion of these issues, particularly the one pertaining to labor standards, of course caused intense debate in Congress and in the US negotiating partners. But the governments of both Colombia (Álvaro Uribe [2002–2010] and Juan Manuel Santos [2010–2018]) and Perú (under Alejandro Toledo [2001–2006] and Alan García [again, 2006–2011]) wanted to consolidate market access to the United States, and were willing to make the concessions Washington demanded.

For the Bush administration, although the FTAA had failed, the agreements with Colombia and Perú were stepping stones toward hemispheric free trade— now in a hub-and-spoke model, one in which Washington was, of course, the former. But even this unbalanced scheme was conceived as a way to instantiate its free trade credo. As president Bush put it in 2007, making the case for the deal with Perú:

> [W]e can send the clear signal to our neighborhood that we want you to be prosperous; that we want to help you realize your potential through trade with the United States of America. Trade agreements are good for both sides—it's good for U.S. workers, and it's good for Peruvians.[24]

Furthermore, the State Department argued, "Approval and implementation of the FTA will demonstrate strong U.S. support for a country and a people who share our values of economic freedom and democracy."[25]

1) 1971–1989

On the same day that the US president pronounced what came to be known as the Nixon Shock, the *New York Times* reported that for treasury secretary John B. Connally Jr.—who would be instrumental in the crafting of the yet to be revealed consequential measure—his country ought to "get though" with countries in Latin America that expropriated US corporations, since "We don't have any friends there anyway."[26] Then came the president's announcement which, as noted, did indeed send shockwaves through the hemisphere. Both the Secretary's opinion and the president's new policy denoted not only a cold-eyed view of international politics, but also a clear (although not necessarily correct in its diagnostic) awareness of the existing continuum between the domestic and the international political economy. In fact, just a few months before Nixon had created the Council on International Economic Policy mentioned in Chapter 4, in order to

> Achieve consistency between domestic and foreign economic policy [and] Provide a clear top level focus for the full range of international economic policy issues; deal with international economic policies—including trade, investment, balance of payments, finance—as a coherent whole; and consider the international economic aspects of essentially foreign policy issues, such as foreign aid and defense, under the general policy guidance of the National Security Council.[27]

The administration's rationale for creating the new office was that "economic interests cut directly across foreign policy considerations and thus bear on military and diplomatic commitments abroad."[28]

Furthermore, related to the issue that treasury secretary Connally most likely had in mind when he expressed his views on the perception of the United States in the hemisphere, to wit, Chile's socialist government's recent takeover of US mining companies, a momentous bureaucratic battle was already boiling within the Nixon administration: whether the Treasury or the State Department was to be in charge of foreign economic policy towards the Western Hemisphere. The former was to emerge victorious, with nefarious consequences, if not for the whole of Latin America, at least for the Allende administration in Chile.[29] Suggesting that there might be a sort of self-fulfilling prophecy in the Secretary's assessment, the *New York Times* warned that "Mr. Connally's dictum about "no friends in Latin America" may assume a newer and richer significance."[30]

But Connally's standoffish approach towards non–market-friendly countries in the region was not based merely on technical economic analysis. It was rather based on a political mentality that considered any policy decision by a foreign government that did not match Washington's canon not only as a sign that such country had gone astray, but also as a potential existential threat to the United States. In the case at hand (Chile under Allende), it was just the continuation of the domino theory applied two decades before in Latin America to the Arbenz administration in Guatemala, as noted in the previous chapter. The domino theory did indeed pervade the US government apparatus. The otherwise moderate career diplomat Edward Korry, who had been appointed as ambassador to Chile by Lyndon B. Johnson, telegrammed Washington on 5 September 1970 about the consequences of Allende's election:

> It will have the most profound effect on Latin America and beyond; we have suffered a grievous defeat; the consequences will be domestic and international; the repercussions will have immediate impact in some lands and delayed effect in others (*sic* [for punctuation marks]).[31]

As Nixon's National Security Adviser Henry Kissinger would later note, "There was no dispute in our government about what Allende stood for. No one challenged Korry's first cable predicting the consequences of Allende's election."[32]

As suggested by the endurance of the anxiety-based, chain reaction belief, the fear of socialists coming to power—even if through democratic means, as Allende had eventually done—in Chile and then taking hold in other countries, was not new in Washington. At least during the preceding decade, the United States had been actively involved in preventing the arrival of a socialist—Allende himself, as he had also ran in 1964 (and in 1952 and 1958)—to La Moneda Palace. Democratic and Republican administrations had spent more than US$3 million to prevent Allende's last two attempts to become president.[33] But on the last occasion it was to no avail:[34] Allende's Socialists emerged victorious with a plurality (36.2%) of votes in the September 1970 elections.[35] The Nixon administration did not give up after the Chilean electoral process' adverse results: it—along with some US corporations with interests in the austral country—maneuvered to prevent Allende from taking office.[36] The rationale, according to Kissinger, was that "Allende's election was a challenge to our national interest."[37] But, to reiterate, it wasn't only him: "That an Allende government threatened our national interests was conventional wisdom when Nixon entered office."[38]

Shortly after Allende took office (3 November 1970), president Nixon issued what his administration's outward position toward the socialist government would be: "correct but cool, to avoid giving the Allende government a basis on which to rally domestic and international support for consolidation of the regime."[39] However, the president directed his administration to enact a host of economic policies intended to pressure the new Chilean government.[40] As the 1975 Senate Select Committee Report on Chile states, "United States foreign economic policy toward Allende's government was articulated at the highest levels of the U.S. government;" president Nixon's indication was to "Make the [Chilean] economy scream."[41]

Economic coercion against the Allende administration actually started before the president-elect took office. Thus, for instance, in October (1970), the US Export–Import Bank downgraded Chile's credit grading rate.[42] Allende, for his part, was fast to act against US companies. In November (1970), the same month he took office, the Chilean president directed the administrative seizure of two US corporations and announced that his government would later expropriate more US assets (as well as other foreign and Chilean ones).[43] The following year, in effect, two US mining companies were taken over, with practically no reparation;[44] Washington then resorted to press the Chilean government on the matter by conditioning future Export–Import Bank support on satisfactory settlement of the recent nationalizations.[45] By that time—August 1971—the United States was confident that the economic difficulties the Allende administration was facing would only worsen, therefore diminishing its approval ratings[46]—a tendency which the Nixon administration considered favorable to its objectives. The economic situation indeed continued to deteriorate in Chile and, in November (1971), Santiago declared a moratorium on its debt.[47] In January 1972, president Nixon issued a strong statement against expropriations and made clear that his administration would grant no more loans to the Allende one.[48]

In addition to the use of overt foreign economic policy tools to undermine the socialist government in Chile, Washington also resorted to covert operations. Thus, for instance, the Central Intelligence Agency (CIA) funded opposition parties, business associations, and the conservative newspaper *El Mercurio*; it also promoted national strikes, one in late 1972, and another in the months before the September 1973 military coup that ended Allende's administration. The CIA spent about US$6 million in its covert operations from 1970 to 1973.[49] Although Washington was not directly involved in the military overthrow in Santiago, it definitively was a contributing factor to it and was certainly not displeased with its occurrence.[50]

Not surprisingly, not long after the armed removal of democratically elected president Allende took place, Washington changed its economic statecraft towards the South American country. Thus, US credit lines were re-established, and economic aid reinitiated.[51] President Nixon's resignation from office was not a major inconvenience to the military dictatorship installed in Santiago by General Augusto Pinochet; his successor, Gerald Ford, kept Henry Kissinger as Secretary of State (he had been promoted to that position by Nixon two weeks after Pinochet's coup; Kissinger kept his role as National Security Advisor until November 1975). Kissinger had become so concerned with the "danger" Allende represented to the interests of the United States that when the planning to prevent him from taking office started in the Autumn of 1970, and an inter-agency group on Chile was created, he had become, in the words of a State Department official, a "Chilean desk officer".[52] The Carter administration, with its already mentioned (in the previous chapter) emphasis on the promotion of human rights, which were flagrantly being violated by the Pinochet regime, in contrast, did represent a serious problem to the latter.

But the cordial relationship between Washington and Santiago returned in 1981, with Ronald Reagan's arrival to the White House. His appointee as UN Ambassador, Jeane Kirkpatrick, who had in 1979 conveniently distinguished between friendly and hostile dictatorial regimes based on their ideology (and therefore their position toward the United States), criticized the Carter administration's promotion of human rights, as this was an "abstract" goal, detached from the US "national interest."[53] It was thus not difficult for General Pinochet to state that same year:

> Seven years ago, we found ourselves alone in the world in our firm anti-Communist position in opposition to Soviet imperialism, and our firm decision in favor of socio-economic free enterprise system ... Today we form a part of a pronounced worldwide tendency – and I tell you, ladies and gentlemen, it is not Chile that has changed its position.[54]

However, the Chilean government's continued abuse of human rights, in the context of Washington's constant accusations of human rights violations in Sandinista, Nicaragua, made it increasingly difficult for the Reagan administration to be partial to the Pinochet regime with favorable economic measures. Thus, by the mid-1980s, the United States was not supporting new credit lines to Chile in both the Inter-American Development Bank and the World Bank on grounds of human rights violations.[55] Santiago was increasingly isolated, as not only Washington was finding it more difficult to support its military regime, but also the rest of the hemisphere and a good deal of capitals in Europe where increasingly ostracizing it. But it wasn't only Chile that was finding itself alone, especially in the Western Hemisphere; the United States was also finding itself progressively isolated in hemispheric affairs. Thus, the *New York Times*' 1971 admonition that former treasury secretary Connally saying of his country having no friends on the region might "assume a newer and richer significance,"[56] was ringing true.

Regardless of its political isolation, with the free market fundamentalism promoted by the "Chicago boys"—the Chilean economists trained in the United States who were to reach the commanding heights of the South American country's economic policy during the Pinochet regime—Santiago had become the Reagan administration's epitome of a well-managed economy. Thus, for instance, Assistant Secretary of State for Inter-American Affairs, Elliott Abrams, told Congress in July 1987: "If our decisions in the international financial institutions were made on economic grounds alone, [their] loans to Chile would generally deserve our strong support and affirmative votes."[57] Similarly, the Reagan administration praised the Pinochet administration for swift renegotiation of its foreign debt that same year (1987)—an issue that was raging Latin America in general, and one in which other South American countries, such as Argentina and Brazil, were fully immersed, finding themselves in constant arrears. I turn to the 1980s debt crisis now.[58]

As previously noted, the Latin American debt crisis erupted in the early 1980s, first in Costa Rica (1981) and then in México (1982). The sudden growth in debt was not limited to those two countries—it was rather a region-wide phenomenon. Latin America's debt went from $12.8 billion in the early 1970s to $315.3 billion the year the crisis emerged.[59] Not surprisingly, as suggested, Brazil in 1983 and Argentina the following year found themselves in serious difficulties to service their debt.

Ironically, a country that was not a protagonist—at least in the economic sense—of the international financial dispute greatly contributed to the burgeoning crisis acquiring increased political salience in 1985: Perú. The Andean country was not an important debtor to private banks, which were the main creditors. During the decade's first lustrum, under the administration of Fernando Belaunde Terry, Lima had been in arrears of its foreign debt service, devoting to it no more than 10% of its export proceeds[60]—and this state of affairs was not cause of grave concern in international financial circles.

But then Alan García, a 36-year-old left-wing politician, came to power in July 1985, and on his inauguration announced to great fanfare that his country would not pay more than 10% of its export earning to service its foreign debt.[61] Furthermore, on his first presidential speech, García also referred to the United States as "the richest and most imperialist country on earth" and exhorted other Latin American countries to unite in their relations with Washington.[62] A couple of months later, at the United Nations' General Assembly, the Peruvian president declared: "debt has become a cause of conflict between the poor South, of which our American continent is a part, and the industrial, imperialist, financial North," and reiterated his call for other Latin American countries to follow his country's lead.[63] As a former US banker noted at the time of García's inauguration, his position on debt servicing was not particularly threatening: "Peru alone will not be enough to sink any foreign bank"; in his opinion the president's announcement was more of a political than an economic shot.[64]

Washington was of course not pleased with Lima's approach to the debt problem.[65] A month after García's UN speech, the Reagan administration announced that it considered the Peruvian debt "value impaired," which severely reduced the possibility of the Andean republic getting new loans (as banks had to put aside more capital), and negatively impacted the banks' earnings; by that time, the IMF had already declared the county ineligible for further loans from the intergovernmental financial institution.[66] Washington suspended economic and military assistance to Lima as well. Also in October, secretary of state George Shultz complained about the "Anti-American" rhetoric of president García in his UN speech,[67] and treasury secretary James Baker took aim at the Peruvian government's stand on debt servicing.[68]

The real concern for the United States was of course not Perú itself but the effect its actions could have in other countries of the region. As former secretary of state Kissinger would put it after the debt crisis had been dragging for several years, "Latin American populism is the last refuge of traditional Marxism … if a new approach to the debt problem does not emerge through imaginative U.S. leadership, it will be shaped in the crucible of confrontation."[69]

Moreover, Perú's attitude and aspirational leadership could endanger the wider international financial system, of which the United States was, in the last instance, responsible.[70] Even if the debt crisis was a matter mainly between private banks and developing countries, Washington's duty was to intervene in order to overcome it. By late 1985, it was clear that things were not improving. Secretary Baker recognized as much in an October meeting with IMF and World Bank executives, and he announced an initiative that came to be known as a plan bearing his last name. The Baker Plan called for indebted countries to reform their economies and for private banks and international financial institutions to lend about US$29 billion in the next three years (with US$20 billion coming from the former and US$9 from the latter) to the 17 top debtor countries, most of them in Latin America.[71]

Although the US proposal was patently insufficient to meet the challenge at hand, it certainly took some of the oomph out of García's call to Latin American concerted action, with most of the region initially embracing the US initiative.[72] Among the developed countries, particularly in the G7, however, the Baker Plan was not welcomed, as it was considered that Washington was passing the buck in order to solve a problem that pertained mainly to its sphere of influence. In the end, while a good deal of debtor countries did carry out economic reforms, neither the banks nor the IMF and the WB followed the Treasury Secretary's exhortations.[73] By the end of the plan's three-year period, at least four South American countries had been in arrears (Argentina, Bolivia, Brazil, Ecuador and … Perú).[74]

The Baker Plan's shortcomings in fixing the international financial atmosphere had indeed become evident not that long after its announcement. But the US Congress was worried as well about the impact that the increasingly grim situation the Latin American countries were going through could also affect the US real economy, to wit, decreased exports to the region. Thus, for instance, in 1987, Senator Bill Bradley proposed what up to then had been anathema to Washington: a debt-reduction plan, in the hope that it would get some traction on the region's depressed economies.[75] The Bradley Plan made economic sense, but it did not materialize. A couple of years later, though, another one that also included debt-reduction crystalized: the Brady Plan (so-called after treasury secretary Nicholas Brady). Announced in March 1989, the new, and, for US-standards, radical proposal, also included market-liberalization conditionality on its beneficiaries, but involved the international financial institutions in both collateralizing the bonds debtor countries would issue, and in providing resources to the insolvent economies so they could buy their debt at a discount from commercial banks.[76] Although skeptical of the new Washington proposal, several Latin American countries also showed their support for this one—particularly important for Washington was the backing expressed by the largest debtors, Brasília and México City.[77] Of the seven countries that would take part in the first round of the Brady Plan, five were South American: Argentina, Brazil, Ecuador, Uruguay and Venezuela; Perú did not participate—but Lima's political and economic relationship with Washington improved substantially in the years to come, during the Washington Consensus' decade—a topic I deal with in the next section.[78]

2) 1990–2000

As noted in the previous section, Chile was able to negotiate its debt problem without much hassle—something that positively impressed the United States. Santiago's approach to the matter had no doubt something to do with its economic model, one that was also valued by the Colossus of the North, as it bore its imprint (after all, as noted, it was the brainchild of the Chicago Boys' instructors); moreover, the Chilean economic system was in a sense the precursor of the hemispheric Washington Consensus that, to different degrees, was to prevail in the Americas during the 1990s. Now, although the Chilean forerunner was designed and implemented during Pinochet's dictatorial regime, the return of democracy to Chile in 1990 after the 1989 electoral process did not translate into its abandonment—particularly as it regarded outward economic openness, especially in trade.[79]

Thus, when George H. W. Bush's administration launched the Enterprise for the Americas Initiative in June 1990 (as we saw in Chapter 2, the US president was to a large extent accommodating a Latin American request), which dealt mainly with the promotion of trade and investment, democratic Chile (president Patricio Aylwin had taken office in March that year) was one of its first and staunchest supporters).[80] It was thus not surprising that, in a following encounter between the two presidents, in December 1990, in Santiago, the US leader told his Chilean counterpart that his country would be the first one in South America with which Washington would negotiate a free trade agreement.[81] It was during that trip that Bush Sr. expressed his objective of constructing a free trade area from "From the northernmost reaches of Canada to the tip of Cape Horn."[82] Eleven months later, in November 1991, Washington informed Santiago that it was willing to start negotiations in February 1992.[83]

Progress toward honoring the promise made to Chile, the role model of the market reform for the region, seemed to be going well—if not necessarily on schedule.

With the 1992 electoral race for the presidency (and Congress) in the United States gathering strength, free trade became a sensitive matter—as it is customary during such episodes. Furthermore, with the NAFTA negotiations heading toward their conclusion, Washington preferred to focus on them. Thus, three months after the negotiations with Chile were supposed to have started, while playing host to his Chilean counterpart in Washington, the US president declared that the two countries would initiate trade talks only after the NAFTA ones had been concluded (something that would happen in August).[84] From then on, the Bush administration largely remained mute regarding the trade deal with Chile.[85]

To complicate matters further for Santiago, the victory in the November elections of the Democratic contender and NAFTA-critic candidate, Bill Clinton, over president Bush meant that the NAFTA episode would not be closed soon—and therefore the Chile–United States negotiations toward a free trade agreement would again be delayed (as discussed in Chapter 6, the North American deal was finally passed in the US Congress in November 1993). But Chile insisted, and, in a May 1993 visit to Washington, president Aylwin brought up the issue again—this time with president Clinton; but the new administration wasn't as enthusiastic about free trade as the previous one. Hence, the former Arkansas governor was more non-committal towards his Chilean counterpart than his predecessor.[86]

Despite the strong dissent brewing within his administration on the matter of free trade, president Clinton decided to include it, with only weeks to go, in the agenda of the December 1994 Summit of the Americas (other topics were the promotion of democracy, sustainable development, and environmental protection). It was at the 34-state gathering in Miami that the launching of the Free Trade Area of the Americas took place. But more significantly for Chile, it was on this occasion that the official start of negotiations leading to its admission into NAFTA—by then almost a year into effect—took place.[87] As Canadian prime minister Jean Chrétien put it, "We have been the Three Amigos ... Now we will be the Four Amigos."[88] Perhaps indecisively and not necessarily following the original design, but the Clinton administration was making good on his predecessor's promise to create a free trade zone, as quoted, "From the northernmost reaches of Canada to the tip of Cape Horn."

By that time, however, the Clinton administration lacked fast-track negotiating authority (it had lapsed in June 1993). The absence of such executive power greatly impacted the potential negotiations with Chile. Hence, despite the cheerful and amicable Miami announcement on Chile's accession to NAFTA, the following year the administration of president Eduardo Frei refused to negotiate with Washington—citing precisely the Clinton administration's lack of fast-track authority.[89]

In the meantime, Santiago had continued (and would continue) to pursue its trade liberalization efforts with what USTR Zoellick would refer to as "can-do" countries—starting with the United States' NAFTA partners.[90] Thus, in 1991 it had signed an agreement with México City, and in 1996 it would sign another one with Ottawa. As the protectionist feeling became again pervasive in the US political environment, the attainment of fast-track authority turned out to be more difficult to achieve for the Clinton administration; it indeed lost the fast-track authority battle in Congress in 1997—with members of his own party voting against it.[91] The US administration's failure was dutifully pointed out by president Frei in 1998, at the second Summit of the Americas, which took place in Santiago. "Be patient with us," Clinton asked of his Chilean hosts; "Just stay with us, we'll get there," the US president said.[92] Later that year, however, the Clinton administration failed again at obtaining congressional authorization to effectively negotiate trade deals.[93]

With the wider WTO trade negotiations stalled, as demonstrated by the 1999 "battle of Seattle," and Washington's making free trade overtures to Jordan and Singapore, the Chilean government changed course regarding its pending trade negotiations with the United States and exerted pressure over it to re-launch their talks.[94] Thus, literally in the last weeks of the second Clinton administration, Chile received what was going to be the final—and definitive—invitation to start negotiations leading to a free trade agreement with the United States. As Osvaldo Rosales, Chile's Director General for International Economic Relations at the time would later note,

> President Lagos welcomed immediately the invitation and a week after the announcement we were already in Washington with a text proposal for 17 of the 19 chapters, bringing in addition another diskette with a comparative analysis of Chilean and American positions in each of the issues covered by the FTAA.[95]

As he observed, "We incurred in the risk of engaging in negotiation with an administration that was ending and we initiated them without a fast track, convinced that the trade agenda would impose it very soon."[96]

[The talks continued during George W. Bush's first months in office, until December 2001. At that point, the negotiators were waiting for Free Trade Authority (as the fast-track process was now called) in order to enter the last phase, consisting of sensitive issues such as labor, environment and dispute settlement procedures.[97] President Bush delivered on his promise to get Free Trade Authority, for which the more homogeneous, pro-free trade team around him contributed a great deal. An agreement was reached in December 2003, and it was signed six months later (June 2003) in Miami—the same city where, almost two decades before, the first formal invitation to Chile to become the United States' trade partner had taken place (although within NAFTA, as the "fourth amigo") *Paragraph in brackets because it falls outside of the section's period*].

On 17 June 1971, a couple of months before the delivery of the Nixon Shock, the president made another announcement that would also have momentous consequences—particularly for South America's Andean Region: what came to be known as the "war on drugs." As president Nixon put it:

> America's public enemy number one, in the United States is drug abuse. In order to fight and defeat this enemy, it is necessary to wage a new, all-out offensive ... this would be a world-wide offensive dealing with the problem of sources of supply.[98]

Since then, Washington's involvement in the Andes, particularly in Bolivia, Colombia and Perú, in the attempt to curtail sources of narcotics supply to the United States, has continued.[99] US intervention in the region increased in the mid-1980s, after president Reagan declared drug trade a national security threat; interestingly, given the already mentioned tense economic relations between Washington and Lima, president García was enthusiastic to cooperate with Washington on the narcotics problem.[100]

Several months after George H. W. Bush came to office, the White House submitted a report to Congress calling for "economic assistance" to cocaine-producing countries in the Andes. Still operating within the framework of the drug problem as a national security threat, the report also justified the proposed support from an economic standpoint; it read: "Few foreign threats are more costly to the U.S. economy."[101] The report also noted that the certification requirement linking US economic assistance and drug control collaboration of the target countries (introduced in 1986) could be "an important tool in motivating foreign governments to help attack the drug trade."[102] Acting on the broad outline contained in the report, president Bush met in February 1990 with the leaders of Bolivia, Colombia and Perú in Cartagena, Colombia. In the declaration that came out of the meeting, the US administration stated its commitment to facilitate increased access of Andean products to the country.

Accordingly, on 23 July 1990—just a few weeks after the unveiling of his Enterprise for the Americas Initiative—president Bush declared his intent to carry out a trade package through the Andean Trade Preference Initiative, a one-way free trade measure, which would benefit the countries of the region. In line with the report sent to Congress, it proposed tariff reduction to some of the area's major exports (e.g., flowers, leather products, vegetables) in order to keep farmers from engaging in coca production. The legislation proposal of the Andean Trade Preference Act (ATPA) was transmitted to Congress on 5 October 1990; in his transmittal message the president stated that the new program would be "patterned after the Caribbean Basin Initiative (CBI)," with the expectation that it would "also increase the prospects for economic growth and prosperity in the Andean countries and throughout the hemisphere;" preferential trade treatment would last for ten years.[103]

During the Congressional Hearings, some private corporations questioned the wisdom of providing economic aid to Perú, given its economic policy during the García administration; the attorneys or American International Group (AIG), which had been expropriated by the Peruvian government shortly after García's arrival to the presidency, for instance, asserted that Lima should not be an ATPA beneficiary.[104] The Act, including Perú, was passed in November 1991, signed by the president in December, and entered into force in July 1992; Colombia and Bolivia were the first beneficiary countries.[105] During the remaining years of the decade (1990s), bilateral trade between the United States and the favored Andean states, to wit, Bolivia, Colombia, Ecuador and Perú, almost doubled; Andean exports increased by 98%, and US exports by 65%.[106]

[When requesting the renewal and expansion of the program in 2001, already (31 January) under Bush Jr. the USTR noted that "ATPA functions as a U.S. trade policy tool that contributes to our fight against drug production and trafficking, and that it has begun to show important success in meeting one of its major goals: contributing to export diversification in beneficiary countries."[107] It also noted that the four favored countries "are working cooperatively with the United States" on the matters established by ATPA.[108] However, ATPA had had very modest effects on one of its main objectives: the reduction of narcotic production in the region, particularly in the case of coca leaf. No doubt as a result of that, in 2000, the Clinton administration launched the already mentioned Plan Colombia. (*Paragraph in brackets because it falls outside of the section's period*)].

3) 2001–2016

United States–Argentina relations underwent a major change during the 1990s. From the Argentinian perspective, at least since the end of World War II, and particularly in the economic realm, the United States had not been a decisive player before the years of the Washington Consensus. As Domingo Cavallo, Buenos Aires' minister of Foreign Affairs (July 1989–January 1991) and minister of the Economy (February 1991–August 1996) put it, "The economic history of Argentina from the mid-1940s, when Juan Domingo Peron [sic—no accent in Perón] came to power, to the end of the 1980s can be narrated without any significant reference to the role of the US government."[109] President Carlos Menem (July 1989–December 1999) carried out a veritable about-face in his country's overall relationship with Washington; his foreign minister for practically his whole tenure, Guido di Tella (January 1991–December 1999), referred to the type of relations he wanted his country to have with the United States as "carnal relations."[110] Even if not that intimate, bilateral relations did become closer; thus, for instance, Argentina sent troops to the Gulf War in 1991 and, at Washington's initiative, became the only country of the Americas to become a non-NATO ally in 1998.

But the most salient rapprochement for this work's argument is the one that took place in the economic front, particularly in the domain of monetary policy. After the traumatic hyper-inflation experience in the 1980s (in 1989 the inflation rate was 3,079%), in 1991 the Menem administration decided to establish a currency board, setting the peso on a one-to-one parity with the dollar. Although the move worked at first, its shortcomings became manifest a few years later. Thus, for instance, with Argentinian exports becoming less competitive, by the end of the decade the country had accumulated a strong current account imbalance: it had also stopped growing.[111] Buenos Aires' giving up of its monetary policy, though, was a homemade choice; in any case, as Cavallo has argued, Washington's influence was indirect: it had to do with the Casa Rosada's embrace—in particular in the aftermath of the end of the Cold War—of the White House's leadership, as well as of its project for what was supposed to be a new world order in general and a new hemispheric era in particular. Buenos Aires' ambitious program of economic reform, of which the currency board was only one component, was not only well-received by Washington—it was also strongly supported by it. US moral and material backing on economic affairs indeed outlasted the years of president Bush in the White House, continuing during the two Clinton administrations.[112]

But things were to change abruptly with the arrival of George W. Bush to the presidency. The financial team of the new president, led by treasury secretary Paul O'Neill, had a very different perspective of how the international finances should work; O'Neill was particularly opposed to the bailout of countries undergoing capital account difficulties (as had happened in México and Brazil during the 1990s). The IMF, over whose decisions Washington had historically exerted great ascendance—the United States had had "a very large role in influencing IMF policy and actions," as the Chairman of the Subcommittee on International Monetary Policy and Trade would put it in 2002[113]—was largely of the same view.[114] Furthermore, partly for political reasons, the Bush administration wanted a clean break from the Clinton administration's take on international economic affairs.[115] Buenos Aires would soon feel Washington's revised economic and political beliefs.

Argentina started to show serious signs of economic crisis shortly after the inauguration of Menem's successor, Fernando de la Rúa, on 10 December 1999. With international confidence in the Argentinian economy evaporating, the IMF agreed to grant the austral country a US$7.2 billion conditioned-loan, after which the de la Rúa administration announced US$1 billion in budget cuts. Since Argentina's standing in the international markets did not improve, in December 2000 Buenos Aires managed to get the IMF to set up a US$40 billion international assistance package. As the economic situation again failed to improve, in March 2001 de la Rúa brought Cavallo—the currency board's architect—to his team as Minister of the Economy. Not long after Cavallo's arrival (in late July), largely in an attempt to satisfy the IMF and the US Treasury, Buenos Aires took another drastic measure: Congress passed the "zero-deficit law."[116] Pleased by Argentina's harsh austerity measures, the IMF doubled its previous US$7.2 billion financing. But all this was, again, to no avail. As a run on the banking system started in November, the government imposed bank withdrawals limits; street protests broke. On 7 December, Argentina declared itself in default—the biggest in history. Within two weeks, both minister Cavallo and president de la Rúa had resigned. An interim administration, led by Eduardo Duhalde was installed on 2 January 2002; four days later, with Congress' enabling legislation, the new administration declared the end of the currency board. As popular protests dragged out, in late January the new Foreign Minister, Carlos Ruckauf, headed north to request political and economic backing from Washington; Argentina's Minister of the Economy, Jorge Remes, made the pilgrimage two weeks later.[117]

But with George W. Bush's administration in office for a little bit more than a year, the odds were against Buenos Aires' requests. In fact, in the months leading to the climax of the crisis—at around the same time when the Argentinian Congress passed the draconian "zero deficit" legislation—treasury secretary O'Neill told *The Economist*: "They've been off and on in trouble for 70 years or more ... They don't have any export industry to speak of at all. And they like it that way. Nobody forced them to be what they are."[118] Using the same ill-mannered tone, a few weeks later O'Neill told CNN:

> We're working to find a way to create a sustainable Argentina, not just one that continues to consume the money of the plumbers and carpenters in the United States who make $50,000 a year and wonder what in the world we're doing with their money.[119]

Although at the 20–22 April 2001 Summit of the Americas in Quebec the US president expressed some sympathy for the Argentinian plight, nothing concrete came out of it.[120] Three months later, National Security Adviser Condolezza Rice made a blunt declaration at the White House: "The best course right now is for Argentina to be able to take the steps that it needs to be able to take at home to stabilize the financial situation"—that is, the Buenos Aires was on its own.[121]

Argentina was not a priority in the United States; it therefore virtually did not get any political or financial support from the Colossus of the North.[122] As a Washington analyst put it at the time, "The Bush II administration and the IMF are comfortable with their tough love rejection of Argentina's carnal embrace because they are persuaded the immediate global repercussions from Argentina's default will be minimal."[123] Certainly, secretary O'Neill pointed out that that "the sheep are not all running for the cliffs" over the Argentinian crisis.[124] As his Undersecretary For International Affairs, John Taylor, would later explain, since the international markets had learned and saw no risk of contagion this time, "this Administration has tried to build on that change"[125]— i.e., the United States saw no reason to come to Buenos Aires' rescue. In 2002

Argentina's economy contracted 11%, inflation rose to more than 40% and unemployment reached 24%.[126]

Ironically, though, Washington's tough love ended up strengthening Buenos Aires' bargaining position vis-à-vis international bond holders.[127] In December 2001 Allan Meltzer, head of the US International Financial Institution Advisory Commission, openly suggested to interim president Duhalde that his country should default on its debt; the president was in accord.[128] Thus, during 2002 and 2003, both the United States and the IMF worked closely with the Argentinian government, even after Nestor Kirchner's accession to power on 25 May 2003.[129] For instance, in March 2004, Roger Noriega, Assistant Secretary for Western Hemisphere Affairs at the State Department, commented on how two months prior president Bush had met with his Argentinian counterpart and asked him to take some measures "to help me help you," referring to the financial negotiations the Kirchner administration was involved in.[130] After Argentina's hard-hitting negotiation with international bond-holders, who took a face value reduction of about 75%, about double what debt reduction had been in the previous decade—what Michael Mussa of the Institute of International Economics described not with the usual buzzword, "haircut," but with the more fatal one "beheading"[131]—Bush took pride on it; he declared: "Kirchner and his government did a good job of negotiating on behalf of the people of Argentina. So we've got a record of involvement."[132] In effect, Buenos Aires' was in the end grateful for Washington's support during the debt restructuring process.[133]

However, this gratitude did not extend to the view most Argentinians, and their left-leaning government, had of their political relation with the United States (only 31% of the population had a positive opinion of the global hegemon in 2005—the lowest percentage in the hemisphere).[134] In the court of public opinion, Washington was still held responsible for the economic collapse of the last years.[135] From Washington's standpoint, supporting Buenos Aires in the debt renegotiation process was partly a strategic move; even if, as noted, it was not worried about the economic contagion of the Argentinian crisis, it was of what a US political commentator called "political contagion" spreading in Latin America.[136] With the "pink wave" rising in the region, the spreading of anti-United States sentiment was, actually, a factor to be reckoned with (for instance, favorable public opinion of Washington stood at 53% in Brazil in 2005 [vs. 65% in 2000] and 39% in Venezuela for the same year [vs. 68% also 2000]).[137] The negative perception of the U.S.' role, at least in the early stages of crisis, was not lost in the Bush administration; Assistant Secretary for Western Hemisphere Affairs, Roger F. Noriega, recognized as much in early 2004.[138] Moreover, with the end of the FTAA negotiating process both approaching—it was scheduled for 2005—and in a delicate situation, Washington needed to cultivate some goodwill in South America. The hemispheric deal was at stake. As a *New York Times* analyst had put it, "The principal beneficiary of any reorientation of [Argentina's] foreign policy promises to be neighboring Brazil."[139]

As noted, the idea of making of the Western Hemisphere a free trade area was first unveiled by president George H. W. Bush in his 1991 Enterprise for the Americas Initiative. Significantly, unlike most Latin American countries, Brazil was not thrilled about the proposal.[140] The significance of Brasília's position was not just its peculiarity, but what it forebode for the future of the hemispheric project. After all, Brazil had historically been an important player in Latin America's political economy.

However, Bush's initiative was certainly short both on details and willingness to spend political capital. On hemispheric trade matters, his administration focused on NAFTA. Ditto for his successor's. Indeed, the Clinton administration decided to include trade, and thus follow up on Bush's initiative in the agenda of the 1994 Miami Summit of the Americas, just days before it took place.[141] It was then that the Free Trade Area of the Americas (FTAA) concrete project, with a 2005 deadline, crystallized. However, with NAFTA already in place, Clinton's idea was to achieve hemispheric trade through a sort of North American agreement writ large. That hub-and-spoke scheme, however, was not agreed upon in Miami, and was put aside at the second Summit of the Americas, in Santiago in 1998; a more decentralized approach was adopted in Chile.[142]

The 1994 Summit had already made clear that the Clinton administration was willing to negotiate the terms of the hemispheric enterprise with the other countries—particularly with Brazil.[143] But even if the NAFTA writ-large approach was not adopted as the roadmap, NAFTA itself became the baseline of the hemispheric project. Thus, strictly extra-trade matters, such as environmental and labor issues, were to be included in the incipient undertaking—much to the discontent of several Latin American countries, particularly Brazil.[144] Now, the United States' conciliatory mood had to do not only with the fact that, for practical purposes, Brasília had veto power over the agreement, but also with one that the Clinton administration's lack of fast-track authority meant a disincentive for the other countries to seriously engage with Washington on commercial affairs. Thus, by 1998, the negotiating parties had agreed that decisions were to be made by consensus, that existing regional agreements within the hemisphere were to remain in place, and that the FTAA was to be a "single undertaking" in which all parties had to concur on all issues before the agreement as a whole could be approved. Significantly, in 1998 the United States and Brazil had been selected by the other countries to co-chair the final stage of the negotiating process.[145]

There remained, however, contentious issues. One of them was agriculture, which Washington did not want to negotiate in the hemispheric project. The United States instead preferred to reserve farming matters for the upcoming (2000) WTO round of negotiations, arguing that it could better use its eventual accommodation of other countries' requests in the wider forum to extract meaningful concessions from the European countries and Japan, thus advancing the cause of world-wide agricultural liberalization.[146] This stance was of course not to the liking of the Latin American countries (again, particularly Brazil) which wanted to secure access to the United States market as soon as possible; in the end, Washington agreed to the creation of an agriculture group within the FTAA negotiating process.[147]

Brasília was able to rally the support of several countries in order to press its stand on agriculture at the WTO ministerial meeting that was to take place in late 1999 in Seattle. Leading a coalition of course strengthened Brazil's position in the WTO, where the important discussions on agriculture were to occur, but it was particularly useful for the pursuit of its political and economic objectives in the hemispheric project. As noted, Brasília had not been particularly enthusiastic of the trade initiative, from its inception. This lack of enthusiasm arose from the sense that Washington's project threatened not only its economic position, but particularly its political leadership in South America. Thus, Brazil's strategy from the get-go—and particularly once the formal discussions started in full in 1998—was to delay the integrative process.[148] As Richard Feinberg, one of the architects of the summitry process born in Miami in 1994 put it, the Brazilians wanted to "render the plan of action more modest in its ambitions, less exact in its objectives, less specific in its timetables, and less accountable in its implementation."[149]

Brasília's stance vis-à-vis the FTAA made sense. In a way, Brazil's position in South America in particular and in Latin America in general is analogous to the one the United States has had in the hemisphere: a large country that does not share the language of the vast majority of the countries in the region. Brazil's identity is that of a middle or regional power;[150] it therefore wants the United States to treat it differently from the way it treats the other Latin American states. To this end, Brasília has been working for decades in consolidating its own regional bloc.[151] Thus, two years after Bush's Initiative for the Americas was launched, then Foreign Minister Fernando Henrique Cardoso referred to his country's region as "a South American platform", and later, as president (1995–2002), indicated that Mercosur was "a pole from which we will organize the South American space."[152] Not that the regional integration efforts had been particularly successful, but on these matters, as Tanja Börzel has put it, "*It is not only the economy, stupid!*"[153]

Brazil's intelligent strategy of not simply rejecting the FTAA but rather engaging it and influencing it from within did not go unnoticed in the United States. Arizona representative Jim Kolbe, at the July 1997 Hearings on the FTAA, lamented the lack of US leadership: "While we wait, Brazil dictates the timetable and structure of negotiations for the FTAA."[154] With Washington and Brasília vying for leadership, formal negotiations were launched at the April 1998 Summit of the Americas in Santiago. Two years later, Chile put forward a proposal—supported by Argentina and the United States—to accelerate the pace of the negotiations, in order to bring them to an end in 2003 instead of 2005, as agreed in the first Summit of the Americas and reiterated at the second; Brazil did not budge.[155] The Cardoso administration was well aware that its distant economic relation with the United States gave it some leeway in the FTAA negotiations; as Rubens Barbosa, its ambassador to Washington put it,

> it is important when one considers the Brazilian position in relation to regional integration, both in South America and the hemisphere, to understand that as far as Brazil is concerned the major trading partner for us is not the United States ... this has to be seen in perspective when one tries to understand our position in relation to the trade negotiation.[156]

Thus, in accordance with its long-standing policy of regional consolidation, in 2000 Brazil played host to a South American Summit—the first of its kind to take place among the 12 countries of the region. For President Cardoso, the Summit was a "moment of reaffirmation of South America's identity as a region".[157]

Brazil's reinforced position by the turn of the century was noticeable in the treatment it received from the United States in the last years of the negotiating process.[158] President Cardoso made clear that the regional trade agreement was just a possibility for his country. As he put it at the third Summit of the Americas held in Quebec in April 2001, "The FTAA is an option, the Mercosur a destiny."[159] A few weeks after the WTO Doha November 2001 ministerial conference, from which his country emerged with a victory over the United States on the issue of drug patents, Brazil's foreign minister, Celso Lafer, stated quite frankly that for the regional trade agreement to progress, "there has to be an understanding between Brazil and the United States."[160]

That is indeed what happened—that is, the understanding, because the advancement of the hemispheric trade project remained unclear. Thus, at the November 2003 ministerial meeting in Miami, Washington gave up on the "single undertaking" principle, and acquiesced to Brasília's preference for an à la carte FTAA. Under this scheme, countries would be able to subscribe sub-regional arrangements with increased benefits and commitments. This turn of events did not please countries such as Canada, Chile and México, but it was clearly a win for Brazil.[161] USTR Zoellick explained his country's concession in terms of the process

> moving from general concepts and people talking past one another to positive realities and opportunities. We're moving into a relentlessly practical stage to be on track and we're at a point where we're negotiating an ALCA [i.e., FTAA] not just seeking it.[162]

Significantly, by the time of the Miami ministerial meeting, Brazil's government had undergone a significant change, as Luiz Inácio Lula da Silva, from the leftist Workers' Party, had replaced Cardoso in January 2003. A former union leader and fierce free trade critic, Lula would nevertheless mostly maintain his predecessor's stance on international commerce (as well as that on domestic macroeconomic policy.[163] Thus, for instance, in his inaugural address, Lula referred to the importance of free trade to his country, and explicitly reaffirmed his administration's intention to remain in the FTAA negotiating process; the United States–Brazil co-chairmanship of the hemispheric pact's negotiations actually coincided with Lula's arrival to power.[164]

Brazil's continued engagement with the FTAA process, though, did not mean that it would lower its guard in the negotiations, as the already-mentioned outcome of the November 2003 ministerial meeting made clear. The United States certainly contributed to the tougher stance of the new administration. In late 2002, in its attempt to get Trade Promotion Authority, the Bush administration had to make some concessions to protectionist members of Congress; some of them had to do with the inclusion of environmental and labor issues in future agreements, something Brazil and other Latin American countries were opposed to. But another concession was one that was anathema to Brasília: the increase in agricultural subsidies. Furthermore, the trade authorization bill also required Congressional approval before the United States lowered tariffs on numerous agricultural products, among them some of Brazil's main exports.[165] To make things worse, in February 2003 the Bush administration announced that it would offer differentiated market access to the negotiating parties depending on the hemispheric bloc to which they belonged—and Mercosur got the least favorable treatment; not surprisingly, Brazil did not take this well.[166]

Additionally, as if to compensate for the major accommodation it had made to Brasília on the hemispheric agreement at the Miami ministerial meeting (the à la carte FTAA), Washington announced a string of bilateral trade agreements with countries of the region (e.g., Colombia and Perú); the United States also revealed that it would start negotiations leading to an investment pact with Uruguay. Not that this move was unexpected or proscribed from the FTAA architecture, but it certainly suggested a sort of divide-and-conquer strategy on Washington's part. USTR Zoellick went on record to defend his country's approach saying: "from the start, the United States has worked on two tracks to create free trade in the Hemisphere."[167]

Regardless of Washington's intentions, the acceptance of a two-tier, light, or à la carte FTAA effectively doomed it. For starters, the initial (at Miami) lack of definition of what the differentiated commitments would entail made ulterior discussions on the matter sterile. Thus, for instance, at a subsequent meeting on the matter a few months later in Puebla (México), the parties, starting with the co-chairs, were unable to reach an agreement on what the baseline "common rights and obligations" for all members were, and how they differed from the increased commitments reached by some countries on a plurilateral basis.[168] The FTAA's stalemate, on the other hand, was perhaps Brazil's best alternative.[169]

Not surprisingly, then, when 2005—the year set for reaching an agreement—came and 34 hemispheric leaders met for the fourth Summit of the

Americas in Mar del Plata (Argentina), the FTAA was a flop. Thus, the Summit's declaration presented divergent views: one of 29 countries stating that they "remain committed to the achievement of a balanced and comprehensive FTAA Agreement," and another of 5 countries which "maintain that the necessary conditions are not yet in place for achieving a balanced and equitable free trade agreement."[170] The dissenting countries were all South American: Argentina, Brazil, Paraguay, Uruguay and Venezuela. The region's pink wave, as instantiated in the Mercosur countries, as well as the more radical position of Venezuela, and not only Brazil, of course played an instrumental role in the FTAA's final demise.[171] But there is no doubt that Brazil was a major force in the hemispheric project's fate. Noticeably, the day after the FTAA's failure, presidents Bush and Lula met in Brasília and expressed their interest in pursuing a broad bilateral agenda of cooperation.[172]

4) Conclusions

The preceding account of US economic statecraft toward South America makes clear that, notwithstanding the larger economic and political distance separating the countries of the region from the United States, the latter has operated under the logic of the "hegemonic presumption." In this case, however, one could argue that there were some signs of diminished US power, as instantiated in the economic realm, throughout the entire period (1971–2016). But this decline did not seem to necessarily correspond to mere material capabilities, as measured by GDP; the ratio of the region's GDP to US' GDP remained largely constant (9.4% in 1971, 16.44% in 2016); South America's trade dependence on the United States also changed, but not by much of a decrease (going from 18% in the first year of the period, to 17% in the last).[173] There is something else then to the power relations between the Andean and Southern Cone countries with the United States than mere material capabilities.

During the first sub-period (1971–1989), popular and academic debate on US decline notwithstanding, Washington managed its economic statecraft toward the region in accordance with the hegemonic presumption. This was the case particularly in the US reaction to the Socialist turn in Chile under Salvador Allende; among other strategies, the Nixon administration resorted to blatant economic coercion. This was of course not the best manner to manage its economic and political relations with Santiago and the region, but the paranoid, domino-theory mentality prevalent in Washington made it seem like the logical way to proceed. The United States' influence attempt was twofold: 1) to prevent Allende from taking office, and subsequently to remove him; 2) to send a message of resolve to the rest of the hemisphere and to the Soviet Union. Washington's target was of course the Allende administration; although the financial costs to achieve the objectives were not high—for US standards—the reputational costs in the hemisphere and abroad were—and the United States was willing to pay them.

Although the demise of the Allende administration was not the direct result of US economic statecraft, it was no doubt a significant contributing factor. From Washington's standpoint, therefore, the influence attempt it deployed through its economic statecraft toward Chile (in addition to the other kinds of pressure, such as covert operations, it resorted to) worked. But the reputational costs the United States had to pay were no doubt high—with much of the international community blaming it, rightly or not, for the coup against Allende's democratically elected government. Furthermore, the abrupt change in foreign economic policy toward the Southern Cone country once General Augusto Pinochet took power only increased the worldwide questioning of US leadership. Somewhat paradoxically, though, US hegemony did not suffer much in Chile's neighborhood, as other countries in South America were also under dictatorial regimes in the 1970s and were not particularly concerned about democracy in the region.

Thus, Perú's challenge to the United States on the debt crisis was not just a wild gamble. It was not only that Washington's role in Allende's Chile was still fresh, but there were other more recent or current examples (e.g., Grenada 1983, Nicaragua, at least since Reagan had taken office), but also the transition to democracy that had taken place in several countries of the region, meant that the United States was not exactly popular in Latin America as a whole. Hence, Washington's concern to president's García's defiance was not limited to the actions of the Andean country, but to potential spread of the challenge to other countries of the region. Hence, the Reagan administration acted to both punish Perú and entice other countries to its successive debt alleviation programs. Washington was willing to incur the necessary financial costs in order to prevent the financial system of which it was, in the last resort, responsible. The US approach, particularly the Brady Plan, worked—at least in isolating Perú and defusing the crisis.

Things only got better for the exercise of the United States' power, as instantiated in the economic realm in South America in the 1990s, the second sub-period of this work. As noted, the Washington Consensus meant that the countries of the hemisphere were largely on board with the Colossus of the North's approach to economic affairs, both domestically and internationally. Thus, even if the United States was not able to make good on president Clinton's promise to bring in Chile to NAFTA, as Santiago had requested, its overall economic liberalization agenda gathered steam with the 1994 Summit of the Americas. Significantly, for domestic reasons Washington did not spend much capital on bringing the South American countries to the fold—one could argue that Chile was already in, but US credence in the region certainly suffered by not being able to fulfill its promise to the region's economic poster child during the unipolar moment.

But it would seem that when matters were more pressing, Washington was able to get its act together. Thus, operating under the logic of the war on drugs, and considering narcotics trafficking as a national security problem,

George H. W. Bush's administration was able to develop the cited economic assistance program to help Andean countries curtail coca production. This was an explicit influence attempt at reducing the supply of drugs by providing one-way free trade access for some products of the beneficiary countries to the US market. Once again, Washington was willing to pay the domestic political price as well as the financial costs involved in granting preferential access to Andean exports. Although the program was not particularly successful in its stated objectives, it certainly gained Washington the good will of the countries involved—to the extent that they would later insist on the program's renewal.

Finally, during the third sub-period considered in this work (2001–2016), United States' economic statecraft was considerably less effective in maintaining the country's power in South America. In the first case reviewed here, it is clear that Washington's radical disengagement from Argentina's plight did not result in increased US influence in the austral country. Although, as noted, Washington's new take on the management of the international financial crisis eventually helped Buenos Aires negotiate with its creditors, Washington saw its standing with the austral country substantially weakened. Thus, US saving of financial resources was not a cheap strategy—it had to pay the price of alienating Buenos Aires in the years to come.

This estrangement was particularly important in the context of the failed FTAA negotiations. As noted, Washington and Brasília were leading the last phase of the negotiating process; in that context, it was particularly important not to alienate the other countries of the region. As it turned out, Argentina was not on the US side. Brazil, on the other hand, true to its identity as a regional power, played its cards with dexterity by engaging the process and building regional support for its cautious approach to the hemispheric trade deal. In the end, despite Washington's concessions to Brasília, the trade project failed. The United States attempt at influencing the trade policy of the hemisphere as a whole failed.

That did not of course mean that Washington's economic influence on the region had vanished—after all 29 out of the 34 countries involved in the negotiations favored the agreement, but with Brazil playing a key role in the last phase of the negotiations, the United States did not get what it wanted regarding the hemispheric pact. In this sense, US power as exercised through its economic statecraft in the early 21st century took a blow.

However, the setback in Washington's power in South America in particular and Latin America in general seems to have been temporary. Soon after the FTAA fiasco, as noted, several countries—some of them in South America—signed FTAs with the United States. Furthermore, as the commodities boom passed, the pink wave lost momentum, and Washington regained the upper hand on the broader economic principles; the arrival of the much less unilateral-oriented Obama administration no doubt contributed a great deal to the change in Inter-American relations as they pertained to economic affairs.

Notes

1   In Dent 1999: 2.
2   In LaFeber 1965: 37.
3   In McDougall 1997, 62.
4   In McCaffrey 1992: 66; McCaffrey's emphasis.
5   Dent 1999: 12–13.
6   Deblock and Turcotte 2005: 17.
7   U.S. House of Representatives 2007: 1.
8   U.S. House of Representatives 2000.
9   Riggirozzi and Grugel 2015: 786.
10   Lowenthal 1976: 201.
11   Viña del Mar 1969: 403.
12   Lowenthal 1976: 208.
13   Hersh 1974: 14.
14   Malamud 2002: 3; Sennes et al. 2006: 2.
15   Wilson 1992.
16   Jordan 1994: 367.
17   Davidow 1997.
18   Rusell and Tokatlian 2004: 18.
19   Zoellick 2003a.
20   Leogrande 2007: 385.
21   Biegon 2017: 82.
22   U.S. House of Representatives 2007: 1–2.
23   Hornbeck 2006: 13.
24   Department of State 2007.
25   Ibid.
26   *New York Times* 1971.
27   Nixon 1971a.
28   In Petras and Morley 1975: 83.
29   Fagen 1975: 305; Petras and Morley 1975: 104–105.
30   *New York Times* 1971.
31   Department of State 2014.
32   Kissinger 1979: 657.
33   Winn 1976; Kissinger 1979: 659; Sigmund 1982: 24.
34   Sigmund 1982: 24.
35   Scully and Valenzuela 1993: 208.
36   Kissinger 1979: 673; Sigmund 1982: 24–25.
37   Ibid.: 654.
38   Ibid.: 661.
39   In ibid.: 681.
40   Ibid.: 681.
41   U.S. Senate 1975: 33.
42   Petras and Morley 1975: 195, note 36.
43   Kissinger 1979: 682.
44   Sigmund 1982: 26.
45   Petras and Morley 1975: 93.
46   Streeter 2004: 10.
47   Sigmund 1974: 325.
48   Sigmund 1982: 26; Petras and Morley 1975: 98; Sigmund 1974: 333.
49   Sigmund 1982: 26–27.
50   U.S. Senate 1975: 2.
51   Sigmund 1982: 29.

52   Fagen 1975: 300.
53   Kirkpatrick 1979; Kirkpatrick 1981: 31.
54   In Sigmund 1982: 36.
55   Bridges 1987.
56   *New York Times* 1971.
57   In Bridges 1987.
58   Ibid.
59   O'Brien 1993: 88–89.
60   Neff 1986.
61   Riding 1985a.
62   García 1985a: 28.
63   García 1985b: 9.
64   In Riding 1985a.
65   McClintock 2000: 5.
66   Neff 1986; Riding 1985a.
67   In Riding 1985b.
68   Roett 1985: 283.
69   In Makin 1989: 11.
70   Katz and Mahler 1992: 197.
71   Hayes 1988/1989: 191-192; Felix 1990: 740–41.
72   O'Brien 1993: 99; McCLintock 2000: 5–6.
73   U.S. Senate 1987; Hayes 1988/1989: 192; Felix 1990: 741.
74   Sachs 1989: 8; Whitehead 1989: 145.
75   *New York Times* 1987.
76   Felix 1990: 744.
77   O'Brien 1993: 86–87.
78   McClintock 2000: 1.
79   Solervicens 2003: 3.
80   Rosales 2003.
81   Wilson 1992.
82   Bush 1991 [1990]: 1738.
83   Jordan 1994: 367.
84   Wilson 1992.
85   Tulchin 1993: 73.
86   Nelson 2015: 76.
87   Ibid.: 79; Poggio 2011: 193.
88   In Sanger 1994.
89   Miller 1996: 155.
90   Zoellick 2003b.
91   *CQ Almanac* 1997.
92   In CNN 1998.
93   Nelson 2015: 92; Hughes 2003: 2; Apple 1998.
94   Arashiro 2011: 99.
95   Rosales 2003.
96   Ibid.
97   Ibid.
98   Nixon 1971b.
99   GAO 2002: 1.
100 McClintock 2000: 39–40.
101 White House 1989: 59, 61.
102 Ibid.: 69
103 In ATPA 1990.

104 U.S. House of Representatives 1991: 140.
105 USITC 1995: 1.
106 USTR 2001: 3.
107 Ibid.: 3.
108 Ibid.: 4.
109 Cavallo 2004: 137.
110 Página/12 2001.
111 U.S. House of Representatives 200: 2.
112 Cavallo 2004: 138, 141–142, 144.
113 U.S. House of Representatives 2002: 35.
114 Corrales 2002: 36; Scoffield 2001; Gerstenzang 2001.
115 Helleiner 2005: 960.
116 U.S. Senate 2002: 40.
117 Ibid.: 6; Helleiner 2005: 951.
118 *The Economist* 2001.
119 In Kahn 2001.
120 Bush 2001; BBC 2001.
121 In Gerstenzang 2001.
122 Rusell and Tokatlian 2004: 20.
123 Felix 2001.
124 *The Economist* 2001.
125 U.S. Senate 2002: 23.
126 U.S. Senate 2004: 7.
127 Helleiner 2005.
128 Cavallo 2004: 147.
129 U.S. Senate 2004: 7.
130 Ibid.: 18.
131 Ibid.: 25; Helleiner 2005: 951.
132 In Setser 2005.
133 Helleiner 2005: 956.
134 Latinobarómetro 2017: 10.
135 Cavallo 2004: 148.
136 In Helleiner 2005: 960.
137 Latinobarómetro 2017: 7
138 U.S. Senate 2004: 10.
139 Rohter 2002.
140 Van Rompay 2004: 120.
141 Arashiro 2011: 33.
142 Nelson 2015: 74, 82.
143 Cardoso 2015: 1504; Arashiro 2011: 100; Nelson 2015: 77.
144 Arashiro 2011: 34–35; Nelson 2015: 85–86.
145 Nelson 2015: 92.
146 Arashiro 2011: 39–40.
147 Nelson 2015: 90.
148 Hirst 2005: 33; Van Rompay 2004: 122.
149 Feinberg 1997: 146.
150 Lafer 2000: 65; Merke 2015 :181.
151 Arashiro 2011: 110; Carranza 2004: 321–322.
152 Both in Poggio 2011: 192.
153 Börzel *et al.* 2012: 258; italics original.
154 U.S. House of Representatives 1997: 10.
155 Van Rompay 2004: 125.

156   U.S. House of Representatives 2000.
157   In Poggio 2011: 203.
158   Corrales 2015: 217.
159   In Briceño 2007: 7.
160   In Rohter with Rich 2001; Rich 2001.
161   Hornbeck 2005: 1; Nelson 2015: 107; Deblock and Turcotte 2005: 29; Poggio 2011: 205.
162   Zoellick 2003c.
163   Williamson 2002: 110; Fishlow 2003: 288, 290.
164   Barbosa 2003: 1018.
165   Poggio 2011: 205; Rohter with Rich 2001.
166   Hirst 2009: 36; Nelson 2015: 106.
167   In Nelson 2015: 108.
168   Hornbeck 2005: 1.
169   Hornbeck 2006: 14.
170   OAS 2005.
171   *New York Times* 2005; Rother and Bumiller 2005.
172   Hirst 2009:38.
173   The countries included are: Argentina, Brazil, Chile, Colombia and Perú. Source for GDP: World Bank 2019. Source for trade: OEC 2019 https://atlas.media.mit.edu/en/visualize/tree_map/sitc/export/

References

Apple, R. W. (1998, September 25). View from abroad: U.S. policy sapped by scandal. *New York Times*.

Arashiro, Z. (2011). *Negotiating the free trade area of the Americas*. New York: Palgrave MacMillan.

ATPA (1990). Andean Trade Preference Act Submitted. *Foreign Policy Bulletin*, 1(3), 75.

Barbosa, R. A. (2003). The free trade area of the Americas and Brazil. *Fordham International Law Journal*, 27(4), 1017–1028.

BBC (2001, April 26). Argentina's struggle to contain crisis. *BBC News*.

Biegon, R. (2017). The United States and Latin America in the Trans-Pacific partnership: Renewing hegemony in a post-Washington consensus hemisphere? *Latin American Perspectives*, 44(4), 81–98.

Börzel, T. A., et al (2012). *Roads to regionalism: Genesis, design, and effects of regional organizations*. Farnham: Ashgate Publishing.

Briceño, J. (2007). *The new regionalism in South America: From SAFTA and the South American community of nations*. Paper presented at the 48th Conference of the International Studies Association, February 28–March 3, Chicago, IL.

Bridges, T. (1987, September 6). Pinochet's reforms boost Chilean economy. *Washington Post*.

Bush, G. H. W. (1991 [1990]). *Public papers of the presidents of the United States: George Bush 1990*. Washington, DC: U.S. Government Printing Office.

Bush, G. W. (2001, April 22). *George W. Bush: The president's news conference with summit of the Americas leaders in Quebec City*. Collection: Public Papers of the Presidents. Retrieved from http://presidency.proxied.lsit.ucsb.edu/ws/index.php?pid=45638

Cardoso, F. H. (2015). *A arte da política: A história que vivi*. Rio de Janeiro: Civilizaçao Brasileria.

Carranza, M. E. (2004). Mercosur and the end game of the FTAA negotiations: Challenges and prospects after the Argentine crisis. *Third World Quarterly, 25*(2), 319–337.

Cavallo, D. (2004). Argentina and the IMF during the two Bush administrations. *International Finance, 7*(1), 137–150.

CNN (1998, April 16) In Chile, Clinton seeks patience on free trade. *CNN – World News.*

Corrales, J. (2002). The politics of Argentina's meltdown. *World Policy Journal, 19*(3), 29–42.

Corrales, J. (2015). Understanding international partnership: The complicated rapprochement between the United States and Brazil. *Political Science Quarterly, 130*(2), 213–244.

CQ Almanac. (1997). 'Clinton Loses 'Fast Track' Trade Bid'. *CQ Almanac.*

Davidow, J. (1997, July 22). *The Free Trade of the Americas.* Ways and Means Committee: U.S. Department of State. Retrieved from https://1997-2001.state.gov/regions/wha/072297_davidow.html

Deblock, C., & Turcotte, S. (2005). Estados Unidos, Brasil y las Negociaciones Hemisféricas: El ALCA en Modalidad Bilateral. *Foro Internacional, 45*(1), 5–34.

Dent, D. (1999). *The legacy of the Monroe Doctrine. A reference guide to U.S. involvement in Latin America and the Caribbean.* Westport, CT: Greenwood Press.

Department of State (2007). *The case for the U.S.-Perú trade promotion agreement.* Fact Sheet, Bureau of Economic, Energy and Business Affairs, Washington, D.C. 13 July.

DOS (2014). *Foreign relations of the United States, 1969–1976, Volume XXI, Chile, 1969–1973.* Washington, DC: U.S. Government Printing Office.

Economist (2001, July 19). How the bug can spread. *Economist, 360* (8231).

Fagen, R. (1975). The United States and Chile: Roots and branches. *Foreign Affairs, 53*(2), 297–313.

Feinberg, R. (1997). *Summitry in the Americas: A progress report.* Washington, DC: Institute for International Economics.

Felix, D. (1990). Latin America's debt crisis. *World Policy Journal, 7*(4), 733–771.

Felix, D. (2001). After the fall: The Argentine crisis and possible repercussions. *Institute for Policy Studies.*

Fishlow, A. (2003). Brazil: FTA or FTAA or WTO? In J. Schott (Ed.), *Free trade agreements: US strategies and priorities* (pp. 277–296). Washington, DC: Institute for International Economics.

GAO (2002). *Drug control: Efforts to develop alternatives to cultivating illicit crops in Colombia have made little progress and face serious obstacles* (GAO Report No. 02.291). Washington, DC: U.S. Government Printing Office.

García, A. (1985a) Mensaje del Presidente Consititucional del Perú, Doctor Alan García Pérez, Ante el Congreso Nacional, 28 de julio.

García, A. (1985b). *Provisional verbatim record of the fifth meeting.* UN General Assembly, New York, September 23.

Gerstenzang, J. (2001, July 14). White House rejects bailout of Argentina. *Los Angeles Times.*

Hayes, M. D. (1988/1989). The U.S. and Latin America: A lost decade? *Foreign Affairs, 68*(1), 180–198.

Helleiner, E. (2005). The strange story of Bush and the Argentine debt crisis. *Third World Quarterly, 26*(6), 951–969.

Hersh, S. M. (1974, September 11). Censored matter in book about C.I.A. said to have related Chile activities. *New York Times.*

Hirst, M. (2005). *The United States and Brazil: A long road of unmet expectations.* New York: Routledge.

Hirst, M. (2009). Las relaciones Brasil-Estados Unidos: Al compass de nuevas coincidencias. *Foreign Affairs Latinoamérica, 9*(2), 33–42.

Hornbeck, J. F. (2005). *A free trade area of the Americas: Major policy issues and status of negotiations* (Report No. RS20864). Washington, DC: Congressional Research Service.

Hornbeck, J. F. (2006). *Brazilian trade policy and the United States* (Report No. RL 33258). Washington, DC: Congressional Research Service.

Hughes, K. (2003). *American trade politics: From the omnibus act of 1988 to the trade act of 2002.* Paper prepared for presentation at the Congress Project/Project on America and the Global Economy seminar on "Congress and Trade Policy" at the Woodrow Wilson International Center for Scholars, November 17.

Jordan, K. M. (1994). Intellectual property under NAFTA: Is Chile up to the challenge. *The Journal of Comparative and International Law, 2*(2), 367–380.

Kahn, J. (2001, August 22). Argentina gets $8 billion aid from the I.M.F. *New York Times.*

Katz, C., & Mahler, V. (1992). Three views of Latin American debt crisis. *Cooperation and Conflict, 27*(2), 191–213.

Kirkpatrick, J. (1979). Dictatorships and double standards. *Commentary, 68*(5), 34–45.

Kirkpatrick, J. (1981). U.S. security & Latin America. *Commentary, 71*(1), 29–40.

Kissinger, H. (1979). *White House years.* Boston, MA: Little, Brown and Company.

Lafeber, W. (Ed.) (1965). *John Quincy Adams and American continental empire: Letters, papers and speeches.* Chicago, IL: Quadrangle Books.

Lafer, C. (2000). Dilemmas and challenges in Brazil's foreign policy. *Estudos Avançados, 14*(38), 63–71.

Latinobarómetro (2017). *La era de Trump Imagen de Estados Unidos en América Latina.* Santiago: Corporación Latinobarómetro.

Leogrande, W. (2007). A poverty of imagination: George W. Bush's policy in Latin America. *Journal of Latin American Studies, 39*(2), 355–385.

Lowenthal, A. F. (1976) Two hundred years of American foreign policy: The United States and Latin America: Ending the hegemonic presumption. *Foreign Affairs, 55*(1), 199–213.

Makin, J. (1989). Developing-country debt problems after seven years. In R. Dornbusch, J. H. Makin & D. Zlowe (Eds.), *Alternative solutions to developing-country debt problems* (pp. 9–20). Washington, DC: American Enterprise Institute for Public Policy Research.

Malamud, C. (2002). México abandona el TIAR: Implicaciones continentales de la iniciativa. *Boletín Elcano,* (5), 1–5.

McCaffrey, J. (1992). *Army of manifest destiny: The American soldier in the Mexican war, 1846–1848.* New York: New York University Press.

McClintock, C. (2000). *The United States and Peru in the 1990s: Cooperation with a critical caveat on democratic standards.* Washington, DC: Department of Political Science, The George Washington University.

McDougall, W. A. (1997). *Promised land, crusader state: The American encounter with the world since 1776.* New York: Mariner Books.

Merke, F. (2015). Neither balance nor bandwagon: South American international society meets Brazil's rising power. *International Politics, 52*(2), 178–192.

Miller, M. A. (1996). Will the circle be unbroken? Chile's accession to the NAFTA and the fast-track debate. *Valparaiso University Law Review, 31*(1), 153–190.

Neff, R. (1986, August 26). A House of cards in Peru. *Washington Post.*

Nelson, M. (2015). *A history of the FTAA: From hegemony to fragmentation in the Americas.* New York: Palgrave MacMillan.

New York Times (1971, August 15). The nation. *New York Times.*

New York Times (1987, February 15). Bradley Warns of foreign-debt impact. *New York Times.*

New York Times (2005, November 6). Negotiators fail to agree on free trade proposal at Americas summit. *New York Times*.

Nixon, R. (1971a). 374. Memorandum by president Nixon. *Office of the Historian*.

Nixon, R (1971b). Press conference: President Nixon declares drug abuse "Public Enemy Number One". *Richard Nixon Foundation*.

O'Brien, P. (1993). The Latin American debt crisis. In S. Riley (Ed.), *The politics of global debt* (pp. 85–112). Houndmills: Macmillan Press.

OAS (2005). *Declaration of Mar del Plata*, Fourth Summit of the Americas, November 5, Mar del Plata, Argentina.

OEC (2019). Visualizations: Export destinations. *The Observatory of Economic Complexity* (Accessed on May 13, 2019).

Pagina/12 (2001, January 25). La frase sobre las relaciones carnales fue una estupidez. *Pagina/12*.

Petras, J., & Morley, M. (1975). *The United States and Chile: Imperialism and the overthrow of the Allende government*. New York: Monthly Review Press.

Poggio, C. G. (2011). Brazil and the instituionaliztion of South America: From hemispheric estrangement to cooperative hegemony. *Revista Brasileira de Política Internacional*, *54*(2), 189–211.

Rich, J. (2001, November 16). Brazil welcomes global move on drug patents. *New York Times*.

Riding, A. (1985a, July 29). Peru's new chief to limit payments on foreign debt. *New York Times*.

Riding, A. (1985b, December 23). U.S. distressed by Peru, but eager to avoid clash. *New York Times*.

Riggirozzi, P., & Grugel, J. (2015). Regional governance and legitimacy in South America: The meaning of UNASUR. *International Affairs*, *91*(4), 781–797.

Roett, R. (1985). Peru: The messege from García. *Foreign Affairs*, *64*(2), 275–286.

Rohter, L. with Rich, J. (2001, December 19). Brazil takes a trade stance and offers a Warning to U.S. *New York Times*.

Rohter, L. (2002, January 20). Argentina and the U.S. grow apart over a crisis. *New York Times*.

Rosales, O. (2003). Chile-U.S. *Free trade agreement: Lessons and best practices*. Paper presented at the American Chamber of Commerce, Washington, April 28.

Rother, L, & Bumiller, E. (2005, November 6). Hemisphere meeting ends without trade consensus. *New York Times*.

Rusell, R., & Tokatlian, J. G. (2004). Argentina, Brasil y Estados Unidos: El desafío de una esfera de cooperación. *Agenda Internacional (Argentina)*, Year 1, No. 2, 16–30.

Sachs, J. D. (1989). New approaches to the Latin American debt crisis. *Essays in International Finance* No. 174. Princeton, NJ: Princeton University.

Sanger, D. E. (1994, December 12). Chile is admitted as North American free trade partner. *New York Times*.

Scoffield, H. (2001, August 22). IMF agrees to Argentine bailout. *Globe and Mail*.

Scully, T. R., & Valenzuela, J. S. (1993). De la democracia a la democracia: Continuidad y variaciones en las preferencias del electorado y en el sistema de partidos en Chile. *Estudios Públicos*, *51*(Invierno), 195–228.

Sennes, R., Onuki, J., & Olveira, J. (2006). The Brazilian foreign policy and the hemispheric security. *Revista Fuerzas Armadas y Sociedad*, *1*(se) [sic].

Setser, B. (2005). Bush has yet to meet a big IMF bailout he does not like. *Council on Foreign Relations*.

Sigmund, P. E. (1974). The "Invisible Blockade" and the overthrow of Allende. *Foreign Affairs, 52*(2), 322–340.

Sigmund, P. E. (1982). Chile: Successful intervention? In R. Wesson (Ed.), *U.S influence in Latin America in the 1980s* (pp. 20–39). New York: Praeger Publishers.

Solervicens, M. (2003). *Impactos del Tratado de Libre Comercio entre Chile y Estados Unidos.* Montreal, QC: CIEM.

Streeter, S. (2004). *Destabilizing Chile: The United States and the overthrow of Allende.* Paper presented at the Latin America Studies Association Convention, Las Vegas, October 7.

Tulchin, J. (1993). La Iniciativa para las Américas: ¿Gesto vacío, astuta maniobra estratégica, o notable giro en las relaciones hemisféricas? In FLACSO (Ed.). *America Latina y la Iniciativa para las Américas* (pp. 53–80). Chile: FLACSO.

U.S. House of Representatives (1991). *Andean trade preference act of 1991.* Hearing before the Subcommittee on Trade of the Committee on Ways and Means, July 25. Washington, DC: U.S. Government Printing Office.

U.S. House of Representatives (1997). *Free trade area of the Americas.* Hearing before the Subcommittee on Trade of the Committee on Ways and Means, July 22. Washington, DC: U.S. Government Printing Office.

U.S. House of Representatives (2000). *U.S. relations with Brazil: Strategic partners or regional competitors?* Hearing before the Subcommittee on the Western Hemisphere of the Committee on International Relations, July 26. Washington, DC: U.S. Government Printing Office.

U.S. House of Representatives (2002). *Argentina's economic meltdown: Causes and remedies.* Hearing before the Subcommittee on International Monetary Policy and Trade of the Committee on Financial Services, February 6 and March 5. Washington, DC: U.S. Government Printing Office.

U.S. House of Representatives (2007). *South America and the United States: How to fix a broken relationship.* Hearing before the Committee on Foreign Affairs, June 19. Washington, DC: U.S. Government Printing Office.

USITC (1995). *Andean Trade Preference Act: Impact on U.S. Industries and Consumers and on Drug Crop Eradication and Crop Substitution (Second Report).* Washington DC: United States International Trade Commission.

U.S. Senate (1975). *Covert action in Chile 1963–1973, Staff report of the select committee to study governmental operations with respect to intelligence activities.* Washington, DC: U.S. Government Printing Office.

U.S. Senate (1987). *Impact of the Latin American debt crisis on the United States.* Hearing before the Subcommittee on International Debt of the Committee on Finance United States Senate, March 9. Washington, DC: U.S. Government Printing Office.

U.S. Senate (2002). *Argentina's economic crisis.* Hearing before the Subcommittee on International Trade and Finance of the Committee on Banking, Housing, and Urban Affairs, February 28. Washington, DC: U.S. Government Printing Office.

U.S. Senate (2004). *Argentina's financial crisis.* Hearing before the Subcommittee on International Trade and Finance of the Committee on Banking, Housing, and Urban Affairs, March 10. Washington, DC: U.S. Government Printing Office.

USTR (2001). *Third report to the congress on the operation of the Andean trade preference act.* Washington, DC: U.S. Government Printing Office.

Van Rompay, J. (2004). Brazil's strategy towards the FTAA. In P. Vizentini & M. Wiesebron (Eds.), *Free trade for the Americas? The United States' push for the FTAA agreement* (pp. 120–148). New York: Zed Books.

Viña del Mar. (1969). Consenso Latinoamericano de Viña del Mar. *Estudios Internacionales, 3*(11), 403–418.

White House (1989). *National drug control strategy.* Washington, DC: U.S. Government Printing Office.

Whitehead, L. (1989). Latin American debt: An international bargaining perspective. *Review of International Studies, 15*(3), 231–249.

Williamson, J. (2002). Lula's Brazil. *Foreign Affairs, 82*(1), 105–113.

Wilson, M. (1992). A U.S.–Chile free trade agreement: Igniting economic prosperity in the Americas. *The Heritage Foundation.*

Winn, P. (1976, May 9). Chile was the Watergate of United States foreign policy. *New York Times.*

World Bank (2019). Gross domestic product [NY.GDP.MKTP.CD]. Retrieved from https://data.worldbank.org/indicator/NY.GDP.MKTP.CD

Zoellick, R. B. (2003a, July 10). Our Credo: Free trade and competitions. *Wall Street Journal.*

Zoellick, R. (2003b, September 22). America will not wait for the won't do countries. *Financial Times.*

Zoellick, R. (2003c). Concluding ministerial press conference, VIII free trade area of the Americas ministerial, November 20, Miami, FL.

Conclusions

In this concluding chapter I undertake three tasks: first, I briefly go over the exercise of US power through its economic statecraft in the different countries and regions covered in the analytical narratives presented above, in each of the three sub-periods established in the introduction; second, I return to the discussion on the nature of power, regional orders and economic statecraft, and, third, I extend the argument to the fate of US hegemony since Donald Trump's arrival into the White House.

On the first assignment, the first thing to note is that during the initial sub-period (1971–1989) material capabilities as measured by the ratio of hemispheric GDP of the countries reviewed to that of the U.S., as well as by the trade dependency (understood as the percentage of exports sent to the United States) of the latter on the former, did not substantially change (22% and 25% for GDP in the first and last years of the sub-period, respectively, and 32% and 43% for trade dependency for the same years, also respectively).[1] There was, however, some variation in the power relationship, as exerted through economic statecraft, between the United States and (some of) the countries covered, as noted in the last four chapters' concluding sections. Something more than brute facts are needed to account for these dynamics.

That something could be the merely strategic approach taken by Washington and the other capitals involved. That is, both the United States and the other hemispheric countries covered here could have approached their broad economic relationship from a purely transactional perspective, without advancing other claims (such as the mutual political relationship, the responsibility and leadership of the United States, or the impact of the economic issue in question on security matters, for instance). As the cases reviewed show, however, non-economic arguments, many of which implied legitimacy, were part and parcel of the power relationship between the United States and the rest of the hemisphere—and not only during the first sub-period, but for the whole period covered (1971–2016).

Thus, for instance, throughout the 1971–1989 span, the United States by and large maintained a liberal trade policy, broadly defined, from which the countries of the hemisphere benefited—and Washington made sure to constantly proselytize the economic benefits of its doctrine, as well as to make his political beneficence known. There were of course exceptions to US economic practice—starting right at beginning of the period, when the Nixon administration imposed the surcharge on US imports, or when the Reagan administration ventured into managed trade—but in general Washington favored free trade. The contentiousness of domestic politics, as well as the protectionist lurches displayed during these years dented, but did not demolish, the US pro-trade identity. Thus, the rest of the Americas looked for United States' leadership on the matter, and demanded Washington be congruous with its stated discourse on commerce. Canada's free trade proposal to its southern neighbor in the mid-1980s was a sign that Ottawa both shared Washington's long-advocated position on the matter and trusted the United States enough to be willing to deepen its economic (and political) relationship with it. Ottawa was confident that something of the postwar special relationship with Washington remained. The United States' protracted influence attempt on the bilateral economic (and political) relationship paid off, and by the late 1980s, the CUSFTA went into effect.

México's conversion to the free trade camp took a little bit longer. In the meantime, the United States by and large exercised restraint so as not to appear like a bully. Thus, when México City first flirted with the idea of joining GATT, Washington encouraged it and offered enticing membership terms. But when the López Portillo administration backed off, the Carter one refrained from pressuring it further. A few years later, when México was certain that it was in its interest to join the international trade regime, the United States did not offer the same terms it had done in the past, but all the same it did not obstruct México's second (and successful) attempt. By that time, Washington had already come to México's rescue in the (1982) debt crisis. It seemed that the United States' neighbor to the South also merited some sort of special relationship.

US discourse on the crafting of the Caribbean Basin Initiative evinces a different type of not strictly economic consideration in the making of Washington's foreign economic policy. In this case, United States' concern with Central American security and stability was paramount, but its role as the patron or tutor of the countries of the region played an important part in creating the unprecedented one-way free trade program. The underlying idea was to "teach" the beneficiary countries how to use "the magic of the marketplace"—on which the United States was of course supposed to be an expert. For all the initiative's limitations, it was clear that the Central American clients were eager to receive their patron's assistance.

In the case of the sweeping debt crisis of the 1980s, the United States devised schemes to help the affected countries put their dire economic situations behind, as well as to put an end to the acrimonious political situation in the hemisphere, to some extent prodded by the Peruvian attitude, particularly its intention to create a front of Latin American debtors to negotiate with their creditors. Thus, with the Baker Plan, but mainly with the subsequent Brady Plan, Washington was able not only to assist the debtor countries, but also to isolate Lima and elicit cooperation and a certain degree of goodwill from the Latin American countries that benefited from the program—several of them South American.

But Washington's main concern was far from gaining the endearment of the countries of the hemisphere. The hostile economic statecraft the Nixon administration undertook in order to make the Allende administration fail made clear that obtaining the region's goodwill was not top on the list of the United States' concerns; the "hegemonic presumption," coupled with a paranoid attitude toward political regimes in the region that might be at odds with its ideological preferences, was prevalent in Washington. An even more extreme case of harsh foreign economic policy pursued by the United States was the one directed toward Nicaragua after the Sandinistas came to power—particularly under the Reagan administration. Although in both instances, but particularly in the Nicaraguan one, Washington's influence attempts through economic coercion eventually worked, its influence in the hemisphere (particularly in the prolonged Central American case) suffered dearly (to say nothing of the legitimacy it lost in the two target countries during the regimes of Allende and the Sandinistas). The United States found itself mostly isolated in the region. Authority is a two-way street, and most hemispheric countries (let's recall that, during the Allende years, several Latin American dictatorships seemed to be in sync with the Nixon administration) did not appreciate Washington's arrogance and blatant interventionism.

Closer to home, Washington's economic statecraft was never as aggressive—if only because neither Ottawa or México City ever adopted an economic and political regime similar to those headed by Allende and the Sandinistas. Thus, after Ottawa's attempt at the Canadianization of its economy in the 1970s, Washington fought back, but in generally politic terms. Furthermore, the United States oftentimes expressed its dismay at its northern neighbor's measures in terms of disappointment at being let down by a (junior) partner (as well as concern about the bad example a country expected to "know better" could set for other less enlightened countries). Canada, for its part, constantly reassured its neighbor—and eventually changed course.

Similarly, when México City adopted a nationalist economic outlook (expressed, for instance, through its foreign investment law, as well through its proposal for the adoption of the Chapters of Economic Rights and Duties of States at the United Nations), Washington refrained from openly chastising it or from enforcing punitive measures. The United States undoubtedly did not agree with its southern neighbor's economic doctrine and policies, but its political stability outweighed the economic damage it could inflict to it, or to the international order it led. Not that Washington failed to engage in tough economic statecraft toward México City during those years (the otherwise friendly and understanding Carter administration did it with the gas episode, for instance) but it generally showed restraint and an awareness of the importance of having México, the country where Latin America starts and an important regional leader, on its side. Thus, if not by accommodating at least by stomaching México's decisions, the United States was able to avoid a confrontation that could have cost it greatly in the hemisphere's volatile political environment of the 1970s and 1980s. Once again, the southern neighbor deserved a differentiated treatment from that granted to other Latin American countries.

Thus, throughout the first sub-period (1971–1989) US hegemony in the Western Hemisphere experienced ups and downs, with the Reagan years being particularly critical, but by its end it was generally in good shape—thanks in part to the return to multilateralism under his successor. As Georges A. Fauriol put it in the 1989/1990 issue of *Foreign Affairs*, under president George H. W. Bush, "the rediscovery of multilateral diplomacy" had taken place.[2] Significantly, by that time it was clear that the United States had emerged victorious from the Cold War, that it was the "lonely superpower"; henceforth, to reiterate, unipolarity does not necessarily yield unilateralism.

During the second sub-period (1990–2000) US hegemony in the Americas only expanded. This expansion had little to do with a noticeable change in material capabilities (27% and 26% of reviewed countries' GDP to that of the United States in the first and last year of the sub-period, respectively; 44% and 52% for trade dependency [i.e., the percentage of exports sent to the United States] for the same years)[3]. The main reasons for the enhancement of US hegemony rather had to do with the end of the Cold War and, relatedly, from the prevalence of the Washington Consensus in the region. US economic statecraft toward the countries of the hemisphere was thus largely carried at a more profound level than that of mere strategic interaction; there was a basic coincidence of interests and values among them. Hence the shared discourse on democracy and economic liberalization, as well as the attempts at deepening hemispheric economic integration, such as the 1994 Summit of the Americas. These were the years of US primacy, hemispheric convergence, and partial restoration of US pro-trade identity.

Thus, beyond some secondary quarrels related to US unilateralist instincts during the unipolar moment (as well as to its domestic politics, as in the case of the Helms–Burton Act), Washington and Ottawa maintained mostly cordial relations; the latter was largely in synch with the former's economic doctrine and practice. Similarly, México's about face in trade policy early in the decade, and the successful outcome of the negotiations that resulted in NAFTA, speak volumes about US ascendancy over its southern neighbor. The 1995 bailout further consolidated US influence over México. Thus, by the end of the century, both countries were the closest they had been in decades.

US statecraft toward Central America, in contrast to the one toward México, was not as active or intense during the interregnum. Without pressing economic, political or security incentives to engage with the region, and with the confidence that it was on board on the prevalent economic model, Washington largely relegated the isthmus in its foreign economic policy agenda. Similarly, although not to the same extent, US economic statecraft toward South America was not particularly active during the 1990s; this was also due, in large part, to its taking of its hegemony over the region for granted. An instance of Washington's confidence (but also of the heated political debate over free trade in Congress) was the inability to finalize the free trade agreement with Chile during those years. This failure, related to the lack of fast track authority, illustrated that on foreign economic policy matters, as Richard Haass lamented toward the end of the sub-period, Washington had "lacked effective leadership"[4] during the post-Cold War. There was, however, at least one more focused and ambitious influence attempt toward the region: the Andean Trade Promotion Act (ATPA). A mixed bag in terms of its objectives, the ATPA's means were clearly economic, and although its performance was far from optimal, it bought Washington some goodwill among the Andean countries. Hence, as in the world at large, in the Western Hemisphere the United States was, as Stephen Walt put it in 2000, "the half-hearted hegemon."[5] Despite Washington's lack of zeal for stewardship, though, at the dawn of the 21st century US hegemony in the region was rather robust.

The last sub-period under consideration in this work (2001–2016) was more problematic for the exercise of US power through economic statecraft in the hemisphere. But again, it is hard to argue that this change had much to do with mere material capabilities (24% and 31% of reviewed countries' GDP to that of the United States in the first and last year of the sub-period, respectively; 50% and 37% for trade dependency [understood again as the percentage of exports sent to the United States] for the same years).[6] Washington maintained a pro-trade policy, but a much more aggressive one, displaying a US-centered trade-hub identity through its competitive liberalization strategy; but this was not, however, the main reason for the heightened difficulties in exerting its hegemony in the Americas. The chief factor arguably had to do with Washington's increased unilateralist tendencies. Thus, on the eve of the start of the George W. Bush era, Condolezza Rice (who, as noted, was to become his National Security Adviser and then Secretary of State) foreshadowed the arrogance of the future administration by remarking: "America's values are universal."[7]

The Bush years (2000–2008), but especially the first four, saw an abrupt surge in go-it-alone US policies in myriad topics; this asocial use of power cost the United States legitimacy worldwide—and the Western Hemisphere was no exception. Furthermore, the economic stagnation (at least in Latin America) that followed the Washington Consensus' decade,[8] plus the opening of alternative export markets (particularly China in the case of commodities), meant that several of the region's countries were more willing to take distance from the United States on economic discourse and practice. The most noticeable case in this respect was South America; for instance, economic and political relations with Buenos Aires deteriorated as a result of Washington's reluctance to help its staunchest ally of yesteryear in the context of its financial crisis at the century's dawn. The United States' low cost and vindictive economic statecraft toward the austral country turned out to be an expensive one, in political terms, for US hegemony in the region.

Not unrelated to the costs Washington had to pay for its arrogant bent in the early 21st century was its inability to carry the day in the Free Trade Area of the Americas' (FTAA) process. Brazil turned out to be a regional leader to be reckoned with. And the United States' reluctance to open the scope of negotiations to matters of vital interest to Brasília, plus the unkind treatment dispensed to the southern giant with the imposition of tariffs and discriminatory treatment, definitively did not help in courting Brazil's support for a successful FTAA—as the fiasco at the Mar del Plata summit evinced.

Washington's failure in the hemispheric project, however, was not synonymous with an overall or permanent decline of US hegemony. As noted, 29 out of the 34 countries represented at the Argentinian city were in favor of the trade deal, and Washington was able to sign bilateral or regional trade agreements with several of them subsequently. Moreover, the boost of the commodities boom, and the political problems several countries of the "pink wave" faced during the Obama years meant that the United States was able to regain some of the influence it had lost during the first half or this sub-period (2001–2016).

Washington was more successful in maintaining its hegemony steady in Central America. There, US acquiescence to the region's request for a free trade agreement helped Washington in preserving its standing—even if the countries of the isthmus were being used as a sort of guinea pig for the broader US "competitive liberalization" trade strategy. However, the region's poor economic performance, along with the rise of an anti-American sentiment in the context of the "pink wave," meant both the increased questioning of Washington's hegemony, as well as the Colossus of the North's need to come up with palliative programs to assist its Central American clients.

US power as effected through its economic statecraft toward México did not suffer major alterations. Both countries were basically in agreement regarding what they considered proper economic policy, both at home and abroad. Noticeably, with its ascendancy on economic affairs over México City well established, Washington even refused to deepen the bilateral economic relationship; the disputes between the two capitals during those years had to do mainly with political affairs, such as the US invasion of Iraq. Similarly, United States–Canada frictions over the period were mainly related to Washington's unilateralist impulses, though toward the end of it there was one that was mostly of an economic nature: the Keystone XL Pipeline. But US economic statecraft toward Canada during those years was, as in the one toward México, generally subdued; Washington's power over Ottawa showed no signs of decline.

Overall, during this 16-year period United States hegemony in the Western hemisphere was much more erratic than during the previous sub-period (1990–2000), and a good deal of this had to with the country's a-social understanding and practice of power. The misunderstanding regarding the appropriate and efficient use of power was clear from the beginning of this sub-period (2001–2016). To quote Rice in 2000 again: "America's pursuit of the national interest will create conditions that promote freedom, markets, and peace. Its pursuit of national interest after World War II led to a more prosperous and democratic world. This can happen again."[9] What she, and the Bush administration in general, missed is that a state's power is more effective when embedded in the larger international community, when the state—particularly if it is a hegemon—possesses an enlightened self-interest.

Having reviewed the exercise of US power through its economic statecraft in the Western Hemisphere, I now turn my the second task in this concluding chapter: revisiting the discussion on the nature of power, regional orders and economic statecraft. As the previous narrative suggests, the exercise of power is a highly relational and contextual matter. Washington's foreign economic policy toward the region certainly corresponded to the country's identity as instantiated through its trade policy in each of the sub-periods. Since the sub-periods were derived from the global debate on the decline of US hegemony (corresponding to the last two decades of the Cold War, the unipolar moment, and the emergence of China), as noted in the introduction, they do not necessarily correspond exactly to the different phases of the wax and wane of US power in the economic sphere in the Western Hemisphere. This realm of power relations was, moreover, shaped by the different administrations' understanding of power. The deployment of US economic statecraft was, *a fortiori*, affected by this contingent fact. As said conception—and practice—changed, so did the authority the United States enjoyed in the region. Thus, for instance, Nixon's, Reagan's and Bush Jr.'s years in office had different effects on US hegemony in the region, from those of the administrations of, say, Carter, Bush Senior and Obama.

Throughout the five-decade period (1971–2016) covered here, though, US power in the economic realm had a distinctive hemispheric twist—and not because, as noted, Washington had deployed a foreign economic policy tailored to the region. There were of course notable exceptions, such as the CBI or ATPA, but the broad contours of US economic doctrine did not differentiate the hemisphere from the rest of the world. The explanation for the hemispheric twist lies in the deeper normative structure that has historically underlain the political economy of the Americas, the Western Hemisphere Idea

(WHI). As discussed in Chapter 2, the separate system of values and interests that evolved in the New World since the early 19th century was an internationally recognized social fact by the early 20th century, and it gained in legal-institutional terms with the 1948 Bogotá Charter.

But beyond the formalization of the regional compact, what mattered for hemispheric economic intercourse were the authoritative elements it contained, to wit, (US) restraint and (Canadian and Latin American) recognition (regarding strictly political inter-American relations, the principles of representative government and non-intervention were central features of the WHI). That is, whereas Washington committed to respecting the rights of its hemispheric neighbors, the latter pledged to acknowledge US leadership. Legitimacy was the glue that held the regional order together. This basic political accord, imbued by the republican legacy according to which sovereign states are linked in a hierarchical realm (one where the leader must utter justifications for its actions), permeated to the economic intercourse among the countries of the Western Hemisphere. Hence not only the non-economic considerations brought to bear in the practice of US economic statecraft, but also the normative and political claims advanced both by Washington and the "target" countries of the Americas in what would otherwise be merely economic interactions.

The wider discussion initiated in the early 1970s on the alleged decline of US hegemony was thus localized in this specific regional order, in the terms shown in the previous chapters; from this vantage point, as illustrated, things looked a little bit different. Although in the early 1980s the declinist proposition was widespread in the Western Hemisphere, later in the decade it had become clear that United States hegemony on economic affairs was still robust. As noted, US economic (and political) leadership in the region, along with that in the wider international context, improved substantially during the interregnum. It was during the last phase (2001–2016), however, that US hegemony in the region became more erratic, declining first and then recovering somehow toward the end of the period covered by this work. This of course had to do with the emergence of the left in Latin America, as well as with the renewed efforts at Latin American-only integration, but also with the noted unilateralist policies of the Bush administrations, the rise of China, and the commodities' boom. The partial recovery of US hegemony in the Western Hemisphere during the Obama years, a period during which a more social understanding of power, one that more closely corresponded to the basic principles of the hemispheric compact, went to some extent against the grain of the alleged downward trajectory of US hegemony worldwide. During these final years, the United States articulated something closer to an enlightened self-interest in the Western Hemisphere, one that included the neighbors' need for more autonomy and respect, which in turn increased its legitimacy in the region.

Throughout the 46-year period covered in this work, as noted in the analytical narratives presented in the previous chapters, US material capabilities vis-à-vis the countries of the hemisphere did not substantially change; that is one reason I have argued resources per se are not very useful in accounting for the wax and wane of Washington's power in the region. This is not to suggest, however, that in the study of international political economy tangible assets are … immaterial. Brute facts of this kind indeed constitute a (very rough) proxy of power relations in world affairs. But a materialist, power-as-an-attribute approach does not get us very far in explaining the intricacies of the political basis of the exercise of both hegemony and political statecraft. Although more sensitive to the social nature of power, a thin relational understanding of power, one that largely focuses on its strategic component, is also of limited use. The thin relational account misses the normative foundations of power, that is, if fails to account for the non-strategic, legitimacy-based and sometimes even deontological aspects of power relations involved in the exercise of hegemony through economic statecraft. That is why a thick relational account of power, along with a thick conception of economic statecraft, can better make sense of the complexities involved in the instantiation of US hegemony in economic affairs.

For economic statecraft, as noted, is not only a set of technical instruments. It reflects the identity of the state, "A," that deploys it; this embedding of identity (as a property concept) is part of what makes the understanding of economic statecraft advanced in this work "thick." That is why, for the most part, the influence attempts implemented in specific foreign economic policies are congruous with the identity of the power wielder. Furthermore, both the identity and the means chosen to effect power appear as social facts to the target state, "B." By the same token, though, B's knowledge of A's identity informs and gives predictability to the power relationship as instantiated in the economic realm. Even if the approach advanced here is less parsimonious than the other approaches, it certainly has some points of convergence with them, as its application in the previous chapters has hopefully demonstrated. The argument presented here is analogous to John Gerard Ruggie's cited analysis (in Chapter 1) on the post-World War II emergence of multilateralism, which he attributed not to the existence of "American *hegemony*" but to the establishment of a particular hierarchical order, "*American* hegemony." It is thus not surprising that the extended existence of United States' hegemony in the New World has patterned power relations in general and in the economic realm in particular.

This of course does not mean that Washington's relationship with its hemispheric neighbors is preordained. There are myriad factors that affect the development of power relationships. For starters, as suggested, state identity, even when disregarding the international-level interaction that goes into it (as done in this work for methodological purposes), is malleable. Thus, although in general terms Washington maintained a liberal attitude toward international trade in the period covered here, as noted in Chapter 4, its identity was not set in stone, as the variations in its economic statecraft suggest. Furthermore, the extent to which other countries bought into US discourse on the matter (whether it was deployed sincerely or for strategic purposes) also sheds some light on the flux of the power Washington was able to exert over the hemisphere. Throughout the 1971–2016 period, though, paraphrasing Dahl's cited definition of power, it is safe to say that the United States' ability to affect the countries of the Western Hemisphere's *actions, or predispositions to act [...] in a direction consistent with—and not contrary to—[its] wants, preferences, or intentions* was mostly preserved.

The previous discussion on power, regional orders and the nature of statecraft leads me to the last task set for this chapter: the extension of the argument to the meaning of the arrival of Donald Trump to power for US hegemony.

In late 2016, when the odds were that US exercise of power under Obama was going to continue on a similar trajectory under the leadership of Democratic presidential candidate Hillary Clinton, Republican contender Donald J. Trump upended the race by winning the election by a margin of minus 2.86 million popular votes—but a majority in the electoral college of 304 (versus 227 for Clinton). Upon taking office in January 2017, Trump started making good on the nationalist and xenophobic promises he had made during his "Make America Great Again" campaign to the presidency. Thus, soon after his arrival to the White House, Trump withdrew the United States from the Trans-Pacific Partnership (TPP), and announced the starting of renegotiations of what he had called the "worst deal ever signed": NAFTA.

On the broader international economic front, the US president has also repeatedly attacked the World Trade Organization, and imposed tariffs left and right (e.g., to Canada, China, the European Union, México and Turkey).[10] It is clear that Trump favors the "revenue" and "restriction" objectives of international trade policy that had characterized US policy in previous eras, instead of the "reciprocity" one that has defined the US approach since the mid-1930s.[11] In the meantime, as Stephen Walt has noted, Washington has followed a "haphazard approach to economic diplomacy," particularly regarding what undoubtedly is its greater challenger: Beijing.[12] Thus, not only Trump excluded his country from the broad political and economic coalition it had built to deal with China's emergence, the above-mentioned TPP, but he also alienated potential allies, such as Canada and the European countries, in its fight against the Asian country. As former treasury secretary Larry Summers noted in the *Financial Times*, a "rule of strategy is to unite your friends and divide your potential adversaries. The US seems to be doing the opposite ... the result has been to cause most of the rest of the world to take China's side against the US."[13]

But since early 2017, the United States has abandoned many other principles that had served as its lodestar since World War II, particularly in the conduct of its diplomacy. Thus, it has repeatedly lambasted its most important security alliance, NATO, criticized the European Union, and even threatened to leave the United Nations. The Trump administration has also snubbed the global threat posed by global warming, as its abandonment of the Paris Agreement on the matter made clear, and has promoted racism, as its travel ban on Muslims, its actions and discourse on its intended "wall" along the Mexican border, or the president's disparaging comments on some Central American and African countries ("shithole" or "shithouse" countries, he called them) have evinced.[14]

In the age of Donald Trump, Washington has privileged the military over the foreign service, pursuing spending increases in the former and cuts in the latter.[15] Confirming the low regard on which the current occupant of the White House holds diplomacy, president Trump has bragged about lying to one of his counterparts (and ally), Canadian prime minister Justin Trudeau.[16] It is clear that no foreign leader would utter about Trump's word what Charles de Gaulle said about president Kennedy's when secretary of state Acheson attempted to show him evidence of Soviet missiles in Cuban soil: "the word of the president of the United States is good enough for me"—and he disregarded the US envoy's effort .[17] As *The Economist* has noted, Trump "treats every relationship as a set of competitive transactions"; according to the English weekly, no other US president "has so conspicuously failed to clothe the application of coercive power in the claim to be acting for the global good."[18] The Trump administration's foreign policy has thus been largely reduced to coercion and rudimentary strategic bargaining[19]—not exactly what US diplomacy in the golden age of US hegemony was about. Hence, as the president of the European Council, Donald Tusk, has observed, "The rules-based international order is being challenged, quite surprisingly, not by the usual suspects, but by its main architect and guarantor, the U.S." (At the 2018 G7 Summit in Canada, the US delegation actually objected to the inclusion of the customary "rules-based international order" in the meeting's communiqué.)[20] In a similar tone, Council on Foreign Relation's president Richard Haass has noted that since the arrival of Trump to the White House "the United States has changed from the principal preserver of order to a principal disrupter."[21]

Now, the observed change in US role, from "preserver" to "disrupter", could be seen as one of degree. For, as noted before, it is not that in preserving the post-World War II international order the United States was doing it for merely altruistic reasons or, more importantly, that it faithfully adhered to it. Washington was acting out of (enlightened) self-interest; in the economic realm, for instance, its (largely consistent) pursuit of the "reciprocity" objective in its trade policy was certainly beneficial to others, but the United States was the main beneficiary. Furthermore, the actually existing international liberal order was rife with "anomalies." A partial list of them would include, on the US part, political assassinations in other countries, over 70 attempts at regime change, support of authoritarian governments, illegal covert activities and torture.[22] There were of course ups and downs in the extent to which Washington followed the liberal order's script; one particularly problematic phase, as noted, was George W. Bush's, with its unilateralist bent.

But still, there has been a category change under the Trump administration. By simply rejecting moral values in the international arena, Washington has taken an unprecedented step. As the liberal weekly *The Economist* put it,

> America's unique willingness to lead by fusing power and legitimacy saw off the Soviet Union and carried it to hegemony. The world order it engineered is the vehicle for that philosophy. But Mr. Trump prefers to fall back on the old idea that might is right. His impulses may begin to impose a new geopolitics, but they will not serve America or the world for long.[23]

Similarly, realist Barry Posen has noted: "Breaking with his predecessors, Trump has taken much of the "liberal" out of "liberal hegemony." [...] Trump has ushered in an entirely new U.S. grand strategy: illiberal hegemony."[24]

But where does this new approach, this understanding of power, come from? It has roots in one of the long-contending foreign policy traditions in the United States, the Jacksonian one, which evinces economic nationalism, populist traits and unilateralism;[25] president Trump has actually acknowledged as much.[26] Just like Argentinian president Juan Domingo Perón's deep, ingrained belief about the pliability of the economy cited in Chapter 4, which guided his approach to economic policy, there seems to be an equivalent deep-seated belief in the US president regarding tariffs and their proper use in economic statecraft; for him, they are an indispensable, all-purpose tool that protect the United States from a world intent on taking advantage of it.[27] There is also a sort of Hobbesian view of international politics at work in the current US administration's understanding of foreign economic intercourse. As Trump's National Security Adviser, H.R. McMaster, and National Economic Adviser Gary D. Cohn wrote in a joint editorial in the *Wall Street Journal* in the context of their boss' first journey abroad,

> The president embarked on his first foreign trip with a clear-eyed outlook that the world is not a 'global community' but an arena where nations, nongovernmental actors and businesses engage and compete for advantage [...] Rather than deny this elemental nature of international affairs, we embrace it.[28]

According to the Trump administration, US material superiority simply means that it should be able to exert more power, at its own discretion. Furthermore, in this understanding, this imbalance should instill anxiety among other countries. For president Trump, as he put it, "Real power is—I don't even want to use the word—Fear."[29] We thus get to the articulation of the Trump Doctrine, as enunciated by a high-ranking White House official: "The Trump Doctrine is 'We're America, Bitch.' That's the Trump Doctrine."[30] Alternatively, a president's friend described the new approach in these terms: "There's the Obama Doctrine, and the 'Fuck Obama' Doctrine [...] We're the 'Fuck Obama' Doctrine."[31]

Graphic language aside, the contrast between the last two president's approach to foreign affairs shows. Take the case of the Western Hemisphere. As noted in Chapter 2, Obama's Secretary of State, John Kerry, declared at the OAS in 2013 that the Monroe Doctrine was no longer US policy. Fast-forward to 2018; secretary of state Rex Tillerson's take on the Monroe Doctrine at the University of Texas at Austin: "I think it's as relevant today as it was the day it was written."[32] For him, though, unlike for the Doctrine's creators, the threat was not coming from Europe, but from China. As the former Secretary of State put it, "Today China is getting a foothold in Latin America. It is using economic statecraft to pull the region into its orbit."[33] Similarly, in 2019, speaking in Miami to a group of Bay of Pigs veterans, National Security Adviser John Bolton said: "Today, we proudly proclaim for all to hear: the Monroe Doctrine is alive and well"; according to him, after all, "It is our hemisphere."[34]

The effects of the Trump administration's raw exercise of power, however, have certainly not been what was expected. Take Latin America again. Washington's renewed arrogant and interventionist approach to the region has not produced increased influence or even apprehension, but rather bafflement. As *The Economist* put it, "A deep perplexity. That, says a senior Latin American official, describes his region's attitude to the government of president Donald Trump. What Latin American leaders do not feel is fear."[35] Washington's asocial conception and practice of power seems thus to be rather ineffectual in the hemisphere. And the same goes for other regions, in the U.S.' dealings with both allies and foes.[36] Particularly in the economic front, as suggested above, US policy has been counterproductive; it has shown Washington not only as selfish, but also as an ineffective leader, thus undermining its legitimacy as a competent hegemonic power.[37]

Beyond purely economic, inter-state relations, the United States has been losing greatly in reputational terms. Compared to Obama's last year in office, the approval rate of US leadership under Trump toward the end of his first year dropped almost 20 percentage points, to about 30, according to a Gallup poll taken in 134 countries.[38] Similarly, a 2018 Pew Research Center survey in 25 countries found that, on average, only 27% of respondents have confidence in president Trump; México had the most negative view of the US president, with only 6% of those surveyed declaring they had confidence in him.[39] Significantly, this is not just foreign perception, US citizens largely agree on the declining image and influence of their country in the world. Thus, according to a 2018 Chicago Council Report, "59 percent of Americans say that the United States is less respected now than it was 10 years ago," and most of those polled "think that the United States is losing global influence."[40]

It is thus clear that the United States has lost influence under Trump. Paraphrasing again Dahl's cited definition of power, we could say that Washington's ability to affect other countries' *actions, or predispositions to act [...] in a direction consistent with—and not contrary to—[its] wants, preferences, or intentions* has taken a severe blow. This does not necessarily mean, though, that the (actually existing) international liberal order is dead. For although Washington is actively undermining the institutions in whose creation it was a leading player, those institutions might as well survive Trump's presidency. Institutions are sticky; they usually do not disappear as a result of one blow. As the literature on international regimes convincingly argued, they sometimes acquire a life of their own.[41] There might be, as Robert Keohane argued long ago, cooperation after US hegemony.[42] And that is exactly the point—it is unlikely that the international hierarchical order will remain being led by the United States. Even if a more enlightened politician wins the 2020 presidential election, he or she will face an extremely uphill battle to recover his or her country's legitimacy in the international arena so as to make it the hegemonic leader again. He or she might manage to regain some of the influence it lost during the last years, particularly during the Trump administration, but that would hardly suffice to place it back at the top of the power pyramid. The damage done to US credibility is probably insurmountable. It might then not be the decline in capabilities that does away with US hegemony, but rather the decline in its ability to properly exert power. For just as in the domestic sphere, as realist author and *realpolitik* practitioner Henry Kissinger noted long ago, "Any system of world order, to be sustainable, must be accepted as just—not only by leaders, but also by citizens."[43] Politics is politics is politics.

Notes

1   Source for GDP: World Bank (2019a). The countries included in Central America are: Costa Rica, El Salvador, Guatemala, Honduras and Nicaragua; the countries included in South America are: Argentina, Brazil, Chile, Colombia and Perú. Source for trade: OEC 2019.

2   Fauriol 1989/1990: 117.

3   Source for GDP: World Bank 2019a; Source for trade: OEC 2019 [Considering same countries mentioned above]

4   Haass 1999: 48.

5   Walt 2000: 64.

6   Source for GDP: World Bank 2019a; Source for trade: OEC 2019 (Considering same countries mentioned above [The most recent available data was used: 2015 for the cases of Guatemala and Nicaragua; 2014 for Honduras]).

7   Rice 2000: 49.

8   For the period 1998–2000 the average growth rate, in percentage points, was 4.5 for Canada, 4.3 for México, 3.9 for Central America, and 1.15 for South America; in the 2001– period, the rate for the same countries changed to 2.2, 0.33, 2.7 and 1.9. For the United States the corresponding numbers are 4.4 and 1.9. The countries included in Central America and South America are the same as above. Source: World Bank (2019b).

9   Rice 2000: 47.

10   Reuters 2019.

11   Irwin 2017.

12   Walt 2019.

13   Summers 2018.

14   Sullivan 2018; Dawsey 2018.

15   Filkins 2017.

16   Walt 2018c: 245.
17   Walt 2018b.
18   *The Economist* 2018.
19   Drezner 2018b.
20   In Shear 2018.
21   Drezner 2018a.
22   Bacevich 2018: 212; Zenko 2019.
23   *The Economist* 2018.
24   Posen 2018.
25   Mead 2005.
26   Friedman Lissner and Rapp-Hooper 2018.
27   Tankersley and Landler 2019; Editorial Board 2019; Irwin 2018.
28   McMaster and Cohn 2017.
29   Woodward 2018: npn.
30   In Goldberg 2018.
31   Ibid.
32   Tillerson 2018: npn.
33   Ibid.: npn.
34   Richardson 2019; Filkins 2019.
35   Lexington 2017.
36   Walt 2018a.
37   Krugman 2018; Drezner 2017; Summers 2018.
38   In Baker 2018.
39   Wike et al. 2018.
40   Smeltz et al. 2018: 13–14.
41   Krasner 1983.
42   Keohane 1984.
43   Kissinger 2015: 8.

References

Bacevich, A. (2018). The "Global Order" myth. In R. Gervis, F. J. Gavin, J. Rovner, D. E. Labrosse & G. Fujii (Eds.), *Chaos in the liberal order.* New York: Colombia University Press.

Baker, P. (2018, January 18). Souring world views of Trump open doors for China and Russia. *New York Times.*

Dawsey, J. (2018, January 12). Trump derides protections for immigrants from 'shithole' countries. *Washington Post.*

Drezner, D. W. (2017, July 10). As it turns out America first does equal America Alone. *Washington Post.*

Drezner, D. W. (2018a, January 9). Is president Trump's foreign policy better than we think? *Washington Post.*

Drezner, D. W. (2018b, October 1). The Trump administration's incomplete understanding of power. *Washington Post.*

Editorial Board (2019, May 31). Tariff man unchained. *Wall Street Journal.*

Fauriol, G. (1989/1990). The shadow of Latin American affairs. *Foreign Affairs, 69*(1), 116–134.

Filkins, D. (2017, October 16). Rex Tillerson at the breaking point. *New Yorker.*

Filkins, D. (2019, April 29). John Bolton on the Warpath: Can Trump's national-security adviser sell the isolationist President on military force? *New Yorker.*

Friedman Lissner, R., & Rapp-Hooper M. (2018). The day after Trump: American strategy for a new international order. *Washington Quarterly, 41*(1), 7–25.

Goldberg, J. (2018, June 11). A senior White House official defines the Trump doctrine: 'We're America, Bitch'. *Atlantic.*

Haass, R. (1999). What to Do With American Primacy. *Foreign Affairs, 78*(5), 37–49.

Irwin, D. (2017). *Clashing over commerce: A history of US trade policy.* Chicago, IL: University of Chicago Press.

Irwin, D. (2018, November 6). Trade under Trump: What he's done so far—And what he'll do next. *Foreign Affairs.*

Keohane, R. O. (1984). *After hegemony: Cooperation and discord in the world political economy.* Princeton, NJ: Princeton University Press.

Kissinger, H. (2015). *World order.* New York: Penguin Books.

Krasner, S. (1983). *International regimes.* Ithaca, NY: Cornell University Press.

Krugman, P. (2018). Leadership, laughter, and tariffs. *New York Times.*

Lexington (2017, August 17). Donald Trump blusters, Latin America shrugs. *The Economist.*

McMaster, H., & Cohn, G. (2017, May 30). America first doesn't mean America alone. *Wall Street Journal.*

Mead, W. (2005). The Jacksonian tradition and American foreign policy. In O. C. Judd (Ed.), *Redefining sovereignty: Will liberal democracies continue to determine their own laws and public policies or yield these rights to transnational entities?* (pp. 307–344). Hanover: Smith and Kraus.

OEC (2019). Visualizations: Export destinations. *The Observatory of Economic Complexity* (Accessed on May 13, 2019).

Posen, B. (2018). The rise of illiberal hegemony: Trump's surprising grand strategy. *Foreign Affairs, 97*(2), 20–27.

Reuters (2019, May 13). Factbox: Tariff wars – Duties imposed by Trump and U.S. trading partners. *Reuters.*

Rice, C. (2000). Promoting the national interest. *Foreign Affairs, 79*(1), 45–62.

Richardson, D. (2019, April 17). John Bolton reaffirms America's commitment to the Monroe Doctrine with new sanctions. *Observer.*

Shear, M. (2018, June 8). Trump attends G-7 with defiance, proposing to readmit Russia. *New York Times.*

Smeltz, D., Daalder, I. H., Friedhoff, K., Kafura, C., & Wojtowicz, L. (2018). *Chicago Council Survey—America engaged: American public opinion and US foreign policy.* Chicago, IL: The Chicago Council on Global Affairs.

Sullivan, E. (2018). Trump denies changing his position on border wall. *New York Times.*

Summers, L. (2018, June 4). Donald Trump's trade policy violates every rule of strategy. *Financial Times.*

Tankersley, J., & Landler, M. (2019, May 15). Trump's love for tariffs began in Japan's '80s Boom. *New York Times.*

The Economist (2018, June 7). Donald Trump's demolition theory of foreign policy won't work. *The Economist.*

Tillerson, R. (2018). *U.S. engagement in the Western Hemisphere.* Remarks at University of Texas at Austin, February 1.

Walt, S. (2000). Two cheers for Clinton's foreign policy. *Foreign Affairs, 79*(2), 63–79.

Walt, S. (2018a, August 13). A playbook for taming Donald Trump. *Foreign Policy.*

Walt, S. (2018b, September 17). Does it matter that Trump is a liar? *Foreign Policy.*

Walt, S. (2018c). *The hell of good intentions: America's foreign policy elite and the decline of U.S. primacy*. New York: Farrar, Straus and Giroux.

Walt, S. (2019, April 26). America isn't as powerful as it thinks it is. *Foreign Policy*.

Wike, R., Stokes, B, Poushter, J., Silver, L., Fetterolf, J., & Devlin, K. (2018, October 1). *Trump's international ratings remain low, especially among key allies*. Washington, DC: Pew Research Center.

Woodward, B. (2018). *Fear: Trump in the White House*. New York: Simon and Schuster.

World Bank (2019a). Gross domestic product [NY.GDP.MKTP.CD]. Retrieved from https://data.worldbank.org/indicator/NY.GDP.MKTP.CD

World Bank (2019b). Gross domestic product growth [NY.GDP.MKTP.KD.ZG]. Retrieved from https://data.worldbank.org/indicator/NY.GDP.MKTP.ZG

Zenko, M. (2019, April 10). Nostalgia is a national security threat. *Foreign Policy*.

Index